2021
SUN SIGN
BOOK

Forecasts by
Alice DeVille

Cover design by Kevin R. Brown
Interior illustration on page 19 by the Llewellyn Art Department

© 2020 by Llewellyn Publications
ISBN: 978-0-7387-5487-1
Llewellyn is a registered trademark of Llewellyn Worldwide Ltd.
2143 Wooddale Drive, Woodbury, MN 55125-2989
www.llewellyn.com
Printed in the United States of America

Contents

2021 Sun Sign Book Forecasts *by Alice DeVille*

2020

SEPTEMBER
S	M	T	W	T	F	S
		1	2	3	4	5
6	7	8	9	10	11	12
13	14	15	16	17	18	19
20	21	22	23	24	25	26
27	28	29	30			

OCTOBER
S	M	T	W	T	F	S
				1	2	3
4	5	6	7	8	9	10
11	12	13	14	15	16	17
18	19	20	21	22	23	24
25	26	27	28	29	30	31

NOVEMBER
S	M	T	W	T	F	S
1	2	3	4	5	6	7
8	9	10	11	12	13	14
15	16	17	18	19	20	21
22	23	24	25	26	27	28
29	30					

DECEMBER
S	M	T	W	T	F	S
		1	2	3	4	5
6	7	8	9	10	11	12
13	14	15	16	17	18	19
20	21	22	23	24	25	26
27	28	29	30	31		

2021

JANUARY
S	M	T	W	T	F	S
					1	2
3	4	5	6	7	8	9
10	11	12	13	14	15	16
17	18	19	20	21	22	23
24	25	26	27	28	29	30
31						

FEBRUARY
S	M	T	W	T	F	S
	1	2	3	4	5	6
7	8	9	10	11	12	13
14	15	16	17	18	19	20
21	22	23	24	25	26	27
28						

MARCH
S	M	T	W	T	F	S
	1	2	3	4	5	6
7	8	9	10	11	12	13
14	15	16	17	18	19	20
21	22	23	24	25	26	27
28	29	30	31			

APRIL
S	M	T	W	T	F	S
				1	2	3
4	5	6	7	8	9	10
11	12	13	14	15	16	17
18	19	20	21	22	23	24
25	26	27	28	29	30	

MAY
S	M	T	W	T	F	S
						1
2	3	4	5	6	7	8
9	10	11	12	13	14	15
16	17	18	19	20	21	22
23	24	25	26	27	28	29
30	31					

JUNE
S	M	T	W	T	F	S
		1	2	3	4	5
6	7	8	9	10	11	12
13	14	15	16	17	18	19
20	21	22	23	24	25	26
27	28	29	30			

JULY
S	M	T	W	T	F	S
				1	2	3
4	5	6	7	8	9	10
11	12	13	14	15	16	17
18	19	20	21	22	23	24
25	26	27	28	29	30	31

AUGUST
S	M	T	W	T	F	S
1	2	3	4	5	6	7
8	9	10	11	12	13	14
15	16	17	18	19	20	21
22	23	24	25	26	27	28
29	30	31				

SEPTEMBER
S	M	T	W	T	F	S
			1	2	3	4
5	6	7	8	9	10	11
12	13	14	15	16	17	18
19	20	21	22	23	24	25
26	27	28	29	30		

OCTOBER
S	M	T	W	T	F	S
					1	2
3	4	5	6	7	8	9
10	11	12	13	14	15	16
17	18	19	20	21	22	23
24	25	26	27	28	29	30
31						

NOVEMBER
S	M	T	W	T	F	S
	1	2	3	4	5	6
7	8	9	10	11	12	13
14	15	16	17	18	19	20
21	22	23	24	25	26	27
28	29	30				

DECEMBER
S	M	T	W	T	F	S
			1	2	3	4
5	6	7	8	9	10	11
12	13	14	15	16	17	18
19	20	21	22	23	24	25
26	27	28	29	30	31	

2022

JANUARY
S	M	T	W	T	F	S
						1
2	3	4	5	6	7	8
9	10	11	12	13	14	15
16	17	18	19	20	21	22
23	24	25	26	27	28	29
30	31					

FEBRUARY
S	M	T	W	T	F	S
		1	2	3	4	5
6	7	8	9	10	11	12
13	14	15	16	17	18	19
20	21	22	23	24	25	26
27	28					

MARCH
S	M	T	W	T	F	S
		1	2	3	4	5
6	7	8	9	10	11	12
13	14	15	16	17	18	19
20	21	22	23	24	25	26
27	28	29	30	31		

APRIL
S	M	T	W	T	F	S
					1	2
3	4	5	6	7	8	9
10	11	12	13	14	15	16
17	18	19	20	21	22	23
24	25	26	27	28	29	30

MAY
S	M	T	W	T	F	S
1	2	3	4	5	6	7
8	9	10	11	12	13	14
15	16	17	18	19	20	21
22	23	24	25	26	27	28
29	30	31				

JUNE
S	M	T	W	T	F	S
			1	2	3	4
5	6	7	8	9	10	11
12	13	14	15	16	17	18
19	20	21	22	23	24	25
26	27	28	29	30		

JULY
S	M	T	W	T	F	S
					1	2
3	4	5	6	7	8	9
10	11	12	13	14	15	16
17	18	19	20	21	22	23
24	25	26	27	28	29	30
31						

AUGUST
S	M	T	W	T	F	S
	1	2	3	4	5	6
7	8	9	10	11	12	13
14	15	16	17	18	19	20
21	22	23	24	25	26	27
28	29	30	31			

Meet Alice DeVille

Alice DeVille is known internationally as an astrologer, consultant, and writer. She has been writing articles for the Llewellyn annuals since 1998. Her contributions have appeared in Llewellyn's *Sun Sign Book*, *Moon Sign Book*, and *Herbal Almanac*.

Alice discovered astrology in her late teens when she was browsing the book section of a discount department store and found a book that had much more astrology detail in it than simple Sun sign descriptions. Bells of recognition went off immediately. She purchased the book and knew she had to have more.

Alice also held credentials as a realtor for twenty-two years in the Commonwealth of Virginia and earned Real Estate Appraisal credentials and certifications in diverse real estate specialties. Her knowledge of feng shui led to the development of numerous workshops and seminars, including those that provided realtors with tips for selling homes and working with buyers.

Alice specializes in relationships of all types that call for solid problem-solving advice to get to the core of issues and give clients options for meeting critical needs. Her clients seek solutions in business practices, career and change management, real estate, relationships, and training. Numerous websites and publications have featured her articles, including StarIQ, Astral Hearts, Llewellyn, Meta Arts, Inner Self, and ShareItLiveIt. Quotes from her work on relationships have appeared in books, publications, training materials, calendars, planners, audio tapes, and world-famous quotes lists. Often cited is "Each relationship you have with another reflects the relationship you have with yourself." Alice's Llewellyn material on relationships has appeared in *Something More* by Sarah Ban Breathnach and *Through God's Eyes* by Phil Bolsta and on Oprah's website.

Alice is available for writing books and articles for publishers, newspapers, and magazines, as well as conducting workshops and doing radio or TV interviews. Contact her at DeVilleAA@aol.com or alice.deville27 @gmail.com.

How to Use This Book

by Kim Rogers-Gallagher

Hi there! Welcome to the 2021 edition of *Llewellyn's Sun Sign Book*. This book centers on Sun sign astrology—that is, the set of general attributes and characteristics that those of us born under each of the twelve particular Sun signs share. You'll find descriptions of your sign's qualities tucked into your sign's chapter, along with the type of behavior you tend to exhibit in different life situations—with regard to relationships, work situations, and the handling of money and possessions, for example. Oh, and there's a section that's dedicated to good old-fashioned fun, too, including what will bring you joy and how to make it happen.

There's a lot to be said for Sun sign astrology. First off, the Sun's sign at the time of your birth describes the qualities, talents, and traits you're here to study this time around. If you believe in reincarnation, think of it as declaring a celestial major for this lifetime. Sure, you'll learn other things along the way, but you've announced to one and all that you're primarily interested in mastering this one particular sign. Then, too, on a day when fiery, impulsive energies are making astrological headlines, if you're a fiery and/or impulsive sign yourself—like Aries or Aquarius, for example—it's easy to imagine how you'll take to the astrological weather a lot more easily than a practical, steady-handed sign like Taurus or Virgo.

Obviously, astrology comes in handy, for a variety of reasons. Getting to know your "natal" Sun sign (the sign the Sun was in when you were born) can most certainly give you the edge you need to ace the final and move on to the next celestial course level—or basically to succeed in life, and maybe even earn a few bonus points toward next semester. Using astrology on a daily basis nicely accelerates the process.

Now, there are eight other planets and one lovely Moon in our neck of the celestial woods, all of which also play into our personalities. The sign that was on the eastern horizon at the moment of your birth—otherwise known as your *Ascendant*, or *rising sign*—is another indicator of your personality traits. Honestly, there are all kinds of cosmic factors, so if it's an in-depth, personal analysis you're after, a professional astrologer is the only way to go—especially if you're curious about relationships, past lives, future trends, or even the right time to schedule an important life event. Professional astrologers calculate your birth chart—again, the "natal" chart—based on the date, place, and exact time of your birth—which allows for a far more personal and specific reading. In the meantime, however, in addition to reading up on your Sun sign, you can use the tables on pages 8 and 9 to find the sign of your Ascendant. (These tables, however, are approximate and tailored to those of us born in North America, so if the traits of your Ascendant don't sound familiar, check out the sign directly before or after.)

There are three sections to each sign chapter in this book. As I already mentioned, the first section describes personality traits, and while it's fun to read your own, don't forget to check out the other Sun signs. (Oh, and do feel free to mention any rather striking behavioral similarities to skeptics. It's great fun to watch a Scorpio's reaction when you tell them they're astrologically known as "the sexy sign," or a Gemini when you thank them for creating the concept of multitasking.)

The second section is entitled "The Year Ahead" for each sign. Through considering the movements of the slow-moving planets (Jupiter, Saturn, Uranus, Neptune, Pluto), the eclipses, and any other outstanding celestial movements, this segment will provide you with the big picture of the year—or basically the broad strokes of what to expect, no matter who you are or where you are, collectively speaking.

The third section includes monthly forecasts, along with rewarding days and challenging days, basically a heads-up designed to alert you to potentially easy times as well as potentially tricky times.

At the end of every chapter you'll find an Action Table, providing general information about the best time to indulge in certain activities. Please note that these are only suggestions. Don't hold yourself back or rush into anything your intuition doesn't wholeheartedly agree with—and again, when in doubt, find yourself a professional.

Well, that's it. I hope that you enjoy this book, and that being aware of the astrological energies of 2021 helps you create a year full of fabulous memories!

Kim Rogers-Gallagher has written hundreds of articles and columns for magazines and online publications and has two books of her own, *Astrology for the Light Side of the Brain* and *Astrology for the Light Side of the Future*. She's a well-known speaker who's been part of the UAC faculty since 1996. Kim can be contacted at KRGPhoenix313@yahoo.com for fees regarding readings, classes, and lectures.

Ascendant Table

Your Sun Sign	6–8 am	8–10 am	10 am–Noon	Noon–2 pm	2–4 pm	4–6 pm
			Your Time of Birth			
Aries	Taurus	Gemini	Cancer	Leo	Virgo	Libra
Taurus	Gemini	Cancer	Leo	Virgo	Libra	Scorpio
Gemini	Cancer	Leo	Virgo	Libra	Scorpio	Sagittarius
Cancer	Leo	Virgo	Libra	Scorpio	Sagittarius	Capricorn
Leo	Virgo	Libra	Scorpio	Sagittarius	Capricorn	Aquarius
Virgo	Libra	Scorpio	Sagittarius	Capricorn	Aquarius	Pisces
Libra	Scorpio	Sagittarius	Capricorn	Aquarius	Pisces	Aries
Scorpio	Sagittarius	Capricorn	Aquarius	Pisces	Aries	Taurus
Sagittarius	Capricorn	Aquarius	Pisces	Aries	Taurus	Gemini
Capricorn	Aquarius	Pisces	Aries	Taurus	Gemini	Cancer
Aquarius	Pisces	Aries	Taurus	Gemini	Cancer	Leo
Pisces	Aries	Taurus	Gemini	Cancer	Leo	Virgo

Your Sun Sign	Your Time of Birth					
	6–8 pm	8–10 pm	10 pm–Midnight	Midnight–2 am	2–4 am	4–6 am
Aries	Scorpio	Sagittarius	Capricorn	Aquarius	Pisces	Aries
Taurus	Sagittarius	Capricorn	Aquarius	Pisces	Aries	Taurus
Gemini	Capricorn	Aquarius	Pisces	Aries	Taurus	Gemini
Cancer	Aquarius	Pisces	Aries	Taurus	Gemini	Cancer
Leo	Pisces	Aries	Taurus	Gemini	Cancer	Leo
Virgo	Aries	Taurus	Gemini	Cancer	Leo	Virgo
Libra	Taurus	Gemini	Cancer	Leo	Virgo	Libra
Scorpio	Gemini	Cancer	Leo	Virgo	Libra	Scorpio
Sagittarius	Cancer	Leo	Virgo	Libra	Scorpio	Sagittarius
Capricorn	Leo	Virgo	Libra	Scorpio	Sagittarius	Capricorn
Aquarius	Virgo	Libra	Scorpio	Sagittarius	Capricorn	Aquarius
Pisces	Libra	Scorpio	Sagittarius	Capricorn	Aquarius	Pisces

How to use this table: 1. Find your Sun sign in the left column.

2. Find your approximate birth time in a vertical column.

3. Line up your Sun sign and birth time to find your Ascendant.

This table will give you an approximation of your Ascendant. If you feel that the sign listed as your Ascendant is incorrect, try the one either before or after the listed sign. It is difficult to determine your exact Ascendant without a complete natal chart.

Astrology Basics

Natal astrology is done by freeze-framing the solar system at the moment of your birth, from the perspective of your birth place. This creates a circular map that looks like a pie sliced into twelve pieces. It shows where every heavenly body we're capable of seeing was located when you arrived. Basically, it's your astrological tool kit, and it can't be replicated more than once in thousands of years. This is why we astrologers are so darn insistent about the need for you to either dig your birth certificate out of that box of ancient paperwork in the back of your closet or get a copy of it from the county clerk's office where you were born. Natal astrology, as interpreted by a professional astrologer, is done exactly and precisely for you and no one else. It shows your inherent traits, talents, and challenges. Comparing the planets' current positions to their positions in your birth chart allows astrologers to help you understand the celestial trends at work in your life—and most importantly, how you can put each astrological energy to a positive, productive use.

Let's take a look at the four main components of every astrology chart.

Planets

The planets represent the needs or urges we all experience once we hop off the Evolutionary Express and take up residence inside a human body. For example, the Sun is your urge to shine and be creative, the Moon is your need to express emotions, Mercury is in charge of how you communicate and navigate, and Venus is all about who and what you love—and more importantly, how you love.

Signs

The sign a planet occupies is like a costume or uniform. It describes how you'll go about acting on your needs and urges. If you have Venus in fiery, impulsive Aries, for example, and you're attracted to a complete stranger across the room, you won't wait for them to come to you. You'll walk over and introduce yourself the second the urge strikes you. Venus in intense, sexy Scorpio, however? Well, that's a different story. In this case, you'll keep looking at a prospective beloved until they finally give in, cross the room, and beg you to explain why you've been staring at them for the past couple of hours.

Houses

The houses represent the different sides of our personalities that emerge in different life situations. For example, think of how very different you act when you're with an authority figure as opposed to how you act with a lover or when you're with your BFF.

Aspects

The aspects describe the distance from one planet to another in a geometric angle. If you were born when Mercury was 90 degrees from Jupiter, for example, this aspect is called a square. Each unique angular relationship causes the planets involved to interact differently.

Meet the Planets

The planets represent energy sources. The Sun is our source of creativity, the Moon is our emotional warehouse, and Venus describes who and what we love and are attracted to—not to mention why and how we go about getting it and keeping it.

Sun

The Sun is the head honcho in your chart. It represents your life's mission—what will give you joy, keep you young, and never fail to arouse your curiosity. Oddly enough, you weren't born knowing the qualities of the sign the Sun was in when you were born. You're here to learn the traits, talents, and characteristics of the sign you chose—and rest assured, each of the twelve is its own marvelous adventure! Since the Sun is the Big Boss, all of the other planets, including the Moon, are the Sun's staff, all there to help the boss by helping you master your particular area of expertise. Back in the day, the words from a song in a recruitment commercial struck me as a perfect way to describe our Sun's quest: "Be all that you can be. Keep on reaching. Keep on growing. Find your future." The accompanying music was energizing, robust, and exciting, full of anticipation and eagerness. When you feel enthused, motivated, and stimulated, that's your Sun letting you know you're on the right path.

Moon

If you want to understand this lovely silver orb, go outside when the Moon is nice and full, find yourself a comfy perch, sit still, and have a nice, long look at her. The Moon inspires us to dream, wish, and sigh, to reminisce, ruminate, and remember. She's the Queen of Emotions, the astrological purveyor of feelings and reactions. In your natal chart, the condition of the Moon—that is, the sign and house she's in and the connections she makes with your other planets—shows how you'll deal with whatever life tosses your way—how you'll respond, how you'll cope, and how you'll pull it all together to move on after a crisis. She's where your instincts and hunches come from, and the source of every gut feeling and premonition. The Moon describes your childhood home, your relationship with your mother, your attitude toward childbearing and children in general, and what you're looking for in a home. She shows what makes you feel safe, warm, comfy, and loved. On a daily basis, the Moon describes the collective mood.

Mercury

Next time you pass by a flower shop, take a look at the FTD logo by the door. That fellow with the wings on his head and his feet is Mercury, the ancient Messenger of the Gods. He's always been a very busy guy. Back in the day, his job was to shuttle messages back and forth between the gods and goddesses and we mere mortals—obviously, no easy feat. Nowadays, however, Mercury is even busier. With computers, cell phones, social media, and perhaps even the occasional human-to-human interaction to keep track of—well, he must be just exhausted. In a nutshell, he's the astrological energy in charge of communication, navigation, and travel, so he's still nicely represented by that winged image. He's also the guy in charge of the five senses, so no matter what you're aware of right now, be it taste, touch, sound, smell, or sight—well, that's because Mercury is bringing it to you, live. At any rate, you'll hear about him most when someone mentions that Mercury is retrograde, but even though these periods have come to be blamed for all sorts of problems, there's really no cause for alarm. Mercury turns retrograde (or, basically, appears to move backwards from our perspective here on Earth) every three months for three weeks, giving us all a chance for a do-over—and who among us has never needed one of those?

Venus

So, if it's Mercury that makes you aware of your environment, who allows you to experience all kinds of sensory sensations via the five senses? Who's in charge of your preferences in each department? That delightful task falls under the jurisdiction of the lovely lady Venus, who describes the physical experiences that are the absolute best—in your book, anyway. That goes for the music and art you find most pleasing, the food and beverages you can't get enough of, and the scents you consider the sweetest of all—including the collar of the shirt your loved one recently wore. Touch, of course, is also a sense that can be quite delightful to experience. Think of how happy your fingers are when you're stroking your pet's fur, or the delicious feel of cool bed sheets when you slip between them after an especially tough day. Venus brings all those sensations together in one wonderful package, working her magic through love of the romantic kind, most memorably experienced through intimate physical interaction with an "other." Still, your preferences in any relationship also fall under Venus's job description.

Mars

Mars turns up the heat, amps up the energy, and gets your show on the road. Whenever you hear yourself grunt, growl, or grumble—or just make any old "rrrrr" sound in general—your natal Mars has just made an appearance. Adrenaline is his business and passion is his specialty. He's the ancient God of War—a hot-headed guy who's famous for having at it with his sword first and asking questions later. In the extreme, Mars is often in the neighborhood when violent events occur, and accidents, too. He's in charge of self-assertion, aggression, and pursuit, and one glance at his heavenly appearance explains why. He's The Red Planet, after all—and just think of all the expressions about anger and passion that include references to the color red or the element of fire: "Grrr!" "Seeing red." "Hot under the collar." "All fired up." "Hot and heavy." You get the idea. Mars is your own personal warrior. He describes how you'll react when you're threatened, excited, or angry.

Jupiter

Santa Claus. Luciano Pavarotti with a great big smile on his face as he belts out an amazing aria. Your favorite uncle who drinks too much, eats too much, and laughs far too loud—yet never fails to go well above and beyond the call of duty for you when you need him. They're all perfect examples of Jupiter, the King of the Gods, the giver of all things good, and the source of extravagance, generosity, excess, and benevolence in our little corner of the Universe. He and Venus are the heavens' two most popular planets—for obvious reasons. Venus makes us feel good. Jupiter makes us feel absolutely over-the-top excellent. In Jupiter's book, if one is good, it only stands to reason that two would be better, and following that logic, ten would be just outstanding. His favorite words are "too," "many," and "much." Expansions, increases, and enlargements—or basically, just the whole concept of growth—are all his doing. Now, unbeknownst to this merry old fellow, there really is such a thing as too much of a good thing—but let's not pop his goodhearted bubble. Wherever Jupiter is in your chart, you'll be prone to go overboard, take it to the limit, and push the envelope as far as you possibly can. Sure, you might get a bit out of control every now and then, but if envelopes weren't ever pushed, we'd never know the joys of optimism, generosity, or sudden, contagious bursts of laughter.

Saturn

Jupiter expands. Saturn contracts. Jupiter encourages growth. Saturn, on the other hand, uses those rings he's so famous for to restrict growth. His favorite word is "no," but he's also very fond of "wait," "stop," and "don't even think about it." He's ultra-realistic and quite pessimistic, a cautious, careful curmudgeon who guards and protects you by not allowing you to move too quickly or act too recklessly. He insists on preparation and doesn't take kindly when we blow off responsibilities and duties. As you can imagine, Saturn is not nearly as popular as Venus and Jupiter, mainly because none of us like to be told we can't do what we want to do when we want to do it. Still, without someone who acted out his part when you were too young to know better, you might have dashed across the street without stopping to check for traffic first, and—well, you get the point. Saturn encourages frugality, moderation, thoughtfulness, and self-restraint, all necessary habits to learn if you want to play nice with the other grown-ups. He's also quite fond of building things, which necessarily starts with solid foundations and structures that are built to last.

Uranus

Say hello to Mr. Unpredictable himself, the heavens' wild card—to say the very least. He's the kind of guy who claims responsibility for lightning strikes, be they literal or symbolic. Winning the lottery, love at first sight, accidents, and anything seemingly coincidental that strikes you as oddly well-timed are all examples of Uranus's handiwork. He's a rebellious, headstrong energy, so wherever he is in your chart, you'll be defiant, headstrong, and quite unwilling to play by the rules, which he thinks of as merely annoying suggestions that far too many humans adhere to. Uranus is here to inspire you to be yourself—exactly as you are, with no explanations and no apologies whatsoever. He motivates you to develop qualities such as independence, ingenuity, and individuality—and with this guy in the neighborhood, if anyone or anything gets in the way, you'll 86 them. Period. Buh-bye now. The good news is that when you allow this freedom-loving energy to guide you, you discover something new and exciting about yourself on a daily basis—at least. The tough but entirely doable part is keeping him reined in tightly enough to earn your daily bread and form lasting relationships with like-minded others.

Neptune

Neptune is the uncontested Mistress of Disguise and Illusion in the solar system, beautifully evidenced by the fact that this ultra-feminine energy has been masquerading as a male god for as long as gods and goddesses have been around. Just take a look at the qualities she bestows: compassion, spirituality, intuition, wistfulness, and nostalgia. Basically, whenever your subconscious whispers, it's in Neptune's voice. She activates your antennae and sends you subtle, invisible, and yet highly powerful messages about everyone you cross paths with, no matter how fleeting the encounter. I often picture her as Glinda the Good Witch from *The Wizard of Oz*, who rode around in a pink bubble, singing happy little songs and casting wonderful, helpful spells. Think "enchantment"—oh, and "glamour," too, which, by the way, was the old-time term for a magical spell cast upon someone to change their appearance. Nowadays, glamour is often thought of as a rather idealized and often artificial type of beauty brought about by cosmetics and airbrushing, but Neptune is still in charge, and her magic still works. When this energy is wrongfully used, deceptions, delusions and fraud can result—and since she's so fond of ditching reality, it's easy to become a bit too fond of escape hatches like drugs and alcohol. Still, Neptune inspires romance, nostalgia, and sentimentality, and she's quite fond of dreams and fantasies, too—and what would life be like without all of that?

Pluto

Picture all the gods and goddesses in the heavens above us living happily in a huge mansion in the clouds. Then imagine that Pluto's place is at the bottom of the cellar stairs, and on the cellar door (which is in the kitchen, of course) a sign reads "Keep out. Working on Darwin Awards." That's where Pluto would live—and that's the attitude he'd have. He's in charge of unseen cycles—life, death, and rebirth. Obviously, he's not an emotional kind of guy. Whatever Pluto initiates really has to happen. He's dark, deep, and mysterious—and inevitable. So yes, Darth Vader does come to mind, if for no other reason than because of James Earl Jones's amazing, compelling voice. Still, this intense, penetrating, and oh-so-thorough energy has a lot more to offer. Pluto's in charge of all those categories we humans aren't fond of—like death and decay, for example—but on the less drastic side, he also inspires recycling, repurposing, and reusing. In your chart, Pluto represents a place where you'll be ready to go big or go home, where investing all or nothing is a given. When a crisis comes up—when you need to be totally committed and totally authentic to who you really are to get through it—that's when you'll meet your Pluto. Power struggles and mind games, however—well, you can also expect those pesky types of things wherever Pluto is located.

A Word about Retrogrades

"Retrograde" sounds like a bad thing, but I'm here to tell you that it isn't. In a nutshell, retrograde means that from our perspective here on Earth, a planet appears to be moving in reverse. Of course, planets don't ever actually back up, but the energy of retrograde planets is often held back, delayed, or hindered in some way. For example, when Mercury—the ruler of communication and navigation—appears to be retrograde, it's tough to get from point A to point B without a snafu, and it's equally hard to get a straight answer. Things just don't seem to go as planned. But it only makes sense. Since Mercury is the planet in charge of conversation and movement, when he's moving backward—well, imagine driving a car that only had reverse. Yep. It wouldn't be easy. Still, if that's all you had to work with, you'd eventually find a way to get where you wanted to go. That's how all retrograde energies work. If you have retrograde planets in your natal chart, don't rush them. These energies may need a bit more time to function well for you than other natal planets, but if you're patient, talk about having an edge! You'll know these planets inside and out. On a collective basis, think of the time when a planet moves retrograde as a chance for a celestial do-over.

Signs of the Zodiac

The sign a planet is "wearing" really says it all. It's the costume an actor wears that helps them act out the role they're playing. It's the style, manner, or approach you'll use in each life department—whether you're being creative on a canvas, gushing over a new lover, or applying for a management position. Each of the signs belongs to an element, a quality, and a gender, as follows.

Elements

The four elements—fire, earth, air, and water—describe a sign's aims. Fire signs are spiritual, impulsive energies. Earth signs are tightly connected to the material plane. Air signs are cerebral, intellectual creatures, and water signs rule the emotional side of life.

Qualities

The three qualities—cardinal, fixed, and mutable—describe a sign's energy. Cardinal signs are tailor-made for beginnings. Fixed energies are solid, just as they sound, and are quite determined to finish what they start. Mutable energies are flexible and accommodating but can also be scattered or unstable.

Genders

The genders—masculine and feminine—describe whether the energy attracts (feminine) or pursues (masculine) what it wants.

The Twelve Signs

Here's a quick rundown of the twelve zodiac signs.

Aries

Aries planets are hotheads. They're built from go-getter cardinal energy and fast-acting fire. Needless to say, Aries energy is impatient, energetic, and oh-so-willing to try anything once.

Taurus

Taurus planets are aptly represented by the symbol of the bull. They're earth creatures, very tightly connected to the material plane, and fixed—which means they're pretty much immovable when they don't want to act.

Sequence	Sign	Glyph	Ruling Planet	Symbol
1	Aries	♈	Mars	Ram
2	Taurus	♉	Venus	Bull
3	Gemini	♊	Mercury	Twins
4	Cancer	♋	Moon	Crab
5	Leo	♌	Sun	Lion
6	Virgo	♍	Mercury	Virgin
7	Libra	♎	Venus	Scales
8	Scorpio	♏	Pluto	Scorpion
9	Sagittarius	♐	Jupiter	Archer
10	Capricorn	♑	Saturn	Goat
11	Aquarius	♒	Uranus	Water Bearer
12	Pisces	♓	Neptune	Fish

Gemini

As an intellectual air sign that's mutable and interested in anything new, Gemini energy is eternally curious—and quite easily distracted. Gemini planets live in the moment and are expert multitaskers.

Cancer

Cancer is a water sign that runs on its emotions, and since it's also part of the cardinal family, it's packed with the kind of start-up energy that's perfect for raising a family and building a home.

Leo

This determined, fixed sign is part of the fire family. As fires go, think of Leo planets as bonfires of energy—and just try to tear your eyes away. Leo's symbol is the lion, and it's no accident. Leo planets care very much about their familial pride—and about their personal pride.

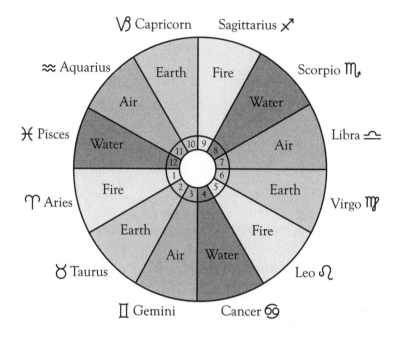

Virgo

Virgo is mutable and therefore easily able to switch channels when necessary. It's part of the earth family and connected to the material world (like Taurus). Virgo energy loves to work, organize, and sort, but most of all, to fix what's broken.

Libra

This communicative air sign runs on high. It's cardinal, so when it comes to making connections, Libra is second to none. Libra planets are people pleasers and the honorary cruise directors of the zodiac, and are as charming and accommodating as the day is long.

Scorpio

Scorpio is of the water element and a highly emotional creature. Scorpio energy is fixed, too, so feelings are tough to shake and obsessions are easy to come by. Planets in this sign are devoted and determined and can be absolutely relentless.

Sagittarius

Sagittarius has all the fire of Aries and Leo but, due to its mutable nature, tends to be distracted, spreading its energy among projects and interests. Think of Sagittarius energy as a series of red-hot brushfires, firing up and dying down and firing up again in a new location.

Capricorn

As the third earth sign, Capricorn is concerned with reality and practicality, complete with all the rules and regulations it takes to build and maintain a life here on Planet Number Three. Capricorn energy takes charge and assumes responsibility quite easily.

Aquarius

The last of the three communicative air signs, Aquarius prefers mingling and interacting with a group via friendships. Freedom-loving Aquarius energy won't be restricted—not for long, anyway—and is willing to return the favor, in any and all relationships.

Pisces

Watery Pisces runs on its emotions—and even more so on its intuition, which is second to none. This mutable, flexible sign is aptly represented by the constant fluctuating movements of its symbol, the two fish.

Aspects

Astrological aspects describe the relationships between planets and important points in a horoscope chart. Basically, they're the mathematical angles that measure the distance between two or more planets. Planets in square aspect are 90 degrees apart, planets in opposition are 180 degrees apart, and so forth. Each of these aspect relationships seems to link energies in a very different way. For example, if two planets are in square aspect, think of what you know about "squaring off," and you'll understand exactly how they're interacting. Think of aspects as a way of describing the type of conversation going on between celestial bodies.

Here's a brief description of the five major aspects.

Conjunction

When two planets are within a few degrees of each other, they're joined at the hip. The conjunction is often called the aspect of "fusion," since the energies involved always act together.

Sextile

Planets in sextile are linked by a 60-degree angle, creating an exciting, stimulating astrological "conversation." These planets encourage, arouse, and excite each other.

Square

The square aspect is created by linking energies in a 90-degree angle—which tends to be testy and sometimes irritating but always action-oriented.

Trine

The trine is the "lazy" aspect. When planets are in this 120-degree angle, they get along so well that they often aren't motivated to do much. Trines make things easy—too easy, at times—but they're also known for being quite lucky.

Opposition

Oppositions exist between planets that are literally opposite one another. Think about seesaws and playing tug-of-war, and you'll understand how these energies get along. Sure, it can be a power struggle at times, but balance is the key.

2021 at a Glance

Meet the new kids on the block in the form of a sign change for a couple of outer planets! Aquarius gets star billing this time around and gets to focus on budding plans, fruitful enterprises, and limiting circumstances that deserve a closer look. Communication, take a deep bow! A new phase dawns on the horizon with expansive Jupiter heralding optimistic vibes in the gregarious sign of Aquarius all year. Jupiter shares the spotlight for part of 2021 with Saturn at the onset of the planet of restriction's two-and-a-half year trek through Aquarius. Jupiter wastes no time moving rapidly through Aquarius before taking on the very different, dreamy energy of Pisces on May 13. Within five weeks of playfully sashaying to this mystical beat, Jupiter turns retrograde in motion on June 20 and heads back into Aquarius on July 28, going direct on October 18 and leaving us with only a teaser taste of what life will be like when this planet returns to Pisces on December 28.

News flash! Transiting Uranus in Taurus is another outer planet still in the early degrees of the sign as we enter a year of eye-opening revelations in major life areas, possibly brought on by the presence of Uranus aiming a few lightning bolts at key areas depending on where the planet of chaos is picking up steam in your birth chart and where natal Uranus resides there. Be prepared for the unexpected, especially if Taurus and other fixed signs are prominent in your chart. In November the third eclipse of 2021 will occur in Taurus in that same area of your life, possibly leading to a shakeup of the status quo and an opportunity to regroup and stabilize plans.

Neptune continues its extensive trip in Pisces that began in 2011, coloring the landscape with bursts of spiritual insight and concern for humanity while simultaneously moving through the fog and confusion that rise up when conflicting information comes to light and sends mixed signals throughout the universe and on an individual level. Those of you with Pisces planets at 18–23 degrees will feel this influence the most. Neptune in this mutable sign will be interacting with three of this year's four eclipses, two in Sagittarius and one in Gemini, sending challenging messages on an emotional level, while the Taurus eclipse, even with its mild volatility, brings a practical side to problem-solving.

Still hanging on and edging its way toward completing its full cycle in the sign of Capricorn is Pluto, the only holdover from the intense Capricorn energy of 2020. No doubt you are used to this planet's slow and insidious presence in the personally highlighted department of life in your birth chart by now. Do you have any late-degree Capricorn planets or planets in the other cardinal signs (Aries, Cancer, and Libra) that may receive a nudge from the hard aspects coming from this Pluto transit? Where's the baggage? What are you releasing that has outlived its usefulness and could benefit from a transformation of attitude, ideas, and solutions? Think of the inner freedom you'll experience when you let go of conditions that restrict the positive flow of energy you desire. Bask in the glow of new awareness as you embrace 2021 and internalize your vision of a better, more fulfilled you.

2021 SUN SIGN BOOK

Forecasts by
Alice DeVille

Aries

The Ram
March 20 to April 19

♈

Element: Fire	Glyph: Ram's head
Quality: Cardinal	Anatomy: Head, face, throat
Polarity: Yang/masculine	Colors: Red, white
Planetary Ruler: Mars	Animal: Ram
Meditation: I build on my strengths	Myths/Legends: Artemis, Jason and the Golden Fleece
Gemstone: Diamond	House: First
Power Stones: Bloodstone, carnelian, ruby	Opposite Sign: Libra
	Flower: Geranium
Key Phrase: I am	Keyword: Initiative

The Aries Personality

Strengths, Talents, and the Creative Spark

Hats off to high-action Aries! Observers say you walk with your head forward and cut a rapid path to your destination. Initiative is your middle name and you don't need a crank to get you going. You're exactly where you want to be as the leader of the zodiac, showing the way and getting there first. Ideas emerge while your inventive mind runs with them, serving up a plan and taking charge of the big picture while saving the implementation details for others.

Mars is your energetic ruler. You don't stop for a rock in the road, and you instantly find a way around barriers. That's because you're impatient and a fast driver, even when it makes no sense to take an unnecessary risk. Impulsiveness is part of your mojo. Others in your circle clean up messes and run interference when you hit a snag. Sometimes verbal messages you deliver startle the recipients, forcing you to double back to do damage control. Likewise, you make snap judgments without processing details, only to have to change your perspective down the road and taking a hit on quality control.

You bubble over with enthusiasm, and few can match the pep talks you give to engage others in your plans. Innovation is your forte. Inventing the future excites you and stimulates your achievement-oriented mindset. As long as the goal holds your interest, you gravitate toward a win and play cheerleader to colleagues. Your fire-sign drive thrives on nonstop action. When you get bored, you're ready for a new beginning.

Intimacy and Personal Relationships

Attraction means the world to you, starting with the picture you present to the world. Your inner warmth longs to find a special someone to shower with your gifts of devotion and passion. Ideally your partner shares a sense of adventure and is not afraid to venture into new territory. As one who likes to drive, you think nothing of traveling a hundred miles with a willing partner for a cup of coffee in a town that you've never visited before to see the highlights and return with something checked off your bucket list. In your maverick mode you may even set off on this type of jaunt at midnight to avoid as much road traffic as possible and get there without speeding, although you have been known to press the pedal hard.

When you find someone to cherish, you pursue the relationship ardently and are faithful and romantic toward your loved one. Although you have a very strong sense of identity, you elevate the sacredness of partnerships and often have long-lasting marriages. You long to be admired by the object of your affection and enjoy the discovery of learning where you have strong similarities or compatible outlooks. Learning to share success with your partner goes a long way in strengthening the relationship. If you get hurt or someone comes between you and your mate, you walk away wounded and rarely come back for more, no matter what the circumstances.

Values and Resources

You were born ready and like to get the show on the road when tackling assignments. Many Aries have phenomenal mechanical abilities. Brilliant ideas lead to a plan of action and development of a timeline that lets you manage the steps to progress. If too much time elapses between start and finish, you lose steam. Sharing the limelight does not come easily to you. Those you admit into your inner circle have to show a willingness to take risks and a commitment to a successful outcome. Your MO is to plunge right in and worry about the consequences later. If a team member makes you wait too long for answers, you get bored and start rattling cages for action. That's because you want a timely wrap-up of the task or project so you can move on to the next opportunity to make a name for yourself. Colleagues complain that you show one-upmanship and want to take over the task. As a reluctant delegator, you don't always follow through with those you leave in charge of the details, and may nitpick the work habits of team members rather than ask questions. Although your temper flares up, you quickly detach from arguments and don't hold grudges.

Blind Spots and Blockages

You often move into spontaneous, passionate relationships that you fail to assess for longevity. You feel the pangs of love at first sight and within a few months decide that you don't know this partner at all. That's because you haven't figured out if you like the person as a friend, let alone a permanent partner. Some of you move into hasty marriages early on in life, only to divorce and take the plunge again. If you don't give the earlier romance a chance to cool off, you will be right back in the same rut.

Professional connections generate wounds when you make decisions quickly yet leave others wondering whether you know what you want. Those on your team can't keep up with your constant shifts in thinking. Don't be shocked if staff members start keeping notes after you reject the results of their work. You changed your mind and didn't tell them. If you're the boss, it's not unusual for staff to bail for greener pastures.

Goals and Success

As the zodiac's initiator, you eagerly accept your mission to set meaningful goals and develop a strategy for seeing them through to completion. You're an explorer type and like to study new concepts formally through coursework or with on-the-job training when you are looking for a new avenue of expression. Creative ideas are your jam, and you look for opportunities to sell their merits to those in charge in the work arena and to family and friends. Few can top your enthusiasm to describe the big picture while sharing your vision with those who benefit from the rewards. Many describe you as fearless in your quest to conquer new fields of action and identify challenges that stand in the way of success. You know you're going to emerge the victor with a sure-fire plan and a team of experts that clear a path for a new beginning. People who know you look to you for inspiration and ideas. With your quick-thinking style, you explore countless possibilities and seldom disappoint your team.

Aries Keywords for 2021
Expansion, expression, exuberance

The Year Ahead for Aries

As you plunge enthusiastically into 2021, do you realize how free you are to express your individuality through your actions, work, and the passion you generate for creative ideas? Get moving! That's what you do best—especially since you took some time last year to bask in the watery daydreams of Neptune in your solar twelfth house of self-reflection. You took a well-deserved sabbatical from the last hurrah of the challenging activity of Saturn in Capricorn in your solar tenth house of career, ambition, and status in life. Start processing any remnants of unfinished business while you eagerly join forces with the compatible energies of both Jupiter and Saturn in Aquarius in your solar eleventh house of associates, friendships, goals, and organizations.

Networking opportunities abound, allowing you to pick and choose among contacts you know and new connections you want to cultivate. Meet, greet, and speak to kindred spirits and eager beavers in search of a new enterprise. Courage becomes you as you sell your skills and services to collaborators, employers, and entrepreneurs. You may be motivating others to acknowledge that meaningful change is an inside job and starts on the inside as it works its way to the arena of activity. This is YOU, INC. showing the way to success. Acknowledge your power and 2021 may be the year when your personal style surges to the top and changes the game beyond your wildest dreams.

Jupiter

Having just survived a challenging passage of Jupiter through your solar tenth house of career last year, you saw how rewards, bonuses, and visibility raised your profile. The path to success was not easy, with rocks in the road as you zigzagged in unanticipated directions. Authority figures recognized your hard work and expertise and your income increased, with the promise of more to come. But your workload ate up so much of your time that you knew by the end of 2020 you wanted a less taxing and more rewarding work and family life.

Enter Jupiter in Aquarius in a shift into your solar eleventh house of plans, goals, associations, and friendships. Networking pays off as you disengage from groups with old or stale ideas and seek organizations with compatible philosophies. Say yes to what truly motivates you and speaks to your soul. If you've ever wanted to lead a group, your connections to new enterprises with a fresh perspective compete for your talent. The money you need to expand educational pursuits appears, as do resources for acquiring work-related products, equipment, and intellectual property. Politics may be a factor for some of you as you hop on the bandwagon of a favorite candidate or run for office in your local district. Budding astrologers among you expand your interest in the field or add these planetary experts to your network for go-to advice and counsel. Implementing humanitarian projects motivates you to do more good in the community and grow personally from the realization that your commitment makes a difference in the world. An added benefit of this transit is a busy social life, with multiple invitations to mix and mingle with group members. Set your aspirations high and enjoy the new affiliations and the pleasure they bring to your emerging vision.

Saturn

Aries, you have a chance this year to sort out your attitude toward the resources related to your job, career goals, and plans for advancement. You will discover just how much your workplace authorities value your ideas and suggestions and how much they are willing to invest in your future. Near the very end of 2020, Saturn moved into Aquarius and your solar eleventh house of organizations, friendships, cherished wishes, and social movements. Review any choices under consideration to maximize your options. Saturn highlights the growth pattern you're leaning toward and helps you compare benefits with the status quo. Although Saturn can tax you mentally with the abundance of available information, you'll be glad you examined the data before committing to a new venture. Responsibilities shift under this transit and test your patience and energy. Those of you born between March 21 and April 3 will be most affected by this Saturn transit during 2021.

Quite often, aspects of discontent lurk in the eleventh house of wishes, making you restless and looking for a shift in dynamics. Saturn transiting here creates conditions that make you take a hard look at what needs to change. What have you discovered about your priorities? Have you set new ones that align with your goals? If there is construction, purchase of new electronic equipment, or a reorganization in your future, you'll be focusing your attention on details and forming or working on a team that implements plans. Those of you in charge of hiring human capital may find your already filled calendar accommodating appointments for highly talented individuals in search of a piece of the action. You'll have success with collaboration this year, so assess the strengths of members and assign tasks accordingly. Those of you on the hunt for replacement vehicles find bargains and favorable loan terms during this cycle. Avoid making your purchase during Saturn's retrograde period from May 23 to October 10. Make your wish list or develop a vision board at the beginning of the year and see how much you achieve by year's end.

Uranus

The solar second house of earned income, financial outlook, resources, development, and values gets a workout during this long passage of Uranus in Taurus. While examining the mundane facets of this transit, with its attachment to the material world, you have opportunities to make spiritual progress as you discard old ideas about accumulating and spending money. Uranus delivers a shock to your system when you're least prepared. That's right! Chaos and angst reign supreme when you forget to breathe. You're not supposed to be working 24/7 creating discord at a frenetic pace when personal self-worth resonates much more objectively with a balanced approach to productivity. Few in your work environment appreciate a relentless dictator who shows irritation at questions related to assignments, frowns on breaks to recharge batteries, or fusses over leave-taking when deadlines loom. Savvy management builds them into the timeline, and work meshes seamlessly while employees enjoy valuable downtime. Instead of creating burnout conditions, build in time for developing new skills, studying innovative procedures, and enrolling in courses that offer a new perspective. Integrate what you learn and share the insights. Those of you born between March 26 and April 4 will be most affected by Uranus this year.

Neptune

If you feel like you've had your head in the fog for a while now, you're correct. Transiting Neptune in Pisces has been occupying your solar twelfth house of atonement, charity, confinement, hospital visits, meditation, mystical outlook, spiritual growth, and secret enemies. Neptune takes many years to move through a house, advancing only 4–5 degrees a year. Neptune moved into Pisces in April 2011, as if in response to your need for a break from high-pressure undertakings—not that you ever slow down completely. Several incidents crept into your life these last few years, creating a reason to set aside some healing time to address what ails you on the physical and mental planes. Among the aggravations you've dealt with are rejection of your ideas by and conflicts with people from your past or current relationships, both professional and personal. You want out but don't know how to get there. Take time to address these vague feelings and determine a plan of action to reduce the tension. Some Aries are taking the time to heal from physical ailments, surgery, and stressful mental health conditions. Secrets are part of this transit, and their disclosure comes out of the blue, demanding discussion and action. A bonus of this period is a stepped-up awakening of your subconscious mind and the gift of intuition. You may wake up one day and simply know the next course of action to take to redirect your life. Those of you born between April 7 and 14 will see the most Neptunian action during 2021. Celebrate enthusiastically!

Pluto

The long passage of Pluto in Capricorn ambles along slowly and insidiously through your solar tenth house of aspirations, career, people in charge, recognition, and the status quo. Those who know you have probably noticed that you have undergone an attitude transformation since Pluto first landed in this department of your life with a teaser debut back in January 2008, challenging you to look more closely at what you want to pursue on your path of attainment. Late in the last decade, your tenth-house ride with Pluto had some company in the form of Saturn, Jupiter, and eclipses in Capricorn in this house. Your comfort zone was clearly out of whack. Many of you left your job, or will do so soon or retire. First, you glimpsed sparks of ideas and perhaps a vision of meaningful goals, although Pluto keeps toying with your self-confidence and dredging up a fear of the unknown. Pluto creeps around cautiously, reminding you that you have to take an inventory of what you already have and then discard what no longer has meaning to make room for your true purpose. You have to do this without leaving any baggage behind. Be aware that Pluto sends in the karma cleaners to make sure you do a clean sweep of toxic energy. Growth means shedding unrealistic goals, letting go of fear that comes with taking the next steps, and embracing the new responsibility by demonstrating high standards of achievement. Fulfillment is your rite of passage to a happy, healthy life—enjoy it.

How Will This Year's Eclipses Affect You?

In 2021, a total of four eclipses will occur. There will be two Lunar Eclipses and two Solar Eclipses, creating intense periods that often begin to manifest a few months before their actual dates. Eclipses unfold in cycles involving all twelve signs of the zodiac, and usually occur in pairs about two weeks apart. Think of eclipses as opportunities to release old patterns and conditions that have outlived their usefulness. Have no fear of them, since they can bring you unexpected surprises and windfalls. The closer an eclipse is to a degree or point in your chart, the greater its importance in your life. Those of you born with a planet at the same degree as an eclipse are likely to see a high level of activity in the house where the eclipse occurs.

The first Lunar Eclipse of the year occurs on May 26 in Sagittarius in your solar ninth house of diverse cultures, foreigners, the higher mind, philosophy, journalism, in-laws, publishing, and long-distance travel. An eclipse here may open up the possibility for advanced educational pursuits, job details or transfers to a different location, travel to the destination of your dreams, visits from in-laws, contracts with those who publish your written material, and interactions with doctors, lawyers, and politicians.

The second eclipse of the year is a Solar Eclipse that takes place on June 10 in Gemini in your solar third house of communication. Cousins, neighbors, and siblings may step up the frequency of exchanging text messages, emails, and phone calls. You may also examine the way your mind is working to resolve anxiety and anger issues. Situations come up that demand solid decision-making on your part. A number of you are in the market to purchase electronic equipment or enter into contracts for services that are personal or job-related. Increased local travel is also a possibility—going back and forth to new work locations, taking classes, visiting relatives, or attending neighborhood meetings.

On November 19, the second Lunar Eclipse of 2021 falls in Taurus and your solar second house, where it hangs out with transiting Uranus in Taurus and highlights income, financial plans, expenditures, and values. Focus your attention on unexpected developments and enjoy the benefits of surprise windfalls.

The final Solar Eclipse of 2021 takes place on December 4 in Sagittarius in your solar ninth house of higher education, religion, foreign countries, medical and legal professionals, interactions with in-laws, and long-distance travel or moves. Decisions you pondered in May are ready for action. If a new job is a possibility, do your research and grab the brass ring. Credentials you've earned recently make you highly competitive for advancement. Those of you applying for graduate school find doors opening and learn more about your chosen field and options for future studies. This year is your opportunity to expand your circle of contacts and find success in a new location.

Aries | January

Overall Theme

The early days of the month begin on an optimistic and celebratory note for you with Jupiter and Saturn in Aquarius in your solar eleventh house helping you expand your goals. An easy connection between the Moon and Venus adds rapport and sociability to the mix. Keep the momentum going by expressing warmth, entertaining friends, and showing appreciation for the little things in life.

Relationships

Connections you share with others show the promise of growth. Avoid intimacy with people in your workplace. With Neptune transiting your solar twelfth house, you could find yourself in an awkward situation or the subject of gossip. Romance blossoms for those desirous of a passionate relationship. With expansion taking place in your solar eleventh house of groups, accept invitations to attend fundraisers or events.

Success and Money

A nice boost from Jupiter sends solid vibes to your financial picture if you were born in the early part of your sign. Career aspects are positive from the 1st through the 19th with planets transiting your tenth house of ambition. Clear thinking aids in goal setting. Network successfully during the first half of the month. The New Moon conjunct Pluto in your solar tenth house creates momentum through serious opportunities for advancement.

Pitfalls and Potential Problems

Uranus may jolt you back to reality on the 14th when it makes an abrupt station in your solar second house of assets. Look at finances carefully. Stay away from signing important documents when Mercury goes retrograde late this month.

Rewarding Days

1, 2, 9, 13

Challenging Days

5, 14, 28, 30

Aries | February

Overall Theme

The romantic overtones in your circle get a boost whether you are in a committed relationship or are single and looking for a partner, especially through February 25. Transiting Aquarius planets are generally compatible with your Sun sign and offer a respite from boredom through group interaction while they converge in your solar eleventh house. Be on the lookout for unplanned expenses or unsettling investment news with Uranus transiting your solar second house of money.

Relationships

Keep Valentine's Day plans low-key and romantic; avoid over-the-top celebrations that could lead to arguments involving expensive purchases. Feelings are very sensitive on February 23 and 24. Those of you born between March 26 and 28 examine old emotional wounds, searching for answers, addressing where you're stuck, and learning to let go of the past.

Success and Money

Tread lightly regarding financial matters in the early part of the month. Make no decisions until you have a chance to get all the facts you need. Arguments arise over existing debt or impulsive spending. A salary dispute is possible late in the month after disappointment leaves you feeling unappreciated. Look at all the angles first before sitting down for a discussion. Optimism returns after February 21.

Pitfalls and Potential Problems

The abundance of air-sign energy puts you in a communicative mood. You have lots to say and want to share news, put out feelers, apply for a new assignment, or make purchases that you postponed while Mercury was retrograde. Resist the urge to move too quickly by waiting until after March 14. In the meantime, do your homework, gather facts, and set up favorable times for appointments for a successful payoff.

Rewarding Days

6, 11, 15

Challenging Days

4, 21, 24, 27

Aries | March

Overall Theme

Mystical memories settle over the mental landscape of your solar twelfth house, sparking an interest in metaphysical topics. You could seem more psychic than usual or be drawn to those who are. Head for the bookstore, sign up for a workshop, or attend an appealing lecture. The first few weeks of the month may be your only downtime.

Relationships

Work collaborators seem unusually needy or sensitive. Of course that could be because you don't mince words when you discover that unfolding situations call for criticism or blunt analysis. Be sure you don't take your problems home with you or the gloom may spread to a cherished relationship, especially around the 30th. Watch for flare-ups with partners at the Full Moon in your solar seventh house on the 28th. A little hand-holding goes a long way in soothing feelings.

Success and Money

Look to the positive vibes on March 1 when the Moon makes beautiful music with Mercury and Jupiter. You'll see business deals that show merit, as well as the start of engaging friendships or personal relationships. A referral may sweeten the deal for a long-desired purchase or travel plans. March 3 is a high-action day with mixed results; make no commitments until you do your homework.

Pitfalls and Potential Problems

Avoid arguments on the 4th when the Moon is in hard aspect to Mars in your solar third house of communication. It's not the best day to schedule important meetings, as feelings run high and ownership of concepts is particularly sensitive to criticism.

Rewarding Days

1, 13, 20, 25

Challenging Days

4, 7, 21, 28

Aries | April

Overall Theme

This month puts you in a celebratory mood, with the New Moon on the 11th in your birthday sign and holidays that lead to reunions, visits, travel, and a break from routines. You could use a change of venue and some recreation after a relentless go at meeting first-quarter deadlines. The new you may be sporting a streamlined body and a few toys, such as a new car, smartphone, or electronic whole-house monitors.

Relationships

Work associates get testy on the 4th over differences of opinion or operating style. Plan presentations carefully. Intimate partners seem touchy-feely on the 18th and 19th and won't be in the mood for either honey talk or money talk until the lunar aspect to Pluto passes. Romantic prospects are stronger on the 2nd, 21st, and 29th. Make dating plans or book a getaway.

Success and Money

The right words come to you, especially from the 5th through the 19th, even if some of them carry contentious connotations. You have the energy to settle differences fairly. Make your pitch to the boss on the 6th or 7th, and be sure to address teamwork in your delivery. Acknowledge stellar performances.

Pitfalls and Potential Problems

What's tempting you to spend money? Take a close look at your debt load and savings to assess viability. Jupiter in your solar eleventh house in hard aspect to the transiting Moon in your solar eighth house brings temptation on the 28th. The 24th relates to issues that crop up in your daily environment, probably your home base.

Rewarding Days

6, 7, 11, 21

Challenging Days

14, 19, 24, 28

Aries | May

Overall Theme

The month starts out with several planets in Taurus—the Sun, Mercury, Venus, and Uranus—adding a touch of pragmatism to the mix and indicating a need for security in financial and romantic matters. The New Moon in Taurus on the 11th in your solar second house calls for comparing costs related to the purchase of household goods or educational venues. Decision-making is strong on the 4th, with an emphasis on manifesting meaningful goals.

Relationships

An appreciation for affection and honest communication strengthens partnership bonds and opens the door for exploring a greater variety of entertainment or recreational pursuits. Talking things out over differences helps, as does sharing views and listening carefully to another's point of view.

Success and Money

Goals get a boost and are under discussion behind the scenes, waiting until the time is right for action. When Mercury moves into Gemini on the 3rd, momentum picks up, something you prefer over dragging your feet and waiting for other minds to catch up with yours. The messenger planet goes retrograde on the 29th for three weeks. Be sure you wait to execute plans or make pending purchases until after June 22.

Pitfalls and Potential Problems

The preponderance of fixed planets in Aquarius in your solar eleventh house and the abundant Taurus planets in your solar second house clash this month, allowing for little wiggle room. Steam builds up and something's gotta give. Just make sure it's not on the day of the first Lunar Eclipse of 2021 in Sagittarius, which occurs on the 26th in your solar ninth house of travel.

Rewarding Days

4, 8, 17, 27

Challenging Days

2, 11, 23, 26

Aries | June

Overall Theme

Communication, coursework, mental outlook, and local travel occupy your time. Enjoy community activities with loved ones and take the time to finalize summer vacation plans. You'll have plenty on your mind this month with a Solar Eclipse in your solar third house on the 10th. Family news takes you by surprise. Relatives put their heads together to share news, discuss problems, and agree on solutions.

Relationships

Messages, phone calls, and visits from cousins, siblings, and neighbors increase this month. Your listening skills get a workout and prove therapeutic for the speaker. Saturn aspects to the Moon favor bookkeeping and financial discussions with family on the 4th. Avoid arguments or tense exchanges on the 5th when the Moon is in hard aspect to Mars. Take a long walk and don't forget to breathe.

Success and Money

Although you have your eye on a new vehicle, postpone the purchase for now. Mercury is retrograde through the 22nd. Research models and compare options. July 7 and 8 may be more advantageous. Service or rental contracts come up for review. You could be dealing with price increases for insurance, cable, and leases. Study clauses and negotiate new terms. Jupiter goes retrograde in Pisces on the 20th.

Pitfalls and Potential Problems

Household disagreements flare between the 1st and the 11th, involving family members or roommates. Sore feelings prevail on the 12th and 13th. Host a meal or gathering. Question information that sounds too good to be true. Neptune aspects with the Moon on the 23rd have confusing undertones. Wait until the weekend to engage in serious discussions.

Rewarding Days

1, 4, 10, 15

Challenging Days

5, 12, 20, 24

Aries | July

Overall Theme

Your family plans may include reunions, parties, vacation ventures, and leisure time this month. If you travel, be sure your arrangements are complete and verified early in the month to avoid confusion. Water sports, swimming, and fishing trips seem like attractive options. If you stay home, why not host a fish fry or holiday barbecue? Participate in Fourth of July celebrations for extra holiday enjoyment and a deeply felt show of patriotism.

Relationships

Planets land in your solar fourth house this month, accentuating visits from family members, intense activity at home base, and household projects. The gardeners among you harvest succulent summer crops such as juicy tomatoes, melons, and corn. Offer summer desserts that feature fruit pies, tarts, shortcakes, and plenty of ice cream to keep everyone cool and happy.

Success and Money

Bonus money is well spent on new furniture and landscaping. Do your homework and shop on July 9. Take on kitchen remodeling projects after Mercury goes into Cancer on July 11. Bankers are more likely to approve your construction or home equity loans. Don't schedule meetings with contractors on the 17th or the 25th to avoid mistakes in measurements and disagreements over building materials.

Pitfalls and Potential Problems

The Moon is in hard aspect to Mars and is conjunct retrograde Neptune on the 27th. You could be so mesmerized by the glamor and glitz of a project proposal that you don't notice the price escalations or add-ons that make your goal more expensive. Be on the lookout for interest rate changes or loan terms that are questionable. Sensitive feelings get in the way of objectivity on the 27th.

Rewarding Days

2, 7, 9, 20

Challenging Days

5, 17, 25, 27

Aries | August

Overall Theme

You deserve a break from routine and the serious side of life. Head for the wide-open spaces, the mountains, or your favorite beach resort this month with the Sun shining in your solar fifth house of children, leisure, amusements, sports, and romance. You have great instincts for booking adventurous vacations that fulfill the wishes of family and friends.

Relationships

Your social life sparkles now. If you're single, step out for fun and you may meet "the one." Get engaged if you're taking an existing relationship up a notch. Parents among you get extra bonding time with children and a chance for one-on-one fun with each child. Wow your partner with a surprise trip, dinner, or entertainment venue. The 18th shows promising vibes for starting foreign travel; delays occur on the 19th when Uranus makes a station in Taurus.

Success and Money

The second Full Moon in Aquarius within a month occurs on the 22nd, conjunct retrograde Jupiter in Aquarius. Earlier discussions of raises and bonuses could be put on hold. Don't let it get you down though, as it could be a signal to make a change. If your entrepreneurial spirit is running hot, now would be a good time to pursue independent contracting or venture into a new career market.

Pitfalls and Potential Problems

Several planets are retrograde right now. Plans need careful review, as do important papers before coming to an agreement. Take security seriously and shred rather than toss old documents. Avoid challenges and unnecessary risks on the 1st. Keep tabs on joint funds and expenditures around the 15th, and don't obligate yourself for big-ticket items on the 29th.

Rewarding Days

8, 18, 25, 30

Challenging Days

1, 15, 22, 29

Aries | September

Overall Theme

Now that your vacation is over and your superior organizational energy emerges, you're ready to move full steam ahead to tackle the lists you made before you took off for a well-deserved vacation. Workplace dynamics are your focus now, including assessing rapport among staff members, assignments, and project launches. If you're thinking about acquiring a new pet, be sure to verify important information concerning breeding and health.

Relationships

Teamwork is a big part of this cycle, along with meetings, synchronizing schedules, and work details. New hires and collaborative ventures eat into the daily routine. Excellent new contacts become part of your resource base. Venus in hard aspect to the Moon on the 2nd hits the sore spots in personal relationships and your solar seventh house. Temper your Aries tendency to say something that sets off an argument; apologize if you do. Intimacy heals your mind and body.

Success and Money

Material benefits and savvy purchases resonate on the 1st, as do lively conversations and amiable online chats or even a reunion. Shop for jewelry between the 11th and 15th. Take care of will updates and estate matters from the 10th to the 22nd while Venus is in Scorpio. Purchase of kitchen equipment is more advantageous between the 15th and 26th.

Pitfalls and Potential Problems

If you're feeling sluggish, be sure to check your nutrition and diet for clues. Avoid fast food just because it's convenient, especially while Mars in Virgo occupies your solar sixth house of health. Do comparison shopping to look at durability and product components of major appliances to avoid purchasing a lemon.

Rewarding Days

1, 6, 15, 22

Challenging Days

2, 10, 20, 27

Aries | October

Overall Theme

Your solar seventh house of personal and business partnerships brings demands on all fronts. Discussion is lively and opinions run the gamut from unifying and supportive positions to scattering discord in diverse directions. With Mercury retrograde, table what you really want to say until after October 18, when clarity emerges and helps you analyze facts to make a good case for your position.

Relationships

Mercury and outer planets Jupiter, Saturn, and Pluto move in forward motion this month, clearing the air, improving communication, taking stuck plans off hold, and lightening the load of baggage you've been carrying around in your career sector. The fall season brings thoughts of holiday entertaining to the forefront and opportunities to include others in celebrations.

Success and Money

Check out jobs in the hottest career sectors where hiring comes back in earnest and alert candidates net the prize positions and a growing salary. Leading the demand list are those geared toward attorneys or experience in legal services, financial expertise, project management, technology (security and software development), and health care. Update your resume and start scheduling interviews. If retirement is in the cards for you in early 2022, schedule time with your organization's benefits professional and start processing the paperwork.

Pitfalls and Potential Problems

Early in the month you may feel unappreciated when you experience opposition and criticism over career initiatives that are unpopular and may not make the cut for inclusion in long-range plans. Sensitivity surfaces when the Full Moon in your sign occurs on the 20th. Ask questions and head back to the drawing board to perfect your product.

Rewarding Days

2, 6, 16, 25

Challenging Days

1, 13, 20, 28

Aries | November

Overall Theme

Curiosity gives you a new mission now. This month focuses on activity in your solar eighth house of depth, investigation, probing, uncovering truth, regeneration, and disposal. The urge to poke around and ask questions about financial matters, joint holdings, debt, insurance, and benefits has been strong for more than a year. New revelations put you in a problem-solving mood. The good news is that you emerge with a workable plan and much better financial prospects.

Relationships

Intimacy is part of this cycle; your psyche appreciates knowing where you stand, how you are valued, and the depth of the love in your life. Keep your eyes open on the 7th to avoid deception. Schedule quality time with your significant other on the 4th, 11th, and 21st, selecting venues away from crowds where you can talk about feelings, declare your love, bond in intimacy, and strengthen communication.

Success and Money

The Full Moon on the 19th is the last Lunar Eclipse of the year and occurs in your solar second house of assets, personal income, resources, and developmental opportunities. It gets a boost from transiting Pluto in Capricorn to highlight your professional prospects that could lead to a new position, bonus, or raise and most certainly more responsibility. Jupiter in Aquarius adds tension to the mix.

Pitfalls and Potential Problems

Uranus in Taurus in your second house opposes transiting Scorpio planets in your solar eighth house of joint finances now. Question transactions that look iffy. Be particularly watchful since this disruptive planet dishes out chaos that affects purchases, investments, salary raises, and resources. The 18th and 19th are vulnerable dates.

Rewarding Days

4, 11, 21, 28

Challenging Days

7, 9, 19, 23

Aries | December

Overall Theme
If you saved your vacation time and long to visit far-off places, now is your chance. Grab those bargain fares and finalize your itinerary. Just don't leave until after the Solar Eclipse in Sagittarius on the 4th. Travel is in the wind, and it could also mean that others visit you for the holidays, including in-laws and those who live in distant locations. Save time for reading, journaling, and writing. Enroll in language classes or study topics that are on your bucket list.

Relationships
Your social calendar is hopping this month. Share holiday customs with visitors, whether in a work or a home setting. Host a cocktail party and invite professional associates. Respond to invitations for feasting and fun before the 18th and late in the month to welcome in the new year with special people.

Success and Money
Cordial relationships bring you the most success this month. Watch spending on the 7th, when you could go overboard on the price of a gift. Set the tone for 2022 by acknowledging blessings and identifying goals for the year ahead. Consider an appointment to chair a committee in the new year that shares your humanitarian interests.

Pitfalls and Potential Problems
Lunar aspects indicate emotional vulnerability on several dates this month. Avoid having serious discussions on the 14th and 19th with individuals in a fragile emotional state. The aspects for the 24th work best with celebratory fare rather than intense topics. Curb expectations and welcome the spirit of the season into your heart and festivities.

Rewarding Days
4, 9, 18, 23

Challenging Days
7, 14, 19, 24

Aries Action Table

These dates reflect the best—but not the only—times for success and ease in these activities, according to your Sun sign.

	JAN	FEB	MAR	APR	MAY	JUN	JUL	AUG	SEP	OCT	NOV	DEC
Move						1		8		2		
Romance		6, 12			27							
Seek counseling/coaching			20						1			9
Ask for a raise	13			6				18				
Vacation							20					18
Get a loan			25								4	

Taurus

The Bull
April 19 to May 20

♉

Element: Earth	Glyph: Bull's head
Quality: Fixed	Anatomy: Throat, neck
Polarity: Yin/feminine	Color: Green
Planetary Ruler: Venus	Animal: Cattle
Meditation: I trust myself and others	Myths/Legends: Isis and Osiris, Ceridwen, Bull of Minos
Gemstone: Emerald	House: Second
Power Stones: Diamond, blue lace agate, rose quartz	Opposite Sign: Scorpio
	Flower: Violet
Key Phrase: I have	Keyword: Conservation

The Taurus Personality

Strengths, Talents, and the Creative Spark

Decisiveness is your strong suit once you commit to a plan and have a firm vision in mind. Those plans always include what you receive in the form of compensation and how you value what you seek or earn in life. Hard work is the vehicle that drives you to success and makes it possible for you to attract security and the material things that increase abundance. You base your personal and psychological self-worth on how well you accumulate personal goods and how they contribute to your happiness. Determination keeps you in the running to succeed and to compete strongly in the job market as well as asset management.

Venus, the goddess of balance and harmony, is your sign ruler and manifests her earthy nature in Taurus, the natural ruler of the second house of income and resources. She's there to remind you to develop your gifts so that you rely on them to provide excellent service to your customers without sacrificing the time to enjoy the benefits you've earned. Continuous improvement in the performance arena is one of your strong suits. You wear achievement proudly. You enroll in courses and go after certifications that add considerable pay value to your skill set. Self-help workshops are another pursuit that makes you promotable in the workplace, and you recommend the best ones to colleagues. As a manager you like to spend money on training to give employees a chance to grow.

You appreciate beauty and art in many forms. Careers that allow you to show your design, decorating, or flower-arranging talent appeal to many of you. Once you take out the paintbrush or the sketchbook, your focused mind spends hours bringing a creative design to life. Another personal gift is your speaking voice, which has a commanding tone and makes you a prime candidate to hit the circuit to showcase products and grow the business. Music appeals to your higher self and you often attend classical, show, or instrumental concerts. Season tickets to a symphony orchestra series are a cherished treat. Singing is another Taurus gift.

Intimacy and Personal Relationships

Sensual and tactile describe your romantic style. Getting there in the early days of pursuit of the object of your affection is not a slam dunk. You like to observe partners in multiple settings and circumstances.

You check them out for good manners, eating habits, communication, and how they handle those unexpected moments. Physical attraction is another matter. You can't get enough of your love once you commit, and shower them with wining, dining, and personal gifts. You have expertise in planning a luxurious event. The reliability you demonstrate is something you expect in return from your love partner. Friends often come to you for advice, especially if you have insight into financial investments or have recommendations for fine dining.

Values and Resources

There is no stone you'll leave unturned in your pursuit of performance excellence. You don't give up on a project or a quest, determined to turn in a quality job by researching all you need to perfect your product. Presentation materials must be top-notch to survive the workout you'll give them to make sure everyone you approach knows what you have to offer. You know how to fill up a calendar and understand the importance of managing rehearsal time and preparation of promotional products. Seat-of-the-pants management is not your style. If you have children, you will be insistent on them getting a good education and will start planting the seeds early in their lives. College funds are high on your list of priorities. You frown on lingering college loans and will encourage any that remain after your offspring graduate to be a repayment priority.

Blind Spots and Blockages

You can't be happy with what you accumulate if you have low self-esteem. If you sacrifice quality of life for attachment to material things, you impede spiritual growth. Some of you become workaholics and seldom take a day off while you pursue opportunities favorable to excessive acquisition of money. Sometimes power and control are your drivers in lieu of monetary compensation when you want to make a viable point. Observers say your neck turns red when you're not comfortable with the direction of a discussion. This is a sign that the anger is building and you're going to blow your stack if you think someone in your circle is way off base and not aligned with the big picture. That's when your stubborn side reaches its peak—you aren't called the Bull for nothing. Those around you note that you pace the floor like a matador facing a bull, only you don't have your cape ready to tame the beast. Critics say you just don't budge, even if you see a hint of logic in what the other party is offering. Most of the time you feel you are correct and keep notes in case you need a backup plan. Negotiation stagnates and meetings often end with the decisions up in the air and the agenda back on the calendar at a future date. Those in your circle go off and talk about the angst from the meeting outcome, but you're likely to return to the drawing board instead of chilling and acknowledging that the end result bombed. Know when to quit and look at the problem with new eyes.

Goals and Success

Solid interfacing with others is a reflection of your communication style, which you spend considerable time perfecting. Financial insight is one of your major gifts, whether you are self-made or inherit substantial holdings. You set your sights on the finer things in life—money, a solid career, high-quality clothing, a beautiful home, and the expendable income to wine and dine others in style, enjoy leisure time and travel, and provide a happy life for your partner and children. Your claim to fame is your pragmatic approach to organizing your ideas and plans and then turning them into a lucrative income stream. Work settings where you have privacy to develop your ideas and tailor the work space to suit your need for security and comfort work best for you. Ideas flow. Channel education, which you highly prize, toward making you the expert in your field—the perfect reward for the services you offer and the benefits you're able to deliver. Contacts see you as loyal, interested in understanding their needs, and thoughtful in managing their accounts.

Taurus Keywords for 2021
Fastidious, flexible, fruitful

The Year Ahead for Taurus

Since the powerhouse planet Uranus entered your Sun sign briefly in 2018 and went full steam ahead in 2019, you've had more success in finding ways to keep the planet of sudden chaos in check during its seven-year jog in Taurus. "Where do I look next?" is a question never far from your mind these days. A few of your contacts have dared to call you rebellious during this period, and you have never been known for taking a radical approach to problem-solving. Other fixed-sign planets, Jupiter and Saturn in Aquarius, line up to create a standoff with your resources. You're usually good at hanging on to stuff, whether it is material or personal, but lately you seem to have no control over your assets and have been scratching your head in search of solutions. Why not take the time this year to plant some positive seeds and mine the aspects that are working for you?

Places to look for optimistic outcomes include your tenth house of career, ambition, and status. Inventory your assets, what you bring to the job, and how you interact with administrators, bosses, and colleagues. What are your recent accomplishments and how have they amped up your role in the power structure? Those of you looking for a raise or promotion succeed when you figure out ways to grab the attention of decision-makers and open their eyes to money-saving or efficiency-oriented proposals that streamline the current way of doing business. If the organization has positions that need restructuring, make recommendations for targeting a few that need individuals with the most relevant skills for today's progressive business market.

Jupiter

The planet of expansion becomes an attention-getter this year as it makes tracks for your solar tenth house of advancement, leadership, career, and status quo through December 28. With Jupiter now in Aquarius, it's time to put your big ideas to work to wow your boss, guide your employees, share with team members, and create a better organization. Every degree of Taurus receives a visit from Jupiter this year, attracting opportunities to your door, increasing the number of important contacts via networking, boosting your visibility, and putting your accomplishments in the spotlight. These successes result in compensation in the form of raises, promotions, bonuses, or awards. Your well-managed goals trigger an appealing growth cycle that adds a layer of security to appease your psyche. With your hard work ethic, you earn every bit of the applause. Important players in your career realm take notice and remember your talent when selecting key individuals for emerging leadership roles. Matters involving family members and parental concerns that generated significant pressure seem headed for satisfactory resolution. Sure, there will be some rocks in the road via retrograde cycles, hits from transiting Uranus, and the presence of restrictive Saturn in this same solar tenth house, but don't let these distractions slow your momentum. The best is yet to come.

Saturn

On December 17, 2020, Saturn moved into Aquarius and your solar tenth house just ahead of Jupiter's entry into Aquarius at the end of that month. These two planets travel in conjunction early in 2021, bringing a serious note to your plans for the year and reminding you of what you have to aim for and issues ripe for elimination on your quest to master your goals. Taurus individuals most affected during 2021 are those born between April 20 and May 3. Saturn wants credit for accomplishments, and your ambitious nature gives you the commitment to work diligently to gain the recognition and rewards you desire. Most of you have the ear of your boss or may in fact be the boss if you own your own firm or are a managing director of one of the firm's divisions. If you let a lazy streak get in the way or have been mean-spirited toward others whom you see as a threat to your turf, the ugly side of limitations and delays could emerge to set you back for part of the year. Put a stop to any undesirable behavior that thwarts your ability as a leader. With Jupiter also present, you hold the cards, and a winning and fair strategy nets the outcome you desire.

Uranus

Nothing spells shakeup like having Uranus in your solar first house or on your Sun for a seven-year stretch. Taurus born from April 25 to May 5 see the most action from this transit at various times this year. The position of your Sun in your natal chart guides the flow of what transpires. Get ready for unexpected shifts in action, surprise visitors, altered plans, health and work shakeups, and deviations from normal operating plans and procedures. Expect others to blow up or engage in heated or bizarre discussions. Uranian energy is reflected in weather patterns, including storm cycles and explosions of all types, including verbal detonations. That means you might encounter normally calm individuals who throw a hissy fit or seem enraged over interactions or opinions that don't match their own. You too could get agitated beyond your comfort zone when Uranus closes in on your Sun and contributes to a nasty eruption of venom. This type of eye-opener gives you a clue about the level of pent-up anger you've been storing internally. Uranus reminds you that you can't pretend that everything is rosy when external evidence tells a different story. Reflect on your values and keep in mind that you may have to tweak them because your inner world is changing and needs your help to build a balanced support network. It starts on the inside and works its way out. Chill out by using yoga or meditation to take the edge off. Be there to catch the wave and make change an adventure.

Neptune

Pisces-ruled Neptune makes its way through your solar eleventh house of friendships, plans, goals, dreams, organizational assets, and groups during 2021. This psychic planet most affects your sign harmoniously this year if you were born between May 7 and 15. As an introspective and somewhat cryptic planet, Neptune's ethereal cycle slows down and includes a retrograde period from June 25, 2021, to January 2022 in your solar eleventh house, giving you time to heal from stressful encounters, recover from medical or psychological traumas, or build relationships with metaphysical communities after moving away from organizations that no longer interest you. A goal leads you to find a worthy outlet serving as a volunteer for a charity or hospital. Promoting a cause without applying hard-sell methods on interested parties appeals to you. Since you like to work with your hands, you could enroll in holistic healing classes that offer reiki or specialized massage certification. Be selective about the venues you choose; watch out for parties who talk a good game and promise the moon but do nothing more than take your hard-earned money. As much as you like personal development, don't pay the price for someone else's greed. Hold your head high and honor your values.

Pluto

In late January 2008, Pluto in Capricorn took up residence in your solar ninth house of the higher mind, advanced education, foreign countries and cultures, in-laws, philosophy, publishing, religion, and long-distance travel. This planet crawls, and does so slowly and insidiously, exposing what you're keeping under wraps in your subconscious. Hidden elements include blocked emotions, secrets about people, debts, fears related to sex and death, and anything mysterious that has you paying a price for stuffing the truth instead of seeking release. In 2021 Tauruses born between May 15 and 17 have a chance to experience a rebirth through the psychological release of old garbage stuck deep within you.

While on foreign travel, it is not unusual to experience a sense of déjà vu when a visit to a place you've never seen, possibly related to a past life, triggers memories and helps you let go of what your soul longs to bring to the surface. Keep the tissues handy; a good cry is cathartic and refreshing. Pluto goes retrograde from April 27 through October 6, giving your inner core a chance to internalize meaningful change. Be ready to view your world with a fresh perspective and feel the relief you have long desired course through your entire being. Viva transformation!

How Will This Year's Eclipses Affect You?

In 2021, a total of four eclipses occur. There will be two Lunar Eclipses and two Solar Eclipses, creating intense periods that begin to manifest a few months before their actual dates. Eclipses unfold in cycles involving all twelve signs of the zodiac, and usually occur in pairs about two weeks apart. Think of eclipses as opportunities to release old patterns and conditions that have outlived their usefulness. Have no fear of them, since they can bring you unexpected surprises and windfalls. The closer an eclipse is to a degree or point in your chart, the greater its importance in your life. Those of you born with a planet at the same degree as an eclipse are likely to see a high level of activity in the house where the eclipse occurs.

Get ready for action, because this year's first Lunar Eclipse occurs on May 26 in Sagittarius in your solar eighth house of joint savings and income, investments, debt, other people's money, wills, estates, birth, death, sex, karmic conditions, psychological matters, and mysterious circumstances. Opportunities arise to assess your debt load, tweak your financial plans, and reduce the amount you owe on a mortgage or other big-ticket item. You may take a hard look at a partner's income for relief from the mounting expenses or take on a second job to apply earnings to loans. If you're named as an executor of an estate, a fair amount of your time may be spent on settlements and disposition of goods.

The second eclipse of 2021 is a Solar Eclipse in Gemini on June 10 in your solar second house of assets, income, money sources, benefits received in the form of bonuses or windfalls, and expenses you undertake for your household or personal development. Watch trends in the employment arena for signs of expansion or reduction of assets or income. Don't be surprised if raises are either eliminated or scaled back from what was promised. On the other hand, you may be honored and surprised by a substantial award, depending on whether you have planets in this house in your birth chart. If you're thinking of applying for new employment, dust off your resume and join the competition. Complete any relevant courses you're taking that will make you a top-tier candidate in the desired applicant pool.

On November 19, the second Lunar Eclipse of the year occurs in your sign of Taurus, signaling a shift that is highly personal since it highlights your solar first house of activity, appearance, initiation, passion, personality, and self-image. By the time this eclipse lands, you'll have a good idea of what you want to change in terms of how you look and what you want to accomplish or implement in your workplace. Eliminate any barriers that stand in the way of your desired goals, and lead the charge for securing your next adventure. Flexibility makes you more attractive in your outlook and generates fruitful results.

Two weeks later on December 4, the last Solar Eclipse of the year takes place in Sagittarius, again in your solar eighth house of joint funds, debts, investments, and estates. You'll have an opportunity to review the path you've taken this year to achieve your financial goals, gain the cooperation of partners, reduce your debt load, and work on healing your psyche. It may be important to draw up a will for your assets or update an existing one. Schedule a session with an estate attorney if you have questions about changing tax laws or provisions that need special handling. Your fastidious nature makes you alert to apply checks and balances to your important undertakings. Know that you have the tools at your disposal to enjoy a very productive year. Welcome the new year with optimism and high hopes.

Taurus | January

Overall Theme

A winter getaway drives your agenda this month, whether for a short or a long-distance trip. You may meet up with those who live in distant places and enjoy the reunion. With Uranus in your sign, this year represents change and you're determined to break out of a rut. Those of you contemplating relocation may be checking out opportunities for a move, a new job, or a sabbatical.

Relationships

Flexibility goes far in healing relationships in need of renewal. Romantic encounters are likely on the 1st, 9th, and 13th and possibly when the Full Moon lands in your solar fourth house of home and family on the 28th. Compliment those who share goals that affect the harmony that surrounds you. You may enjoy how much your investments in self-improvement, organizational savvy, and entertainment affect the attitude and behavior of dear ones.

Success and Money

The eclipse in Sagittarius in December 2020 left you with extra cash after you reconciled your debt load, giving you the funds for travel and purchases you were postponing. It helped that transiting Jupiter in your solar ninth house gave your health and mental outlook a big boost. Jupiter and Saturn now in your solar tenth house of career create reasons to renegotiate employment conditions or stabilize family matters.

Pitfalls and Potential Problems

Examine all the options in front of you as you face the new year. Which ones tie strongly to your goals? Embrace them and make things happen rather than holding fast to a fear of the unknown. Think of Uranus as shaking things up rather than taking a bite out of your self-confidence. Avoid major transactions when Mercury goes retrograde on January 30.

Rewarding Days

3, 5, 13, 22

Challenging Days

8, 14, 28, 30

Taurus | February

Overall Theme

The month gets off to a productive start with well-planned meetings that shed light on upcoming projects and plans. You're feeling industrious. If possible, put in a bid for a part of the work that showcases your talents. Follow up with colleagues and collaborate on strategies that point to success. Activity heats up in key solar houses of your chart this year, setting up demands for your time and a pressing schedule. Take time to relax and build in recreational enjoyment.

Relationships

A meetup of Venus and Jupiter in your solar eleventh house holds the promise of a romantic interlude with the right partner on the 11th. That same day, the New Moon in your solar tenth house of status shines on both business and personal connection. Accept invitations and take advantage of offers of support that come your way.

Success and Money

Make suggestions about the type of human capital that gets the job done. Learn what you can about hiring plans. Funds may be allocated for organizational or personal expenses when Mercury goes direct on February 20. Shop for loan terms on the 9th. Order your own annual credit report to get a leg up on your credit status.

Pitfalls and Potential Problems

Don't sign loan papers until February 24, a day when lunar aspects in your solar third house of agreements and contracts favor your plans. Avoid the 25th, though, when hard aspects dominate the planetary landscape. Avoid heated exchanges on the 5th or 6th, when Venus dances with Saturn and Uranus, resulting in ruffled feathers or an impasse.

Rewarding Days

1, 9, 15, 24

Challenging Days

5, 18, 25

Taurus | March

Overall Theme

You may be feeling a bit edgy due to restrictive influences that emerge compliments of the lineup of Aquarius planets occupying your solar tenth house of career, some of which are receiving a harsh aspect from transiting Uranus now. Sudden events keep you on your toes looking for immediate solutions to unraveling problems.

Relationships

Those of you contemplating getting engaged may find the middle weekend of the month a good day to pop the question or say yes to your partner. Blending of families takes center stage, giving you time to celebrate the happy occasion or a birth, milestone birthday, or important anniversary. Argumentative types surface around the 12th and the 25th of the month. Duck and run.

Success and Money

Home decorating and gift giving are on your mind, creating a much needed diversion from the intense work cycle as you shop and search for the perfect goods. Compare loan terms and settle or sign contracts around the 18th. Enroll in classes on the 22nd and service your car on the 27th. Watch spending from the 5th to the 7th to avoid going over the limit with your use of credit cards.

Pitfalls and Potential Problems

The work environment seems like an out-of-control arena for part of this month. Every few days, another communication issue or crisis emerges, largely due to unclear roles or new assignments that beg for clarification. The 4th and 5th are particularly contentious. Household disagreements escalate and parties reach an impasse, especially around the Full Moon on March 28. Talk things out the following weekend when cooler heads prevail.

Rewarding Days

8, 9, 13, 18

Challenging Days

4, 5, 12, 25

Taurus | April

Overall Theme

Just when you start to breathe normally again, the wheel of restriction and limitation enters your sphere of action, especially your solar tenth house of career, delaying your plans and escalating your level of impatience in getting the job done with precision. Remember that ambition is a good thing as long as you don't go overboard thinking "it's my way or the highway" when the schedule doesn't meet your expectations.

Relationships

Some of the rifts are on the mend in family and personal relationships, especially around the 4th and 5th of the month. Contacts are in a festive mood, and it spills over to you when you agree to take a work break and enjoy the diversion. The 9th and 10th are good party or entertaining dates. Stay flexible if plans need adjustments.

Success and Money

Reflect on current goals by enjoying downtime on the New Moon of April 11. Some facet of your work needs tweaking, and the calm retreat gives you the passion and enterprise to figure it out far from the madness of the polarizing workplace. Enjoy the harmonious aspects of April 22, when the Moon in Virgo opens up the possibility for smooth dialogue with your Sun, Mercury, and spontaneous Uranus.

Pitfalls and Potential Problems

Cooler heads do not prevail on the 2nd or 3rd, and these are not the best days to conduct meetings or interviews or shop for electronic goods. Arguments flair up, schedule coordination is unlikely, and key people are missing from the cadre of support players. Cranky people show up on the 26th, and Pluto shifts and goes retrograde on the 27th, leaving unfinished agendas and indicating that it's time to rethink plans.

Rewarding Days

4, 9, 11, 22

Challenging Days

2, 3, 26

Taurus | May

Overall Theme

How nice to have the world ready for your energy this month! You are raring to go and are enthusiastic about beating the odds that a Uranus flare-up will throw a boulder onto your path. Aquarius amps up the volume from your solar tenth house of career. By the 3rd, Gemini brings lightning-speed ideas into the mix, along with much-needed humor that you relish to break up the monotony of pressing issues.

Relationships

Harmonious aspects on the 2nd from the Moon in Taurus to Venus, Neptune, and Mercury give you opportunities to enjoy the company of cherished companions and partners. Your own birthday celebration may take place over several days, with separate meals, outings, and entertainment. Conversations and events that spark emotional feelings occur on the 6th and bring passion and commitment to the mix.

Success and Money

The New Moon in Taurus on the 11th reminds you that you have ownership of the creative plans that are unfolding in your solar first and fourth houses. Review the budget and the details you developed. Be mindful that shifts in planets' directions occur this month, with Saturn going retrograde in Aquarius in your solar tenth house of career on the 23rd and Mercury beginning a three-week slide into Gemini on the 29th, slowing down financial transactions and calling for further insight before committing.

Pitfalls and Potential Problems

Acting hastily around the first Lunar Eclipse of the year in Sagittarius on May 26 leads to regrets, especially since it occurs in your solar eighth house of debt, loans, and other people's money. Note the challenges indicated by the harsh aspects from Saturn to the Sun and Moon on the 3rd, a day that is best used to research problem areas.

Rewarding Days

2, 6, 11, 17

Challenging Days

1, 3, 5, 26

Taurus | June

Overall Theme

Mental acuity and communication set the tone for June's planetary activity. Air signs dominate the landscape, suggesting that rapid thought processes count in a pinch when an information overload occurs. A competitive press may be behind mass reporting of incidents, political decisions, and challenges to citizens. On a personal level, the first three days of the month invite social discourse, meetings with kindred groups, and get-togethers.

Relationships

The 12th is perfect for graduation parties, strengthening loving relationships, planning or scheduling weddings, and hosting home-based events. You feel like you're getting somewhere in discussions you had tabled, especially after Mercury goes direct on the 22nd, as affected parties show a greater interest in participating. Work connections move in sync with business plans and build confidence in teamwork.

Success and Money

Evidence of strategic planning and results-oriented outcomes is strongest during the first half of the month. High-five when you learn that profit margins are up on a business level and personal debt shows significant reduction. Jupiter, now in the teaser degrees of early Pisces, goes retrograde on June 20 for the next four months, indicating that goals require more research before implementing action.

Pitfalls and Potential Problems

Rejection in social circles is likely on the 3rd, when the Moon is in hard aspect to Venus. Concentration may be impeded on the 10th due to distractions or lack of sleep. The first Solar Eclipse of 2021 occurs on this date in Gemini in your solar second house of income and assets. Wait until the 12th to get back on track.

Rewarding Days

1, 12, 22, 29

Challenging Days

3, 10, 15, 24

Taurus | July

Overall Theme

Whether for a few days or a couple of weeks, schedule some well-deserved vacation time this month and enjoy the break in routine. Your racing mind will thank you for finding a relaxing beach location or a mountain retreat to ditch the pressing schedule you've maintained for the first half of the year. Why not treat your inner child to a visit to an amusement park to ride the latest high-tech rollercoaster and try your hand at arcade games?

Relationships

Family factors into this month's activity, whether they show up for a reunion or you visit relatives in distant places or schedule an anticipated vacation in a fun environment for your significant other and/or children. High energy and romance are probable on the 13th, with Venus and Mars in starring roles and the Moon and Mercury aligned with Jupiter. Steer clear of arguments on the 5th that may arise over your unwillingness to say no to an unexpected work assignment or a schedule change that affects the departure date for your vacation.

Success and Money

The 13th is perfect for purchasing household goods, baby equipment, or office furnishings. Moon-Jupiter connections on the 21st put you in touch with key business people in long-distance locations, and you benefit from substantial discounts and attractive terms.

Pitfalls and Potential Problems

Around the 19th, you learn the hidden cost of goods or loan terms that was withheld during negotiations that took place around the 1st of the month. Major players with involvement in the action may have been missing due to holiday closings. Wait until after the Full Moon on July 23 to request new numbers.

Rewarding Days

9, 13, 15, 21

Challenging Days

1, 5, 19, 23

Taurus | August

Overall Theme

Surprising facts come to light as the month gets underway. The topics involve both personal and business arenas. Some days are just plain mixed bags from a planetary standpoint and generate confusion. Be prepared to double-check and cancel transactions and don't let any time elapse once you know the truth. With four planets retrograde for most of the month, the best option is to retreat during the dog days of summer and decide on which issue needs the most attention.

Relationships

A greater than usual number of problems creep up this month that affect people at home base. Hasty choices are at the root of the personal issues. The work environment also manifests evidence of premature decisions that call for an audit of financial matters. Ruffled feathers accrue when power players request reports of activities and involvement to get to the heart of the problem. With vacation season in full operation, a wait is likely before solutions are fully realized.

Success and Money

The New Moon in Leo in your solar fourth house on the 8th highlights activity at home base. Purchases go smoothly if done before Uranus goes retrograde on August 19. A jewelry purchase could be in the wind. Shop on the 20th when the Moon's harmonious aspect to Venus and meetup with Saturn calls attention to the need to examine cost and value.

Pitfalls and Potential Problems

Be on the lookout for a tall tale or fraud on the 4th, if subject to a manipulative telemarketing call or an offer that looks too good to be true. Missing or vague information could lead to a skewed decision on the 11th. Check paperwork carefully. Do not respond to calls from unknown parties in pending business transactions. Initiate correspondence personally to check sources and the validity of data.

Rewarding Days

1, 2, 8, 20

Challenging Days

4, 11, 22, 25

Taurus | September

Overall Theme

After staying flexible for most of the summer, your mounting schedule calls for a fastidious account of action items. The New Moon on the 6th in your solar fifth house of evolving enterprises and social outlets calls for a change of pace and a visit with key contacts who support your income-generating ideas. Perhaps you're interested in starting a new business. Be sure to network to maximize success.

Relationships

Entrepreneurial connections and leaders in their fields take center stage in the relationship realm this month. Seek out idea people, brainstorm with members of your team, or visit organizations that have restructured the work environment. See what business owners are doing to rejuvenate human capital and increase their bottom line. Make visibility a priority while the Sun makes favorable connections to your sign this month.

Success and Money

Your eye for detail results in lucrative leads this month beginning on September 1. A nice Moon-Jupiter connection on the 13th puts you in touch with investors in your own ideas or those of your organization. Arrange meetings and initiate opportunities to speak about your vision for an innovative workplace. Check out candidates that fit the model for the emerging enterprise.

Pitfalls and Potential Problems

A lack of focus on the 3rd and 12th puts you behind the curve when sleep deprivation catches up with you and you miss key points with major players or team members. If you confuse your audience, get back on the bandwagon. Review your plans and budget details that need clarification. The Moon is full on the 20th and Mercury goes retrograde on the 27th.

Rewarding Days

1, 6, 13, 28

Challenging Days

3, 12, 17, 20

Taurus | October

Overall Theme

You start the month with an abundance of energy. The earth is deep and rich and ready for harvest—the ideal time to reap what you've sown in terms of accomplishments. Be sure you have your timeline ready for review, with a possible performance reward from managing authorities. Congratulate yourself on progress you've made with health and nutrition goals. With disruptive Uranus nipping at your heels, the road hasn't been easy.

Relationships

Rapport increases among coworkers, teams, and collaborators. The New Moon in your solar sixth house on the 6th stimulates discussion and the drive to exceed deadlines. You're so excited about the extra cash in your wallet that you invite family and friends to celebrate at a trendy restaurant or host a fall party in your home environment.

Success and Money

Productivity peaks on the 2nd and 10th, and the momentum flows into your workplace, especially after the 10th, when Saturn goes direct in motion. Fresh approaches to goal implementation ignite passion and competition. Handle suggestions fairly and be sure to acknowledge participants' contributions on work or sports teams. Avoid a spending spree on the 3rd or you'll have items to return. Jupiter goes direct on the 18th, joined later in the day by Mercury moving direct.

Pitfalls and Potential Problems

Misconceptions or confusion surface on the 5th and may involve those who do not have the facts to make a corrective decision. On the 20th you may be wrestling with a power struggle that results in a sleepless night while you regurgitate details. Seek advice from experts for a new perspective.

Rewarding Days

2, 6, 10, 31

Challenging Days

3, 5, 20, 29

Taurus | November

Overall Theme

You can feel a difference in the air right from day one of this month. Anticipation abounds with talk of approaching holidays and the desire to complete implementation of loose ends on professional projects. Despite improved communication and successful meetings with principals and partners, a few rocks block the road. Be prepared for surprise announcements, unplanned travel, and unexpected expenses.

Relationships

November 1 adds a note of spontaneity to the mix, along with aha moments and revelations about emerging plans that affect your future. Some of you welcome children, new grandchildren, or the newly engaged to your circle. Discussions with personal and business associates succeed on the 13th and 24th. The New Moon conjunct Mars on the 4th has an intense tone and gives mixed signals.

Success and Money

Negotiators hang tough to win favorable contracts and settle salary and benefits issues for the coming year. Be prepared to spend more than one day to achieve a favorable outcome by the middle of the month. Enlist the aid of specialists to support arguments where certain factions want to debunk the merit of higher wages and retirement funds, especially from the 11th to the 16th.

Pitfalls and Potential Problems

Naysayers rear their stubborn heads in both personal and business arenas. The most intense evidence of unyielding positions occurs between the New Moon in Scorpio on November 4 and the Lunar Eclipse in Taurus on November 19. The energy is one of contraction rather than expansion of effort, and stifles enthusiasm. Look for relief on November 22–25 or on the 29th.

Rewarding Days

1, 8, 13, 24

Challenging Days

4, 11, 16, 19

Taurus | December

Overall Theme

Wrapping up pending details and unfinished work occupies your mind so you can free up time to finalize plans for the holidays and schedule special events. Your organized approach to tackling the to-do list helps you stay ahead of the game. Offer assistance to others who may have fallen behind the curve. Surprise a pal or embrace the spirit of giving by making a contribution to a worthy cause around December 11.

Relationships

During the month that we set aside to reflect on those we cherish and what we admire about them, our thoughts turn to how we can allocate significant quality time to spend with loved ones. Venus in Capricorn goes retrograde on December 19 for the next six weeks. Those of you with a late Taurus Sun work through relationship challenges.

Success and Money

You seldom make holiday shopping a last-minute chore and probably have the gifts carefully selected, wrapped, and mailed early. The budget you set aside for this annual custom reflects your good taste and attention to the preferences of loved ones. Jupiter moves into your solar eleventh house on December 28 in Pisces and opens the door to successful accomplishment of desired goals in the new year.

Pitfalls and Potential Problems

Failure to take inventory of progress you made in the goals and plans you established for 2021 could leave you unprepared to jump unencumbered into the balanced, creative energy called for in 2022, a year that sheds light on important relationships. Remember that Uranus is still in Taurus and retrograde until January 18, 2022, and is making a statement to those born around May 1.

Rewarding Days

4, 7, 11, 28

Challenging Days

2, 13, 17, 18

Taurus Action Table

These dates reflect the best—but not the only—times for success and ease in these activities, according to your Sun sign.

	JAN	FEB	MAR	APR	MAY	JUN	JUL	AUG	SEP	OCT	NOV	DEC
Move			9			2			1		13	
Romance		11					13	1, 20				7, 28
Seek counseling/ coaching	5				17				9			
Ask for a raise				10			9			2		4
Vacation			25								24	
Get a loan				1					28			

Gemini

The Twins
May 20 to June 20

Ⅱ

Element: Air

Quality: Mutable

Polarity: Yang/masculine

Planetary Ruler: Mercury

Meditation: I explore my inner worlds

Gemstone: Tourmaline

Power Stones: Ametrine, citrine, emerald, spectrolite, agate

Key Phrase: I think

Glyph: Pillars of duality, the Twins

Anatomy: Shoulders, arms, hands, lungs, nervous system

Colors: Bright colors, orange, yellow, magenta

Animals: Monkeys, talking birds, flying insects

Myths/Legends: Peter Pan, Castor and Pollux

House: Third

Opposite Sign: Sagittarius

Flower: Lily of the valley

Keyword: Versatility

The Gemini Personality

Strengths, Talents, and the Creative Spark

Life is a learning experience for you through diverse classrooms and appealing forms of education. Your quick mind cycles through challenging topics until you become a sought-after fountain of information, mastering all the basics before embarking on the journey of your higher mind. You have no fear of the unknown and seek to gather wisdom and build expertise in emerging career fields. Not surprisingly, you are an avid book collector and outfit your home with an abundance of bookcases and shelves to house your print book collections and reference materials. Since you like two of everything, you probably have more than one electronic reader so that you are never far from the latest novel, biography, or nonfiction bestseller when you have scheduled appointments, and you use this convenient tool to digest interesting facts while you manage considerable wait times or travel between destinations.

Mental versatility is a key asset. You resonate proudly with most forms of communication, and your talent for conversational ease is the perfect ice-breaker at meetings, parties, and social gatherings. Equipped with stellar presentation skills, you get the nod to showcase important facets of your work or your organization's mission. Writing and editing are skills you have meticulously polished and may represent a key component of your career. Another of your gifts is a sense of humor with perfect memory and timing to deliver the punch line for the jokes you tell. You know a little about a lot and are often the winner of trivia games and challenging word games. You're a confident soul who solves crossword puzzles in ink.

Assignments that allow you to use your stellar interviewing skills give you personal satisfaction. You enjoy analyzing qualifications and facts about others, and your sharp mind aids in putting all the parts together quickly. Employment as a media relations specialist, a commentator, or a reporter satisfies your quest for putting your power of observation to the test.

Intimacy and Personal Relationships

At the top of your list in choosing a loving partner is one who has a highly evolved intellectual capacity. You want someone who talks to you, listens to what you have to say, and shows a willingness to routinely explore new avenues of interest. The object of your affection must learn right away that you love to talk and will leave no moments of silence until the last bit of fascinating information you want to share has run its course. That's a tall order and means that no silent type with more mundane interests in discussing the daily grind will be able to keep up with you. Fragile types need not apply; you would exhaust them. You fall for your loved one's mind first, and if the rest of the chemistry is there, you engage in the pursuit of happy adventures. Mental restlessness means your partner will have to adjust to sharing you with individuals who have creative minds and spend considerable time discussing details of their experiences.

Values and Resources

Knowledge is one of your most treasured resources. You place a great deal of value on what your fertile mind absorbs and how you use the information in competitive settings, through your work, with family relationships, and when studying new perspectives. Acquisition of important information comes through a variety of modalities, including early education, advanced degrees, certification programs, online coursework, seminars, workshops, on-the-job training, and cross-training opportunities, including work details to another location. You've never met a bookstore you didn't like nor passed by a library that didn't attract your interest. Book sales and auctions fascinate you, and you grab the bargains to add to your collection. You look for notes in used books to see what has been written on the introductory pages. People are your favorite resources, and you join networks of all types to build links to your community, circle of friends, and social or work environments. The expertise you have for information sharing makes you a popular party guest. You admire the talents of relatives and often form close bonds with siblings, calling on them to help you solve dilemmas or just hang out for a weekend get-together.

Blind Spots and Blockages

You pursue topics or hobbies enthusiastically once you discover an interest and then drop them like a hot potato when you become bored. Storage areas fill up quickly with unfinished projects, which you hesitate to throw out or give away in case you ever decide to finish them. Don't worry, you probably won't! Losing track of time is often problematic. You get sidetracked when running errands and arrive late for appointments or meetings. Your Achilles' heel is overtalking and missing clues that you're spending too much time on a subject. Another is that you forget to give others a chance to speak during conversations and interrupt them frequently when they have the floor. Avoid poking fun at others in the room under the guise of using humor. Show others you care by listening to what they have to say.

Goals and Success

As the chief communicator of the zodiac, you passionately embrace the role of your sign's ruler, Mercury, as the messenger of the gods. You look for ways to breathe life into diverse avenues of expression, often multitasking to keep up with the number of irons you have in the fire. You're cut out for dual careers and often hold down more than one job at a time. If you're organized, you can pull it off beautifully. You're attracted to positions in the field of talent management, such as recruiters, scouts, interviewers, or providers of employee orientation after the hiring process takes place. You're known for speaking your native language eloquently, and a good number of you are accomplished linguists, speaking multiple languages fluently. You may excel as a translator, bridging language gaps between parties who speak other languages or find themselves in need of interpretive skills in decoding or explaining the meaning of documents. Teaching is another field that draws your attention, as do related fields such as events management, which includes facilitating meetings and running training sessions, especially those that offer travel opportunities. Adaptability is the key to your success.

Gemini Keywords for 2021
Dexterity, discovery, diversity

The Year Ahead for Gemini

Be sure you get in great shape in 2021 so that you readily display dexterity and grace in physical activity, the type you need when you hit the road on a speaking tour to a number of cities. It's likely that you'll make your mark in a slightly different playing field this year, with eclipses throwing a charge your way and transiting Jupiter in your solar ninth house of the higher mind, travel, and distant experiences. Communication will remain a huge part of the action regardless of which personal assets you want to draw into service. Perhaps you'll study a new language or take courses to build qualifications for an anticipated job promotion. You'll be using your hands a lot, whether in demonstrating a product you sell or making a point while delivering important strategic information about your firm's mission. In response to the mental restlessness that never seems far from your soul, you'll explore diverse career options, even facets of work in your current company that you hadn't previously considered for a job change. Those of you in the acting field are adept at developing the mental adroitness to remember lines or ad-lib intuitively, along with using the right body moves to tell your story.

With a number of planets in your solar ninth house this year in Aquarius, you won't get to push pending items aside and ask for a pass instead of taking action. Ditch the lazy streak and the reputation for being a procrastinator. For example, you have the know-how to write that book you've had on the back burner for years. With your dual energy, you probably have at least two book topics you've considered. Come on, Gemini, you know you love to write. This year you'll narrow down your options for identifying the perfect publisher and sign a contract to deliver the goods. Ignite your creative spark and watch how quickly the missing pieces fall into place. With your flair for diversity, you could wind up with a long-term contract or agree to write a series of articles for magazines, periodicals, or websites. Those of you with experience in the commercial field may land a contract writing ads and or apply for a position to run the advertising campaign for a prominent firm.

Jupiter

The planet of benevolence and expansion occupies your solar ninth house of the higher mind in compatible Aquarius for most of the year, moving through the first few degrees of Pisces starting on May 14 and then going retrograde on June 20 and making its way back to Aquarius in late July before resuming direct motion on October 18. You'll have ample opportunity to work on key goals that may include going back to school for an advanced degree or acquiring certification for credentials that raise your profile for a promotion. You may discover new perspectives on philosophical or religious interests that claim your attention and put you in touch with spiritual leaders. The ninth house represents long-distance travel, which may appear in the form of a job offer to relocate to a distant location, a trip of a lifetime to another country, participation in a cultural exchange program, or a visit from relatives or in-laws who live in a foreign country. Jupiter in the ninth house puts you in touch with principals in the journalism and publishing fields, helping you expand your contacts for marketing and sell your written material. Jupiter has company this year, with Saturn in Aquarius present in the same solar ninth house all year and Mercury entering Aquarius on January 9 and then going retrograde on January 30.

Saturn

In the sign of Aquarius, Saturn partners favorably with your Sun to give your projects a boost of support. During this transit of your solar ninth house, Saturn settles in for a 2½-year stay and lives up to its reputation as a stern taskmaster, reminding you to consult with doctors and other medical professionals about current medical conditions so you have the stamina to achieve the goals you have on the drawing board. Be sure to have checkups and tests as warranted. Some of you bypass yearly exams, using a crowded schedule as an excuse for creatively avoiding your medical team. See the dentist too, because that jaw-clenching you do at night emanates from the hectic schedule you're juggling on the road to success. Certain individuals take a sabbatical from routine when Saturn comes calling on the ninth house. You'll have no time to do so with the sheer volume of goals you have set. Previous encounters with Saturn netted powerful lessons in overcommitment of time that left you physically spent or resulted in missed deadlines. Avoid that scenario this time around by carefully choosing work or home projects and committing to travel or coursework that can be successfully integrated into your schedule. No double-entry meetings on your calendar! Accountability is a reality you can't afford to ignore. Include others in your plans to make sure all the bases are covered. Watch expenditures as well.

Uranus

In 2021 you are a couple of years into the current seven-year transit of Uranus in Taurus in your solar twelfth house of confidential matters, confinement, escapism, inner changes, and meditation. If you have early-degree Taurus planets in this house in your birth chart, you already know that Uranus is here to shake up the status quo, your quiet time, and the secrets you're keeping. This year, if you were born between May 28 and June 5, the planet of disruption and chaotic behavior visits your Sun. Planets in Taurus are incompatible with the two Aquarius planets that are currently occupying your solar ninth house, Jupiter and Saturn. The energy can be harsh. Take no risks in travel by avoiding hazardous driving and flying conditions. Be prepared for a break in the activities you have planned. You or others around you may spend time recovering from illness or broken bones. If you deliberately planned a period of seclusion to work on your book, develop user manuals, or take a mental health break to process an emotional setback, Uranus may intervene and challenge you to move in an unforeseen direction. Don't be discouraged. Use the time to analyze the flow of events and let go of the urge to blame yourself or others for the outcome. Focus on a cherished goal instead and visualize a win.

Neptune

Neptune in Pisces first entered your solar tenth house way back in April 2011 when it made a teaser appearance in this department of your chart related to authority, ambition, career, and recognition. Planets in Pisces challenge your Gemini Sun. In the tenth house, they either add a note of spirituality to your work routine or confuse you with a complex agenda. Neptune here is a great place for those of you who use your imagination to create new products or concepts that increase the tempo of the workplace. Each week could bring a new discovery about the direction the organization is taking. Sometimes it means that a new leader throws the baby out with the bathwater. Change is good but is not easy to adapt to when most of the players misunderstand the message or don't know how to play the game. Daydreaming could have a life of its own without a firm work plan to separate ideas from goals and could interfere with accomplishment efforts. You'll know if this is the case now. Be sure to avoid exaggerating the facts about what you're actually doing or withholding information that would add clarity to the process. On a personal level, you may have moved to another job or undergone a career shift since Neptune appeared in this house. If you're contemplating a move, be sure to do your research and get the inside scoop on any organization under consideration. Many individuals with Pisces on the tenth-house cusp seek work in medical fields, with elderly people, in metaphysical practices, or as entertainers, actors, or writers of poetry and prose.

Pluto

By now you are used to transiting Pluto in Capricorn meandering through your solar eighth house since 2008, making sure to clean out every shred of accumulated karma and highlighting the nature of the fear you're eradicating. This house is important now because it has been the scene of fiscal battles over the last two years via eclipses in Capricorn, which gave you a new perspective on joint assets, debt, and financial management. Death, either actual or symbolic, may have been a factor in accelerating movement here and calling attention to your fragile psyche and the need to keep control of pain rather than release it. Be sure to acknowledge lingering grief and then let it go. You may have added responsibility now in settling an estate and distributing goods to heirs. Although you and your partner may be in a better place economically, fragile connections remain. Examine the big picture for any fragments of baggage that create tension. Perhaps you still have intimacy issues to acknowledge. Consider finding a therapist who can help you work through them so you and your significant other can enjoy your relationship. The 2021 Pluto transit most affects Geminis born between June 15 and 19.

How Will This Year's Eclipses Affect You?

In 2021, a total of four eclipses occur. There will be two Lunar Eclipses and two Solar Eclipses, creating intense periods that begin to manifest a few months before their actual dates. Eclipses unfold in cycles involving all twelve signs of the zodiac, and usually occur in pairs about two weeks apart. Think of eclipses as opportunities to release old patterns and conditions that have outlived their usefulness. Have no fear of them, since they can bring you unexpected surprises and windfalls. The closer an eclipse is to a degree or point in your chart, the greater its importance in your life. Those of you born with a planet at the same degree as an eclipse are likely to see a high level of activity in the house where the eclipse occurs.

For Gemini, the first eclipse of the year falls on May 26 in your opposite sign, Sagittarius, a Lunar Eclipse in your solar seventh house of personal and business partners. Activity revolves around the nature of your relationships. If they are positive, you benefit from strengthening bonds and fulfilling mutual goals, forming a loving connection or getting married or engaged. When challenging aspects occur, painful issues meet you head-on, calling attention to rifts in the quality of demonstrative love and communication. If contentious exchanges have been escalating, it could mean a breakup or separation from your partner or a parting of ways with business affiliates.

Two weeks later, the first Solar Eclipse of the year occurs in Gemini on June 10 in your solar first house of action, assertiveness, passion, and self-interest. Focus on the message you want to share with others. How do you feel about the quality of your life, your self-image, your health, and the direction your life is taking? What personal matter most needs your attention right now? Take preventive measures to make sure you solidify plans, cherish special relationships, and nurture your body, mind, and spirit.

On November 19, the second Lunar Eclipse of the year falls in Taurus in your solar twelfth house of healing, hidden matters, hospital visits, metaphysical practices, widows, orphans, secret enemies, and charities. Events may occur that call for rehabilitation or recovery from an illness, accident, or emotional setback. In some cases the stress level intensifies, and you need a sabbatical from the daily grind and choose to work from home, away from the hub of intensity. Writers use the seclusion of the twelfth house to churn out assignments, and this eclipse aids in illuminating brilliant ideas.

The final eclipse of 2021 occurs two weeks later on December 4 in Sagittarius and your seventh house of partners, highlighting what you discovered about relationships back in June. Assess the status quo to determine the current conditions and any progress you've made in reinforcing connections, strengthening collaborative ventures, dealing with the public, or taking on roommates. If you're still on rocky ground, be sure to schedule serious discussions and work through the issues. Mediation may be a fair option if differences involve joint assets or intellectual property. Truthful communication clears the air.

Gemini | January

Overall Theme

You begin the year with a strong sense of anticipation, a feeling that discovery is in the air and that you're a major player in manifesting it. Curiosity buoys your spirit, lifting it toward socializing, travel, and a change in routine. Now that eclipses have begun to occur in your sign, a wide range of possibilities emerge. What will it be—a new job, relocation, an unexpected windfall, long-distance travel, or a new direction in communication? Your wish list overflows with prospects.

Relationships

Socializing energizes you. Grab the brass ring and enjoy connections and events with favorite people on the 6th, an excellent day to begin a vacation. Others may be drawn to you on the 24th and seek your advice or pick your brain for solutions. Manage alcohol consumption on the 1st to avoid criticism and heated discussions.

Success and Money

After the first full week of January, showcase your ideas for projects and present their cost-effectiveness and benefits. Excellent lunar energy on the 14th gives you the inside track for making a clear presentation that you'll be able to act on in the days following Uranus's direct motion early that morning. Around the 15th, you get help funding specialized training or travel for business to scope out new territory for possible work expansion.

Pitfalls and Potential Problems

Watch what you say on the 4th when lunar aspects take a hard hit from Mercury and Pluto. Exchanges flare with children or romantic partners. Words sting and can't be easily revoked. Indifference is wounding. Arguments over expenses occur on the 28th. Be careful how you spend money. Include your partner in determining allocation of joint funds. Mercury goes retrograde on the 30th.

Rewarding Days

6, 14, 15, 24

Challenging Days

1, 4, 17, 28

Gemini | February

Overall Theme

With your mentally restless nature, you find it boring to get into a tight groove. Somehow it seems a little easier this month to pace yourself and listen to what others have to say. You have the dexterity to make proficient use of concepts that enhance the quality of your work and improve teamwork. Identify performance areas in need of training for you and colleagues.

Relationships

Enjoy loving moments with your significant other on the 2nd. Talks about jewelry or home decor generate excitement and lead to a firm purchase. Make plans for a Valentine getaway between the 11th and 16th. Don't let loose lips spoil a surprise. Keep secrets regarding gift giving.

Success and Money

You'll get the go-ahead for your well-developed plans related to hiring and staffing after Mercury goes direct on the 20th. Don't be in a hurry to implement them while you wait for vital information to surface. Look for news of a raise or award around the 21st, a stellar day for communicating accomplishment details.

Pitfalls and Potential Problems

Mixed messages populate the landscape on the 7th, when conversation may be misconstrued. Avoid gossip or starting a rumor that will reverberate and cause a major flare-up by the time of the Full Moon in Virgo on February 27, when the planetary lineup challenges the flow and integrity of communication. Avoid evasive tactics when briefing authorities or your credibility will suffer.

Rewarding Days

2, 11, 16, 21

Challenging Days

7, 27, 28

Gemini | March

Overall Theme

The plans you've been mulling for the last few months are ready for action. The bulk of a laborious project nears completion. You're working on reports that are due to present authorities with accomplishment results. Vested employees show excitement about the details of upcoming assignments and eagerly await news of them. You could be tasked with identifying how to allocate talent in this emerging venture.

Relationships

The New Moon in Pisces on the 13th favors travel or contact with people at a distance. Messages pop up from old friends wanting to set up lunch or dinner dates. Members of professional organizations approach you for ideas on how to better use targeted funds to increase visibility, select projects, and add to the membership base. Election to a leadership post is possible this spring.

Success and Money

Seed money is available to fund your goals and commit to purchases of big-ticket items. Sign contracts on the 2nd and celebrate at a favorite haunt. Include a trip, if you can get away for a few days, while the Moon favorably transits your fifth house on March 1 and 2.

Pitfalls and Potential Problems

Choose your words carefully in conversations with partners on the 5th. One wrong word could ignite the flames of anger and misunderstandings. A date to use caution in workplace communication is the 12th, when egos clash, stymieing action. Suggest a roundtable discussion of critical points to get a handle on differences in approach to the work. Confusion reigns at home base on the 27th, creating tension around the approaching Full Moon in Libra on the 28th.

Rewarding Days

2, 13, 14, 20

Challenging Days

5, 12, 19, 27

Gemini | April

Overall Theme

The long parade of planets going retrograde starts on April 27, when Pluto takes the lead in your solar eighth house of joint funds and loans. Examine any irons you have in the fire related to activity in this complex space and take inventory of the issues. Set priorities for addressing each problem. Temper the pace to do a thorough clearing of clutter that blocks progress so that you experience long-anticipated relief.

Relationships

Your work environment dominates the essence of communication this month. The powers that be in your work world discuss organizational resources and allocation of assets around the New Moon on April 11, highlighting promising expansion with opportunity for advancement. Camaraderie improves collaborative enterprise and leads to development of stable team assignments. Cheerleaders set the tone and harmony works wonders.

Success and Money

Those of you who filed tax returns early see more money in your checkbook in the form of a refund, even if it's not as large as you had hoped. Good news about scholarships and tuition costs comes through around the 17th, lessening the anticipated burden. An employer may offer to foot the bill for specialized coursework as part of your continuing education benefit.

Pitfalls and Potential Problems

Cooperative work goes off course on the 3rd, suggesting the need to regroup and examine priorities. Romantic partners show skepticism regarding upcoming plans and seem confused over how far away the two of you are from consensus. Confusion delays execution of management plans around the 9th, not a good day to hold major meetings to discuss details, work adjustments, and assignments.

Rewarding Days

6, 11, 17, 23

Challenging Days

3, 9, 24, 26

Gemini | May

Overall Theme

Don't feel the need to rush into making any changes this month. Your efforts will get caught up in two key planets turning retrograde: Saturn in Aquarius on May 23, which places limitations on your unfolding plans, and Mercury in Gemini on May 29, which causes delays in timing and confusion with messages.

Relationships

Matters connected to your closest partners—romantic or business—are under the microscope now with the Lunar Eclipse on May 26 in your solar seventh house of partnerships. Information comes to light that opens the door for discussion about feelings. Determine what you value about your partnerships and where they need an adjustment. If you've been haggling over differences, negotiate a win-win solution.

Success and Money

You'll enjoy success in seeking medical or legal advice on the 5th. Reach out to long-distance connections on that date as well—you'll learn the truth about someone's health or financial status. Work with children and their interests on the 13th, or apply for a new job if you're in the market. Attend sports events on the 24th or examine investment opportunities when your solar fifth house opens doors.

Pitfalls and Potential Problems

Despite the retrograde planetary energy that is skewing the flow of activity right now, positive leads are coming your way. Avoid taking action, though, on the retrograde station days already mentioned, the Lunar Eclipse on May 26, or the challenging dates listed below. Spend the time doing your homework and strengthening prospects to maximize success.

Rewarding Days

5, 9, 13, 24

Challenging Days

1, 14, 21, 26

Gemini | June

Overall Theme

Why not honor your Sun sign with a special birthday bash? Others in your circle will schedule celebratory meals, parties, and outings at your favorite haunts. Make a wish that your fondest dreams come true, and spend the next year directing the flow of energy in the direction you desire. The Solar Eclipse in Gemini on June 10 fills your spirit with creativity, enthusiasm, and innovative ideas.

Relationships

You have a strong desire to hang out with your closest relatives and friends this month. Reunions are likely. You will hear from people near and far who reach out to touch base. Phone calls and text messages abound. The neighbors drop in to wish you well and your work colleagues celebrate with cake and gag gifts. Harmonious days are the 15th, 23rd, and 28th, when lunar aspects provide a cordial aura perfect for feasting and fun.

Success and Money

Ask for feedback or provide authority figures with a status report at least a day after the Solar Eclipse on the 10th. Entertainment and travel bargains are yours for the asking. Request upgrades and the best discounts possible on the 28th. Skip the 3rd and 6th for requesting a raise or budget increase.

Pitfalls and Potential Problems

Misplaced humor lands you in the doghouse at home on the 18th. Sensitive housemates stay in a funk for the weekend. Watch spending and splurging on the 24th, when the Full Moon in Capricorn weakens your resolve to limit the use of credit cards. The Moon in Pisces on the 3rd in your solar tenth house of career reminds you to check your facts before rushing in with professional insight that doesn't hold up.

Rewarding Days

10, 15, 23, 28

Challenging Days

3, 6, 18, 24

Gemini | July

Overall Theme

Social invitations arrive from all over. Friends host multiple holiday get-togethers from the 2nd through the 5th. Immediate family members have the limelight the following weekend, with a leading role for you, while cousins and neighbors are on board for hosting middle-of-the-month action. Work associates celebrate success and acknowledge teamwork during the last week of the month. Decisions require cooperative enterprise to succeed.

Relationships

Although harmony reflects the overall tone of the alliances in your life this month, the most difficult day could be the 4th, when sensitive feelings surface and flare-ups occur over tension that has been simmering for far too long. Use some private time to sort out what you believe to be the issue. You'll be surprised by what you discover to be the root of the problem. Don't make light of another's angst. Once you discover the source, be proactive about apologizing.

Success and Money

You find a few unanticipated bargains and unusual foods when you shop for holiday fare on the 2nd. You could splurge on a gift for yourself when you spend the birthday money you put aside to buy a long-desired object. Others benefit from a substantial reduction in the price of tickets for an entertainment venue that gives you and those you treat access to a high-quality, memorable event.

Pitfalls and Potential Problems

Incomplete information and poor communication are the culprits around the 15th, when offended parties argue for diverse strategies. Things are not much better when you return to the work environment on the 19th and note the stubborn standoff that remains. Solve it before the Full Moon in Aquarius on the 23rd.

Rewarding Days

2, 9, 12, 28

Challenging Days

4, 15, 19, 23

Gemini | August

Overall Theme

Uranus has been creating unstable conditions in your solar twelfth house of secrets, incomplete plans, and healing all year. The edginess you've been feeling is a reality check. The planet of unexpected eruptions goes retrograde on August 19, warning you not to divulge sensitive information at this time. Sudden glitches may appear, making it evident that you need a more advantageous time to fine-tune and reveal details of your big picture.

Relationships

You're interested in reaching out more to those you cherish and those you'd like to reconnect with on a friendship basis who have disappeared from your radar screen. You'll have success on the 2nd if you remember to share the floor with others and assimilate the perspectives they describe. Reuniting with others works best if you make phone calls to check mutual calendars and set times to meet over a drink or a meal. Avoid the 1st, 4th, or 7th, when difficult aspects deter smooth communication.

Success and Money

The New Moon in Leo falls in your solar third house on the 8th, facilitating the installation of software or the purchase of electronic equipment or a new vehicle at an agreeable price, especially before August 19. Sign up for or start educational classes around August 10, when favorable Mercury aspects support the learning experience. If you teach classes, the students enjoy your style and the subject matter.

Pitfalls and Potential Problems

Sharing secrets prematurely leads to conflicts with confidants and hurt for loved ones. Keep anger in check on August 18, when testy Mercury-Mars aspects aggravate parties. Avoid sarcastic exchanges that day, when irritation and annoying barbs could creep unnecessarily into conversations.

Rewarding Days

2, 10, 11, 19

Challenging Days

1, 4, 7, 18

Gemini | September

Overall Theme

Air-sign Moons work favorably for you all month to keep communication and humor flowing, especially before Mercury goes retrograde on September 27. The diversity of intelligent ideas charges your batteries. You activate your networks by sending out feelers for interest in staffing professional projects, various memberships, food clubs, sports teams, and alumni associations. Be on the alert for telemarketing scams early in the month and block offending phone numbers.

Relationships

Learn all you can about relationships this month—new and existing ones—because building solid connections serves you well in light of shifting responsibilities. Analyze why you think critical relationships are important to you. What do you like best about them? What needs work? Review memberships you hold with organizations. Are you energized by these associations? If not, consider sampling at least one new group with a philosophy that interests you. Join if you like what you see.

Success and Money

Those of you in sales reconnect with old clients and set up meetings to showcase new products. Assess how current products are working and determine what management would like to change. Go to the drawing board and prepare a presentation that highlights potent possibilities, and you could see a fat commission in your paycheck this quarter.

Pitfalls and Potential Problems

Enjoy social gatherings on the 2nd, but don't whip out your checkbook to spend money on a whim. The 7th draws attention to household goods and appliances that need replacement. Shop to compare products and prices, but wait until after the 9th to make purchases. The 18th is a good day to research college options.

Rewarding Days

1, 10, 18, 28

Challenging Days

2, 7, 20, 24

Gemini | October

Overall Theme

This month you have a surplus of ideas filling your mind with nervous energy, and you must decide what to tackle first. Stick with the plan that provides your bread and butter and select one or two new directions to explore for exciting possibilities. Saturn, Mercury, and Jupiter all turn direct this month in air signs, creating shifting energy that requires a close look at progress. Be sure to leave some wiggle room in your calendar.

Relationships

Your social life takes off this month, with parties, dinner dates, and sporting events that include a mix of relatives and friends. Two days that stand out are October 6 and 15. Offer choices for entertainment venues and be flexible if the group prefers a different direction. The 3rd is not the best date for a night out, as moodiness could get in the way of enjoyment.

Success and Money

Celebrate on the 1st when good news about raises or bonuses unfolds at the end of the workweek. Spread the word to team members and acknowledge stellar performance by organizing a presentation ceremony. Cyber-shopping works on the 15th, and you can resume auto shopping on the 24th. Personal vibrations pick up momentum and call for action. Plan festivities for family birthdays, weddings, or engagements.

Pitfalls and Potential Problems

Be aware of a hard ad campaign for sales of inferior goods or prices that are far below those of competitors. Especially examine the quality of appliances on the 3rd and 5th. The Full Moon in Aries on the 20th stifles fluid communication when anger issues erupt and reveal that parties have been withholding the depth of their true feelings.

Rewarding Days

1, 6, 15, 24

Challenging Days

3, 5, 20, 25

Gemini | November

Overall Theme

Holiday excitement takes over the water-cooler chat this month, with colleagues sharing plans, trips, and traditions in merrymaking. Clear your space of unfinished tasks over the next two weeks so you can thoroughly enjoy the downtime. Make provisions to put off less pressing tasks until early December, including cleaning and decorating for upcoming gatherings.

Relationships

You know so many people. Why not invite someone to your holiday dinner who may be alone or recovering from an illness or setback and could use a cheerful emotional lift? Do your homework to learn favorite dishes and find the recipes. Pay it forward for past kindnesses and watch the glow of pleasure from tablemates at your Thanksgiving feast. Tantalizing aromas from special dishes take the ambience to a whole new level.

Success and Money

Right before mid-month, certain Geminis hear news of exciting changes in organizational advancement. You'll learn of changes in authority that emerge, along with exciting innovations and additional funding to support the expanding mission. Enjoy shopping for items for children and holiday gifts on the 3rd. Review mailing lists and wrap presents to be mailed early.

Pitfalls and Potential Problems

Harmony hits the skids at home base on the 1st when emotional outbursts erupt early in the day. The misunderstanding may revolve around information that had not been previously known. Later the heat is still on until cooler heads prevail. Talk it out. Romantic exchanges reach stressful levels on the 7th, when challenges arise over disclosure of facts.

Rewarding Days

3, 13, 24, 25

Challenging Days

1, 7, 19, 21

Gemini | December

Overall Theme

The Lunar Eclipse in Sagittarius on the 4th ushers in a breath of fresh air in your solar seventh house of partnerships and encourages heartfelt discussion of mutual goals. Break out the music and the holiday games and have a blast when visitors pop in for a meal or a cookie exchange.

Relationships

During the Balsamic Moon on the 2nd, you bump up against work colleagues who are in a snit and pick an argument late in the day over conditions they don't like. Suggest a review of current procedures and schedule a discussion for the 9th, when others have a chance to gather concerns. Family relationships blossom this month, except for the 25th, when key individuals feel tired and tense, including you. Plan a family night out on the 27th.

Success and Money

Make lists and buy all the gifts and goods you need, especially jewelry, before Venus goes retrograde on December 19. Careful shopping nets quality products and bargains on the 7th. Curb the use of credit cards so you'll have fewer bills in the new year. Enjoy a gift you receive from a special someone in a distant location who conveys a loving message.

Pitfalls and Potential Problems

If you're a baker, watch the oven on December 3, 17, and 19, when sweet treats could be too hot to handle. The Full Moon in Gemini on December 18 brings mixed signals. Details you're working on seem to go smoothly until out of the blue, you wrangle with misleading information and an outright fib. Check facts and ask for proof.

Rewarding Days

4, 7, 9, 27

Challenging Days

2, 17, 19, 25

Gemini Action Table

These dates reflect the best—but not the only—times for success and ease in these activities, according to your Sun sign.

	JAN	FEB	MAR	APR	MAY	JUN	JUL	AUG	SEP	OCT	NOV	DEC
Move	14			6		28			1		3	
Romance		2			13		2					7
Seek counseling/coaching			21					10		24		
Ask for a raise				23					18			9
Vacation	6							2			25	
Get a loan		21					9			1		

Cancer

The Crab
June 20 to July 22

Element: Water

Quality: Cardinal

Polarity: Yin/feminine

Planetary Ruler: The Moon

Meditation: I have faith in the promptings of my heart

Gemstone: Pearl

Power Stones: Moonstone, Chrysocolla

Key Phrase: I feel

Glyph: Crab's claws

Anatomy: Stomach, breasts

Colors: Silver, pearl white

Animals: Crustaceans, cows, chickens

Myths/Legends: Hercules and the Crab, Asherah, Hecate

House: Fourth

Opposite Sign: Capricorn

Flower: Larkspur

Keyword: Receptivity

The Cancer Personality

Strengths, Talents, and the Creative Spark

With one of the best memories in the zodiac, you take in enormous amounts of information and share it well when others pick your brain. Cancers have a photographic memory and recall where in a book, paper, or program they found certain facts—some of you even cite the page number. Many consider you the institutional memory of an organization, an asset your boss wholly appreciates. Once you learn a birthday, you remember it for life and often send a note to acknowledge celebrants. Both male and female Cancers have strong nurturing genes. Males frequently run the household, prepare the meals, and take the lead in household chores such as cleaning and laundry. They may also be the parent who gets up in the middle of the night when the children are sick or takes on diaper duty for the babies.

The Moon rules your water sign, the first of three in this element to appear in the twelve-sign lineup. You are extremely intuitive and know the scoop deep inside, fully understanding what is going on instantly. Sometimes cohorts call you a human lie detector. Many of you show the depth of your feelings and life experiences through work. You make excellent leaders, managers, and supervisors and understand the psychology of the workplace, what it needs to thrive, and how to integrate the talent pool to strengthen goal accomplishment. You'll fight for the underdog to make sure fair business practices are part of the institutional framework and distribute the workload to maximize opportunities for employee growth.

You often follow unconventional paths and make excellent entrepreneurs or business owners. Among the businesses in which you excel are those that include metaphysics, astrology, and various forms of intuitive art. If you teach these topics, your students are in for a treat since you develop excellent, often colorful training materials and use case studies to drive home important points.

Intimacy and Personal Relationships

Love runs deep for you, and when you first recognize that you've met the person of your dreams, you go running back to your safe, protective shell to sort out your feelings before making any declarations. When you fall in love, you fall hard. Once you're sure, you don't want to let go of the object of your affections. You hug and kiss them every chance you get. You're loyal and put your cherished one on a pedestal to be adored up close or from a distance, believing the two of you want the same type of intimacy. You're extremely sensitive and pick up on slights or sudden shifts in the level of affection. If you find you've landed a cold fish instead of a touchy-feely type, the relationship is headed for the sand pile. Word on the street is that you're overly possessive. Maybe some of you are, but the truth is you like to show that you care, and reinforce it frequently. You're not the type who is satisfied with a significant other who tells you once or twice in the early stages of the relationship that they care and then later tells you you're insecure because you like to hear "I love you" often.

Values and Resources

The fourth house of home and foundations means the world to you. This includes family members and those you treat like family. You want people you care about to feel welcome and comfortable in your home, and that means showing your nurturing side, listening to their troubles, and feeding them delicious meals. You value your parents and their wisdom and traditions, incorporating many of them into your family routines, especially during holidays. Many of you enjoy the parenting role and cherish closeness and affection with your children, building trust and encouraging them to form their own opinions about life and to learn from mistakes along the way. You value commitment and loyalty in others and seldom make promises you don't intend to keep. A priority for you is owning a spacious, lovely home, with beautiful landscaping, a welcoming front door, and a kitchen with multiple ovens and state-of-the art equipment that make meal preparation a pleasure. Viva connection!

Blind Spots and Blockages

Although you are very action-oriented and accomplish much, you often let others get away with bad habits in managing tasks at home or at work. Instead of calling attention privately to slackers' lack of follow-through, you do the work personally without acknowledging the performance shortfall that needs to be addressed in the present moment. You prefer to keep matters private and not make a scene. That doesn't mean you forget about the anger or disappointment you're stuffing inside of you; in fact, you get cranky and no one knows why. You let others get away with their behavior without admonishment until your threshold for tolerance reaches the boiling point. Then you let the person know what you really think, living up to your reputation for being a crabby Cancer. Ideally, you would address the matter and request corrections before accountability and deadlines prove embarrassing. You are also very sensitive to criticism and will lose sleep over encounters that leave you feeling vulnerable or slighted. Learn to chill and file these incidents under "so yesterday."

Goals and Success

Since you're good at so many things, the biggest dilemma you face is narrowing down your options or you'll work day and night to get everything done. You are very service-oriented, and the security of government employment attracts you at an early age. When asked if you're a morning or a night person, you often answer "both." Most of you enjoy two or more careers during your lifetime and sometimes hold two jobs simultaneously. Self-employment appeals to you, including engaging in freelance contracts, writing, and training. You may excel in multiple facets of food management connected to restaurant management, catering, developing recipes, and writing and publishing food articles. Social issues hold your interest. You use your expertise in analyzing problems, creating and conducting workshops and seminars, writing about personal and business relationships, and providing advice in a consulting practice in various fields of expertise. With the Moon as your ruler, you enjoy professions linked to fourth-house matters such as real estate—your own or others. Examples include decorating and remodeling homes, home appraisals, home inspections related to closing on a sale, landscape design, and feng shui.

Cancer Keywords for 2021
Receptive, reflective, reliant

The Year Ahead for Cancer

With Jupiter and Saturn in Aquarius in your solar eighth house in 2021, your analytical side gives financial management, estates, and joint funds much-needed attention. You'll understand early in the year where to identify issues and what it takes to produce a plan that stabilizes income, assets, and retirement funds. Uranus in Taurus tests friendships and group endeavors in your solar eleventh house, while favorite humanitarian projects stimulate your passion to take the lead in doing as much good in the world as your nurturing heart can manage. Neptune in Pisces stimulates your higher mind in your solar ninth house of travel and awakens your intuitive gifts and dream state. A trip to a distant country ties in with a need to lift the spirits of those who have experienced natural disasters and economic downturns. Both personal and professional partnerships undergo excavation of sorts as you dig through layers of complications courtesy of Pluto's long transit in Capricorn in your solar seventh house of relationships. Know that with your sensitivity and smarts, you'll tune into the truth and implement winning solutions in 2021.

Jupiter

With last year's passage of Jupiter in Capricorn through your solar seventh house of partners, you made progress in the quality of relationships that brought you greater satisfaction through stronger bonds of commitment. These changes strengthened both your personal and your professional connections. For some of you, that means marriage plans advance, while others dissolve long-standing partnerships. In 2021 Jupiter begins the year in Aquarius in your solar eighth house of partnership funds, money from new sources, joint ventures, and investments. You and a partner may be contemplating the purchase of a new home by shopping mortgage rates, examining real estate values, and selecting the perfect location. Those who marry draw up wills, examine joint assets, and adjust tax structures. It's possible that the self-employed among you seek legal advice while taking on a business partner in a collaborative enterprise. Other possible outcomes include accepting new employment offers, holding down more than one job, expanding your role in freelance consulting, and receiving unexpected windfalls or assets from a settled claim, estate, or will. The eighth house represents extractions that include acknowledging problems buried deep in your psyche or intimacy-related fears. Jupiter's presence here helps bring on the karmic release that allows you to experience the healing you desire along with more fulfilling relationships. Don't be afraid to probe—the truth will set you free.

Saturn

Cancer, you have another player in your solar eighth house this year in serious-minded, responsibility-obsessed Saturn in Aquarius, whose arrival in December 2020 stakes a claim on your financial outlook and joint ventures for the next 2½ years. Take this visitor seriously, since the stern taskmaster insists that you reflect strongly on money management through debt repayment, purchasing priorities, partnership assets, and investments, including savings and retirement funds. If you have played loose with your budget or don't really have one (normally not a Cancer habit but often related to out-of-control relationships that add financial burdens), new procedures are in the wind. Saturn has a way of calling attention to the need to pay down debt, get rid of excessive credit card balances, and examine the volume of random spending. If you're addicted to online shopping and don't know where the debt came from at the end of the month, Saturn is about to treat you to a reality check. The last thing a cozy, comfy Cancer needs is sleepless nights and fretful dreams brought on by whip-cracking Saturn putting you on a guilt trip for loading your credit cards with debt, living beyond your means, or letting out-of-control conditions skew your judgment. Who needs roadblocks that force you to deal with the consequences of your actions when you could be reaping the benefits of sound financial plans and the rewards they bring? Investigation succeeds when you are willing to probe within and identify what holds you back. If you need help getting on track, seek the advice of well-qualified professionals to look at reliable options. Those of you born between June 21 and July 5 are most affected by Saturn's transit this year.

Uranus

Your solar eleventh house of friendships, plans and wishes, groups, organizations, and employer's assets hosts transiting Uranus in Taurus all year in a generally harmonious aspect to your Cancer Sun. Uranus acts up periodically this year when it clashes with transiting Jupiter and Saturn in Aquarius in your solar eighth house, bringing unpredictable outcomes to financial dealings such as salary negotiation, estate settlement, mortgage loans, joint expenditures, and partnership assets. Cancers born between June 26 and July 7 experience the most intense activity. Be on the lookout for telltale signs of discord over activities in professional organizations, leadership direction, and planned projects. On the fence about retaining membership in a longtime affiliation? A meaningful way to tap into Uranian energy is to analyze a group's productivity and examine the philosophy to see if humanitarian trends are in sync with needs. What is the status of membership—gaining or losing? Find out why shifts occur. Your assessment may lead you to a leadership role and deep satisfaction that your contributions open doors for organizational growth and result in goal accomplishment that increases benefits for stakeholders. Your attention to detail may lead you to a new career.

Neptune

Opportunities abound with options to expand your vision as Neptune in Pisces makes harmonious aspects with your Cancer Sun as it moves through your solar ninth house of the higher mind, travel, new thinking patterns, spiritual insight, and foreign cultures. If you've been waiting for a solid breakthrough or evidence of truth, validation is possible this year when you activate your plans and step outside your comfort zone. Idealism is magnificent, but not when it blurs the facts and leads to faulty decisions. Admit it: you have been struggling with conflicting thoughts and confusing evidence, sifting through lies and feeling deluded by information you thought was valid but turned out to be more fantasy and fiction than your logical mind wants to handle. You have been slowly discovering the truth about friendships, career management, family issues, and long-term goals. Every time you think you're going to implement a change, new facts come to light to cloud the images you have of people and their behavior. Then you take a long breath instead of acting on what you've discovered. That's the Neptune lazy streak at work, feeding you the message that it's okay to escape from reality. Even though you know the truth and your intuition is right on the money about these matters, you benefit from extra insight and clarity with this transit. Just make sure you don't spend too much time daydreaming. This year Neptune most affects Cancers born between July 9 and 16, as it travels over degrees that create a harmonious trine aspect with your Sun and puts you ahead of the curve in discovering kindred spirits and members of your soul family. Use this gift wisely.

Pluto

Your solar seventh house of intimate and business partners is almost taking on a lighter feeling these days after surviving several intense eclipses in Capricorn in 2019–2020, as well as Jupiter and Saturn leaving Capricorn last December. You're not quite out of the woods yet since Pluto has been in residence in your solar seventh house since 2008, reminding you of any relationship issues you still have to address. No doubt some of your seventh-house baggage has disappeared over the course of this long-term transit. These recent eclipses and planets stirred the pot when they connected with Pluto, pushing concerns you have been repressing to the surface. Now it's time to face the music and dance to the tune of the karma cleaners. What have you discovered lingering deep in your psyche that conjures up fear instead of confidence in putting your cards on the table and speaking up? You could be paying the price for keeping too much angst inside that suppresses your light in a variety of ways. You may be dealing with intimate relationships that do not meet your needs, work partners who stifle your independence and drive, roommates whose bad habits keep you on edge because responsibility is too one-sided, or collaborative ventures that suck the air out of you instead of giving you large doses of creative energy to successfully sustain momentum and keep passion alive. Start asking questions and schedule serious discussions. You could find the pot of gold at the end of the rainbow. Cancers born between July 15 and 19 see the most action from this opposition transit of Pluto in 2021. All you have to do to seed your new beginning is say these magic words: "This isn't working for me."

How Will This Year's Eclipses Affect You?

In 2021, a total of four eclipses occur. There will be two Lunar Eclipses and two Solar Eclipses, creating intense periods that begin to manifest a few months before their actual dates. Eclipses unfold in cycles involving all twelve signs of the zodiac, and usually occur in pairs about two weeks apart. Think of eclipses as opportunities to release old patterns and conditions that have outlived their usefulness. Have no fear of them, since they can bring you unexpected surprises and windfalls. The closer an eclipse is to a degree or point in your chart, the greater its importance in your life. Those of you born with a planet at the same degree as an eclipse are likely to see a high level of activity in the house where the eclipse occurs.

May 26 ushers in the year's first Lunar Eclipse in Sagittarius in your solar sixth house, reminding you to get medical and dental checkups, work on fitness and eating habits, and keep records of progress on goals you've developed to live a healthier life. Tests may uncover the need for surgery or specialized treatments. Preventive measures provide relief and mitigate uncertainty. You could be involved in organizing a project or installing a more efficient communication system. If your job has been upsetting your equilibrium, you might be searching for new work after getting hints that conditions have become untenable for you after last year's Sagittarius eclipses.

On December 4, another eclipse occurs in Sagittarius in your solar sixth house. This time it's a Solar Eclipse that elaborates on current matters related to everyday routines, workplace dynamics, organizational projects, health, medications, and nutrition. Some Cancers may be investing in kitchen equipment, especially products that aid in meal preparation and streamline the time you spend on this chore. Dietary concerns have you tracking your food choices and balancing the types of foods you eat to increase your energy level.

The year's first Solar Eclipse occurs on June 10 in Gemini in your solar twelfth house of privacy, contemplation, and work that is percolating on the back burner. You experienced a Lunar Eclipse in this house last year in Gemini, and now you're ready to act on information you've been mulling over, hoping to make important decisions and make your new intentions known. Those of you with ill family members or close friends rally support for critical care and spend more than the usual amount of time visiting medical facilities. Meditation has a calming effect and aids in finding solutions.

The second Lunar Eclipse of 2021 takes place on November 19 in Taurus in your solar eleventh house of friendships, goals, plans, associations, and group endeavors. This department of life is fortuitous for bringing solid new relationships into your life and helping you discard the ones that no longer have relevance. With a little help from Uranus in Taurus in this house, you start taking inventory of your memberships in personal and professional groups. The opportunity to review the organizations' philosophies and goals sheds light on how much involvement you wish to have or whether you want to disconnect. With growing awareness of your desire to find new challenges, you are drawn to insightful humanitarian initiatives and meet new contacts who welcome you to participate, take on a leading role, or engage in fundraising drives to raise the profile of meaningful causes.

Cancer | January

Overall Theme

A strong need to communicate with diverse contacts dominates the landscape this month. Earth and water lunations provide positive vibes that help you direct your feelings and state what is on your mind. Negotiating may be a factor in getting the best price for services and signing contracts for electronic equipment, vehicles, or appliances. Your neighborhood may be the location of extended holiday celebrations.

Relationships

With more frequency than usual, you interact through phone calls or visits with siblings and other relatives. Excellent dates to share news or personal thoughts are the 4th, 12th, and 17th, when you meet with neighbors, share intimate moments with your partner, or visit in-laws or special friends who live at a distance. You might take a post-holiday trip with your significant other to celebrate the new year.

Success and Money

Visibility adds to your popularity with collaborators who value your talent and invite you to participate in new projects. You may be offered a personal or professional partnership on the 12th or be invited to address a work-related group in another city around the 17th. Avoid asking for raises on the 20th or asking for funding increases for work initiatives on that date or the 30th.

Pitfalls and Potential Problems

Acting prematurely leads to a disappointing outcome if you're competing for an assignment or waiting to hear about a loan. Essential data may be missing, or financial reports critical to a decision may be late. Check with colleagues who may have key material that will help to expedite the outcome. Stay away from making a final pitch on the 20th; the 27th looks better for you.

Rewarding Days

4, 12, 17, 27

Challenging Days

1, 7, 20, 30

Cancer | February

Overall Theme

Mid-winter demands put you in the mood for a short vacation or a romantic getaway to celebrate Valentine's Day or take you away from mentally challenging work. Friends may ask to join you or invite you to an enjoyable event. The New Moon on the 11th is a favorable time to obtain estimates for home improvements or refinancing rates. Contact three firms to see what competitors can do to win your business.

Relationships

This month's aspects draw intimacy and lighthearted discussions into the limelight to strengthen partnership communication. Some of the discussion revolves around spending joint funds, offering each of you a chance to weigh in on decisions. Single Cancers may experience a canceled date or rough patch with a prospective partner, especially around the 4th. Anticipate a positive experience around the 24th, when dreamy, harmonious vibes open the door for a deeper relationship.

Success and Money

Workplace routines feel more coordinated and increase rapport among teammates. Goal alignment ensures cooperation and awareness of pending deadlines. Good vibes aid in reviewing assignments, shifting roles, and scheduling meetings to put everyone on the same page, especially from the 8th to the 12th. Avoid arguments in professional groups or among friends around February 18, when focus can be an issue and immovable thinking patterns prevail.

Pitfalls and Potential Problems

Signing documents without reading the fine print or understanding the details of contracts could lead to stressful moments this month, especially around the Full Moon on February 27. Succumbing to pressure from peers or your significant other leads to agreeing to participate in something you don't really want to do. Stall until you have clearer information.

Rewarding Days

1, 6, 11, 24

Challenging Days

4, 7, 18, 27

Cancer | March

Overall Theme

The month begins and ends with matters connected to home base and the people who live there. Expect both laughter-filled moments and emotional outbursts. When you're feeling out of sync, be sure you don't fall into a crabby funk and kill the joy that others are feeling. Whatever you do, don't bring your disappointments into the workplace. Be receptive to modifying plans related to unforeseen weather conditions, event cancellations, and health matters.

Relationships

You'll find that family members and intimate partners have plenty to say about conditions in your household. Unfolding scenarios revolve around children's activities, recreation choices, space modification, and investments. Set the stage for compatible interactions around March 1 to show you're willing to listen and that each family member's opinion counts. Plan surprises inclusive of each person's preferences, even if you have to select different dates to accommodate choices.

Success and Money

Use the time between the 5th and the 9th to shop for goods and make product comparisons. Don't rely on cheap imitations to get the job done if you're in the market for new appliances—the low price may be more expensive in the long run. After the New Moon on the 13th, you're ready to make your purchase. Your talent may get you a raise or promotion this year.

Pitfalls and Potential Problems

With the Full Moon in Libra and your solar fourth house of home on the 28th, your best strategy is to avoid sulking or becoming overly emotional when discussing issues with family members. Keep a cool head when workplace snafus mean extra work for you and coworkers. Take the lead in making adjustments.

Rewarding Days

1, 6, 8, 13

Challenging Days

4, 12, 18, 28

Cancer | April

Overall Theme
Your social life could use a pick-me-up this month. An abundance of options draws your attention. Pick one or two and chill. Even though most days this month call for your attention to duty and escalating responsibilities, go ahead and book an enjoyable weekend getaway and come back energetically charged to manage pressing issues. Clear it with your boss first and then ask your most reliable coworker to cover for you while you spend quality time experiencing a new adventure.

Relationships
Spend quality time with your significant other on April 1, 7, and 23. Include your children in recreational or sports venues to establish bonding time. The New Moon favors professional relationships on April 11–12, indicating that harmony dominates the workplace. Avoid arguments with members of groups or organizations and steer clear of a standoff with a friend on April 14.

Success and Money
Start planning a successful strategy to implement right after the New Moon on the 11th. Your intuitive mind attracts all the components and the positive energy necessary to bring plans into alignment. Excellent vibes in your solar third house at the end of the month favor signing contracts and having meaningful conversations that unite efforts and showcase a win.

Pitfalls and Potential Problems
Personal attacks on others' opinions cloud the integrity of group accomplishments. Take a breath if your feelings get hurt over criticism. Take the high road by asking questions that show you're open to improving the outcome. Don't make money decisions on April 26–27, when Full Moon energy dominates the flow of communication and expression is testy.

Rewarding Days
1, 7, 12, 23

Challenging Days
3, 14, 21, 26

Cancer | May

Overall Theme

With two critical planets turning retrograde this month and the first Lunar Eclipse of the year on May 26 in Sagittarius, you'll have to take a hard look at how quickly you want to proceed with pending decisions. Saturn shifts direction on May 23, lending an air of uncertainty to long-term plans for nearly five months. Mercury turns retrograde on May 29 and spends three weeks delaying plans, sending confusing messages, and messing with the operation of equipment.

Relationships

After starting the month on a challenging note, affection and heart-to-heart talks with partners revive the love theme and lead to suggestions for spending quality time together or planning vacations. The New Moon on the 11th favors interaction with friends, reviewing goals, and meeting with those involved in humanitarian projects. Turnover is occurring among officers in professional organizations, opening the door to run for office or offer your time to chair a group.

Success and Money

The first three quarters of the month favor getting the job done, outlining future plans, and engaging in group endeavors. From the 23rd on, the energy becomes erratic and slows down the pace of your can-do attitude. Watch what you spend during the last full week of May. Start researching and comparing costs the first weekend of the month and again around May 18–20 to see what the competition offers.

Pitfalls and Potential Problems

Don't even think about signing important legal documents, home purchase agreements, car loans, or contracts for other pricey investments after the 22nd. You could overlook the fine print or misunderstand the terms. Put fresh eyes on the details through the help of a partner, business advisor, or attorney.

Rewarding Days

2, 7, 11, 23

Challenging Days

1, 16, 26, 27

Cancer | June

Overall Theme
Travel may be part of the landscape this month and may include business trips to locations at a distance, vacations to foreign countries, or visits to relatives at a distance. Some of you have to cram for exams if you're seeking new credentials and enrolled in higher education classes. Simultaneously, career demands accelerate, with authority figures demanding accountability reports and requesting details about staff performance.

Relationships
Connections with friends and groups take on a celebratory tone. You could become closer to people at a distance and may possibly enjoy new respect for colleagues in distant locations, your in-laws, or those with the gift of intuition. You could experience a breakthrough and take on a new awareness of the relationship you have with yourself when you stop demanding perfection in everything you do.

Success and Money
An eclipse on June 10 in your solar twelfth house of reflection and behind-the-scenes planning may open the door to a promotion or raise. Discuss the prospect with your boss after the 12th, especially if you've been discussing moving up the chain of command. Be sure to have a clear understanding of the timing of events. Ask questions about your role and new responsibilities.

Pitfalls and Potential Problems
Avoid discussing anything to do with assignments or work-related problems on June 4–6. Authority figures may be dealing with challenging money disclosures or shortfalls in funding or fielding outside complaints about the quality of the work. Be alert that you may be called to meetings later in the month. Start taking inventory of accomplishments in the interim. On June 21, steer clear of jealous competitive types who cause trouble by embellishing the facts.

Rewarding Days
3, 7, 10, 12

Challenging Days
4, 6, 21, 26

Cancer | July

Overall Theme

Grab your beach blanket and head to the shore for some well-deserved sun and fun. Join the festive crowds for holiday venues and celebrate summer attractions to the max. Visit favorite amusement parks or state fairs for a change of pace. Take time to reflect on your blessings and clear your head, and return from your getaway prepared to launch your next venture. The 2nd is a good day to begin a trip.

Relationships

People at home base claim your attention as travel mates or adventure seekers. Work mates extend invitations for company parties that may include a ballgame or picnic. Steer clear of arguments with friends on the 4th and with children or younger contacts on the 16th, when communication could break down over a desire to take unnecessary risks. You love company, so host a get-together or visit relatives you seldom see.

Success and Money

July 2 is a good day to lobby for a raise or bonus or to submit a resume if you're seeking new employment. Be patient for the next few weeks while those in authority enjoy vacations and table hiring decisions. Use purchasing power on the 12th to snag a luxury item at a great price. You and a partner disagree over plans and serious decisions on the 23rd. Review financial matters and investments on the 24th.

Pitfalls and Potential Problems

You can get caught up in the glamour of an over-the-top vacation without considering the financial burden that results. Be sure to get more than one estimate for a comparable adventure or for high-end appliances or vehicles. Examine your values, especially on the 24th and the 4th, when the deal looks too good to be true.

Rewarding Days

2, 9, 12, 18

Challenging Days

4, 16, 23, 24

Cancer | August

Overall Theme

Diversification and reliability are key words this month. With remote work becoming more popular than ever, you may want to brush up on some of your interpersonal skills to get ahead of the competition. Seek opportunities that allow you to apply excellent collaboration strategies with team members across the globe or within your employer's network. Creativity spans the product universe and contributes to your desire for security. The talent pool resonates to high-level performance. Stay true to your action-oriented point of view.

Relationships

Get ready for the retrograde motion of Uranus in Taurus on August 19, when the mission or philosophy of important groups shifts. How will change affect your attitude and continuing membership? Check the status of personal and business partnerships. Siblings show caring ways on August 11; children need attention on the 15th.

Success and Money

Work on your image and wardrobe on August 6, and take care of health matters on the 17th. You may not agree with solutions to medical or work problems at this time. Say no to a financial proposal on the 8th that comes to you unexpectedly. Contracts work favorably on the 11th after you weigh options carefully. Spend time strategizing privately on the 31st for matters that need a decision next month.

Pitfalls and Potential Problems

Enjoy travel with romantic partners around the 23rd and 24th, but watch intake of alcohol or recreational drugs that affect judgment. The Full Moon on the 22nd in your solar eighth house has you examining proposed expenses and pondering whether the value of what you get is worth it; expect an escalation clause or some type of unplanned fee.

Rewarding Days

6, 11, 24, 31

Challenging Days

8, 15, 17, 22

Cancer | September

Overall Theme

Your intuition is strong this month, and your hunches are right on target. You put them to good use early in the month assessing romantic relationships and options for travel. A workshop or seminar at a distance is a good bet. Reading and study material includes metaphysical works and spiritual journeys. Those of you engaged in business management have job-related trips that may take you to more than one city.

Relationships

The 3rd, 9th, and 30th favor social interaction of a romantic nature—dates, vacations, entertainment venues, and surprise gifts or engagements. Invitations come from distant locations asking for a commitment for holiday gatherings. Be sure to discuss details with your significant other. Interaction with international visitors may claim a slot on the calendar after mid-month.

Success and Money

Speculation related to investments calls for a decision before the 27th and may come about through the suggestion of a contact at a distance. Work with a trusted financial advisor before agreeing to a money transfer, avoiding action on the 7th or 11th. Postpone talking about the workplace budget until after September 7, when new reports shed light on availability of operating capital.

Pitfalls and Potential Problems

Use that intuition of yours to identify spinners of tales who exaggerate returns on investments around the time of the Full Moon on the 20th. Be sure to get bids on contracts for pending work in either business or personal space. Look over warranties—length and what is included in the coverage.

Rewarding Days

3, 5, 9, 30

Challenging Days

2, 7, 11, 20

Cancer | October

Overall Theme
It is an opportune time for you to follow up on seeds you have planted for your future security. Areas of interest to you are likely to be employment venues, opportunities for advancement, and your plan to escalate savings in retirement and household funds. Schedule time with authority figures to discuss performance, goals, and meaningful next steps that keep you in alignment with your desired career path. At home base, talk over savings plans with your family to strengthen options.

Relationships
This month offers abundant opportunities to interact harmoniously with neighbors, siblings, and other relatives. Work colleagues and team members claim your time starting on the 11th and for the next few days, when deep discussions cover assignments and strategic timelines that define the plan of work and integration of key roles. If you want to set a team meeting, this is the week to do it. By the 15th, everyone should be on board and enthusiastic about the project, especially you.

Success and Money
Information becomes available regarding raises for the year ahead and possibly awards for bonuses earned in 2021. Make sure your record of accomplishments is available, and be sure to acknowledge members of your team and how pooled resources brought success. Check health insurance for ways to improve coverage and keep costs down.

Pitfalls and Potential Problems
Credit checks are more essential than ever, with identity theft and front-porch bandits making off with ordered goods. Be on guard on the 1st, 2nd, and 20th when managing transactions. Make special arrangements for delivery of online orders. Say no to dating sites that want to connect you to potential partners from outside your country of origin.

Rewarding Days
5, 11, 15, 22

Challenging Days
1, 2, 17, 20

Cancer | November

Overall Theme

Overcommitment is the word of the month, even though it starts out showering you with abundant energy and excitement. You have high expectations to finish major tasks and get a jump on holiday plans, especially with the last Lunar Eclipse of the year on November 19 in your solar eleventh house. You'd like to take some time off, yet guilt over unfinished business holds you back. Let this be the year when you ask for help instead of absorbing the workload and ending up exhausted.

Relationships

Family harmony is powerful and bonds are strong around the time of the New Moon in Scorpio on the 4th. A sense of sharing envelops those in your circle, and everyone wants to talk more about expectations and gratitude for life's blessings. The 9th highlights bonds with personal partners, and those of you who are not in a relationship have unanticipated opportunities to meet a new special someone either locally or while traveling.

Success and Money

Curb spending on gifts without doing your homework on November 11 and 26. A shopping spree could have you dipping into your savings or overpaying for an appliance or household item. Collaborative work nets praise on the 9th and could lead to a windfall or bonus in the coming weeks. The 9th is a good day to play the lottery or treat your loved one to a dinner out.

Pitfalls and Potential Problems

Behaving like a workaholic is the big caution for you this month. Be astute in assessing where roadblocks pile up with the workload. Team members start using leave or scheduling vacation dates. Coordinate with them so nothing slips between the cracks and you don't have to pick up the slack. Don't travel on the 19th.

Rewarding Days

4, 9, 13, 24

Challenging Days

5, 11, 19, 26

Cancer | December

Overall Theme

Go off the grid and celebrate seasonal bliss with all your favorite people. That suggestion might seem like an impossible dream with all you have on your plate. Consult your timeline, blitz on the most pressing tasks, and proceed to schedule enjoyable events for those you cherish. Scatter the dates to bond with your partner, children, siblings, neighbors, and work colleagues and you'll experience a month of happy memories.

Relationships

The first half of the month seems reserved for get-togethers with business colleagues and professional groups. Schedule these right after the Solar Eclipse on December 4 in Sagittarius. Take time for adventure and camaraderie with partners and visit public places and gatherings. Enjoy special bonding time with family members on December 25–26 and with children or romantic interests on the 30th.

Success and Money

Unexpected gifts and compliments come your way from the 4th through the 7th, when conversations highlight accomplishments and contributions. You could win a door prize or raffle at a party. During the same period, you may learn of a promotion or bonus or a boost in your retirement annuity. True feelings surface and bonding is lovely to experience at gatherings around the 26th, a perfect day to communicate love.

Pitfalls and Potential Problems

The two days before the Solar Eclipse, December 1–2, reflect poor timing in communicating or hosting events, leaving people confused about the message. The 14th is a day when tension escalates at the workplace and staff members may push back over criticism, real or perceived, that they lack understanding of the details of tasks. Venus goes retrograde on December 19, right after the Full Moon in Gemini on the 18th. Be sure to soothe any hurt feelings.

Rewarding Days

4, 7, 26, 30

Challenging Days

1, 2, 14, 19

Cancer Action Table

These dates reflect the best–but not the only–times for success and ease in these activities, according to your Sun sign.

	JAN	FEB	MAR	APR	MAY	JUN	JUL	AUG	SEP	OCT	NOV	DEC
Move			13				18				4	
Romance	12			1	23	12				15		7
Seek counseling/ coaching		6				3		11			13	
Ask for a raise			6				12			5		
Vacation	17				7		2	24				30
Get a loan		11		7					5			

Leo

The Lion
July 22 to August 22

♌

Element: Fire

Quality: Fixed

Polarity: Yang/masculine

Planetary Ruler: The Sun

Meditation: I trust in the strength of my soul

Gemstone: Ruby

Power Stones: Topaz, sardonyx

Key Phrase: I will

Glyph: Lion's tail

Anatomy: Heart, upper back

Colors: Gold, scarlet

Animals: Lions, large cats

Myths/Legends: Apollo, Isis, Helios

House: Fifth

Opposite Sign: Aquarius

Flowers: Marigold, sunflower

Keyword: Magnetic

The Leo Personality

Strengths, Talents, and the Creative Spark

You are the roaring lions, capricious cats, and playful kittens of the universe. No singular personality fits magnetic Leo, ranging from the exuberant type who naturally takes over the room to the quiet cat who knows everything that's going on but prefers to lead behind the scenes. Many perceive you as the zodiac's ruling royalty, strutting your stuff dressed in your preferred luxurious fabrics, decorating with regal furnishings, and accenting your wardrobe with gorgeous jewelry. Your Sun sign enjoys bold color and favors jewel tones such as purple, deep jade, magentas, and striking blues. As the owner of a sparkling personality, you bring drama and excitement to interactions with family, friends, and associates. The Sun rules your sign and your fifth house of adventure, fun, games, social life, children, lovers, dating experiences, freelancing, sports, exercise, romantic interludes, speculation, risk-taking, and entrepreneurial enterprises. How delightful that your flair for individualism meshes with your passionate expression of the qualities most affiliated with Leo, such as entertaining, acing challenging projects, and showing loyalty to others.

Any planets residing in the fifth house of your birth chart describe the complexity of emotions and the range of creative and recreational interests you have. Yours is the second fixed sign and the second fire sign of the zodiac. A number of you are huge sports fans—active participants or spectators—while others prefer entertainment, showmanship, and leadership.

Intimacy and Personal Relationships

Generosity is your middle name, prompting you to spend time selecting thoughtful gifts and sharing your caring spirit. You absolutely adore your love interest and do everything to make sure the object of your affection knows it. You understand how to say it with roses, books of poetry, passionate love notes, and candlelight dinners. An intuitive sense of what your partner needs leads to a long-lasting and successful relationship. Finding a true partner means the world to you. You appreciate a lover who both listens and shares information freely. Nothing holds you back when you commit to a person or an idea except a bruised ego. When someone rejects you or bashes your ego, you retreat, licking your wounds and sometimes pretending it doesn't matter. If the relationship can't be salvaged, you eventually find someone new. Yours is one of the few signs who can marry the same sign and enjoy happiness, although you may fight over who's the boss.

Leos are dedicated parents who are adept at directing their children's interests, often coaching their teams and sharing their accomplishments with others. You encourage music lessons and spend freely on concerts, stage shows, and musicals. Nieces or nephews enjoy spending time with you, remembering the fun everyone shared for years to come. You thoughtfully treat them to special adventures or vacations and take them out to chill when they are down or upset.

Values and Resources

You have quite a flair for creativity, and what you express often highlights your magnetic Leo qualities, including pride of accomplishment, commitment to goals, development of plans, leadership, social finesse, and a passion for achieving life balance by including work and play in the mix. As a connoisseur of elegance and comfort, you've never met an office environment you couldn't turn into a throne room. Loyalty is one of the attributes you prize most in others, and you offer it in return. If you're in charge, you throw inclusive parties and welcome visitors, colleagues, and employees to your home. Entertainment and amusements are very important to you to give your brain some downtime and turn the heavy mental analysis into free-flowing fun and magic.

You'll take the starring role in any business enterprise, desiring recognition for what you do as a leader, director, manager, owner, or star. If your career involves work with children, it's often as a coach, agent, teacher, physician, or guidance counselor. Leo is often called "lucky" because winning streaks seem to find you wherever you go—the door prize, lottery, contest, or vacation getaway. Although you normally know your limit and watch your spending, you like gaming and sometimes play the slots at gambling meccas, another fifth-house affiliation. You convert any wins into gifts for loved ones or creature comforts for your home.

Blind Spots and Blockages

Very few would accuse you of having low self-esteem. Instead, you can be overly self-confident, believing the roses will bloom above the thorns and remove all traces of any setbacks you encounter. The trap of unfulfilling life work may haunt you at some point if you choose salary over goodness of fit. Even when your career is on the right track, you have to make sure the compensation, including salary increases and tangible benefits, reflects your worth. The fixed-sign attribute of stubbornness is one to overcome when it periodically rattles your cage in both personal and professional arenas. It can surface because of rejection or disrespect for ideas or individual style. Don't bury it. Anger builds up and affects your health when you ignore the truth. Ignoring tension in the workplace can lead you to develop unhealthy habits such as becoming a workaholic, drinking too much, or overeating. Your sign rules the back, blood, circulatory system, heart, spine, and metabolism. Illness connected to these areas often results when your emotions are blocked or when you don't know how to release your anger. Unlike the other fire signs, you hold grudges way too long when you have determined that you have been aggrieved. Internalize healthy habits and stick with a routine that works for you. See a comedy act instead of a heart surgeon.

Goals and Success

Success is yours if you find the perfect job and put passion into all you do. Become the master in your chosen field and capitalize on your entrepreneurial spirit. Understand that leadership becomes you when you acknowledge your talent and spirit, whether you run the show or play a supporting role. Engage in fitness routines and prevention measures to stay healthy and build up the energy to manage your diverse responsibilities. Delegate authority and share accountability with others so that you develop the most insightful and inspiring team possible. Create an environment that welcomes new ideas and values feedback. You excel at coaching a team to a winning, successful outcome. Make use of timelines to keep everyone informed of key accomplishment dates and track the deliveries. Be sure to include celebration dates to acknowledge stellar performance.

Leo Keywords for 2021
Magnificent, masterful, motivated

The Year Ahead for Leo

"What am I waiting for?" could be your mantra for 2021. The Moon in Leo starts off the new year, igniting your passion for beating all odds to create a masterful life phase and filling you with growing anticipation to exceed goals. You'll have no time to coast and daydream about napping on the beach. Just look at the array of planets that is setting up challenges for your enterprising spirit: Jupiter and Saturn newly arrived in Aquarius oppose your Sun from your solar seventh house of committed partnerships; Uranus in Taurus jars your equilibrium from your career-driven tenth house and throws authority and family issues into the mix; and Neptune in Pisces weaves a cloud of financial confusion in your solar eighth house of shared resources and debt. Roll up your sleeves, examine these momentum drivers, and take the lead in generating solutions.

For the last few years, one of your busiest houses has been your solar sixth house of health, daily routines, work environment, and the people you interact with on a regular basis. Not surprisingly, you may have spent considerable time visiting doctors and undergoing treatments or surgeries, including dental work, while outer planets piled in and reminded you of limitations in one way or another. Several eclipses plus Jupiter and Saturn in Capricorn kept you hopping along, with Pluto also in this sign dropping abundant hints about facing the music, clearing out old baggage, and giving the atmosphere a lift. Eclipses moved to mutable signs, and Jupiter and Saturn completed their cycles, saying goodbye to slow-moving Pluto, a subtle invader that gets the point across slowly but surely until you take action to change conditions that appear stuck. You're not a big fan of holding patterns, feeling restless and ready to roll as the new year gets underway. Since you hold the key to the executive office, all you have to do is focus on the vision that brings your plans to life and take charge of implementation. Inner joy motivates you and moves you to the height of fulfillment.

Jupiter

There are memorable times ahead this year with Jupiter, the planet of expansion, moving into Aquarius and your solar seventh house of relationships, where it influences activities through December 28. Although it takes about a year to get through a Jupiter cycle, sometimes the planet travels at a rapid pace and advances to the next sign very briefly, only to turn retrograde and go back over already traveled degrees. This year Jupiter moves into early Pisces degrees on May 13 and turns retrograde on June 20, moving back into Aquarius on July 28 while it covers familiar degrees until turning direct on October 18. You could be making big plans with your partner, starting a business, or celebrating a wedding, anniversary, or graduation. Collaborators in your professional world seem enthusiastic about taking on a project or entering into a cooperative agreement that has long-term potential. Those of you looking for a room-mate to share expenses hit the jackpot, with several contacts competing for the opportunity. You could be in the public eye and be called on to accept speaking engagements, appear at book signings if you are a writer, advertise products or services in expanding markets, or build a better web presence in your field. Professional connections steer new advisors, consultants, medical experts, or attorneys your way to help you through planning phases, personal dilemmas, illness, or legal matters. Timing is everything, so get a jump on plans. Attention to detail brings fulfillment of dreams and goals and happier relationships.

Saturn

The new year starts with Saturn in Aquarius joining Jupiter in your solar seventh house of personal and business partners. Saturn repre-sents the cement that helps to bind those promises you make while you're creating joyful memories. The message seems to be to think big (Jupiter) while you watch your step (Saturn). If anything has seemed amiss in the relationship arena, Saturn will exert discomfort in the form of nagging, a sinking feeling, or an outright dispute. Remember, the planet of restriction is opposing your Leo Sun. Let nothing you cherish fall under a dark cloud or push you toward a depressed state of mind and a decision you'll regret. Be tactful in communication and draw oth-ers into insightful conversations. Standoffs won't cut it. Those of you born between August 15 and 22 see the most action this year through May 23, when Saturn turns retrograde until October 10 and resumes the challenge of pushing you to examine the full gamut of relationships: depth, goals, desired outcomes, rewards, standards, and consequences of actions. Pay attention to the body language and attitude of partners in both business and personal life. Review your feelings and own up to disappointments or identify areas that would benefit from discussion. If you feel stuck, seek advice and weigh your options. You have the lion's courage and willingness to shape meaningful change.

Uranus

Look who's taking up space in your solar tenth house of ambition, business objectives, career, authority figures, and life status: Uranus in Taurus, the planet of sudden shifts in direction, ready for another year of shakeups. This volatile visitor to your house of reputation first made a teaser appearance in May 2018 that has made you aware of the need to set high standards of conduct and performance to achieve vital goals that affect your income and your standing in the world. Uranus begins 2021 in retrograde motion and goes direct on January 14. This year it will most affect Leos born between July 28 and August 8, calling attention to comfort levels in your career arena before going off the grid in retrograde motion again on August 19 for the rest of the year. Some Leos change jobs or careers more than once during this cycle; others get laid off or fired as organizations restructure or downsize. Extreme restlessness may send you on a quest to find the perfect job. Deep down you're not happy at work. Don't even think about pretending you get along with your boss when you don't. You've had heartburn over it for a couple years and it's time to ditch the antacids and search for a better fit. Make a magnificent pitch to the hiring authorities at your organization of choice and wait for the offer. You'll be setting new trends in an exciting and compatible environment.

Neptune

The musical notes of the year are coming from your solar eighth house of intimacy, shared resources, and psychological depth. In 2021 Neptune most affects Leos born between August 11 and 16, who experience an irritating inconjunct aspect to their Sun. The mystical planet goes retrograde from June 25 to December 1. The first tune being played is all about examining your finances, eliminating confusion over who owns what in partnership funds, and cleaning up the debt load that has you frustrated with the mixed signals you get after you pay off the debt but then it suddenly escalates out of the blue due to hasty purchasing choices you and your partner make. Time to review your budget to get off the runaway train of impulse spending. Stick with the plan and enjoy financial freedom. The second melody revolves around your attachment to your partner and the lovely bonds you've created through understanding the inspiration that drives your emotional connections. While they are truly masterful and romantic in validating your choice of a partner, you sometimes miss the details of behavior that throw you off track while producing an illusion that clouds objectivity in personal and financial matters. Seek out advice for practical solutions that keep you solidly on track, and at the end of the year you'll be able to answer the question "What's in your wallet?" with your favorite saying: a whole lot of cash.

Pluto

Way back in 2008, Pluto in Capricorn began invading your solar sixth house of activity in your daily environment, health, work and those you interact with in your workplace, nutrition, and pets. You would think by this time that matters connected to sixth-house themes where you have felt stuck would have morphed into the patterns you desire, especially since the last few years featured eclipses in Capricorn that triggered unplanned events and Saturn in Capricorn finished its 2½-year cycle here as well. In 2021 Leos most affected by Pluto's transit are those born between August 16 and 20 as Pluto makes an inconjunct aspect to your Sun. The probing planet keeps you motivated to deal with inner struggles and master health issues that may have sidelined you recently. Typically, Pluto could be applying pressure to anxieties you have about the management of your organization. Perhaps a new boss or owner takes over, breaking up the pattern of your work, shifting responsibilities, or replacing members of your team. If you've been ill, consult with new medical professionals, seeking relief from pain and a cure for longtime health problems. You could be starting a different fitness routine or changing eating habits. Once you're on a roll, the crystallized habits fall by the wayside and the new you finds stimulating interests to fill the void.

How Will This Year's Eclipses Affect You?

In 2021, a total of four eclipses occur. There will be two Lunar Eclipses and two Solar Eclipses, creating intense periods that begin to manifest a few months before their actual dates. Eclipses unfold in cycles involving all twelve signs of the zodiac, and usually occur in pairs about two weeks apart. Think of eclipses as opportunities to release old patterns and conditions that have outlived their usefulness. Have no fear of them, since they can bring you unexpected surprises and windfalls. The closer an eclipse is to a degree or point in your chart, the greater its importance in your life. Those of you born with a planet at the same degree as an eclipse are likely to see a high level of activity in the house where the eclipse occurs.

The first Lunar Eclipse of the year occurs on May 26 in Sagittarius and your solar fifth house of children, entertainment, risk-taking, romance, social life, speculation, and sports. Opportunities abound for you to bond more closely with your children, get pregnant, or accelerate your social life by accepting invitations, hosting parties, or scheduling a dream vacation. Coaching or teaching opportunities may appear out of the blue. If you have children, support for their activities increases. Your love life is in high focus and you may meet the person of your dreams or become engaged.

The second eclipse is a Solar Eclipse in Gemini that takes place on June 10 in your solar eleventh house of friendships, professional affiliates, groups, organizations, hopes, dreams, and goals. Expansion of contacts becomes a reality as you receive numerous invitations to meet friends for meals or get-togethers, join clubs, accept a membership in a prestigious organization, or consider running for office in one of your preferred groups. Opportunities through these connections may be life-changing and could lead to a new career, mentorship, or source of success. Humanitarian causes may attract your interest and shift the way you spend your time. Some of you volunteer or engage in political campaigns.

On November 19, the second Lunar Eclipse of 2021 falls in Taurus and your solar tenth house of career, authority figures, ambition, organizational direction, leadership, and life status. Uranus in Taurus is also transiting your solar tenth house, adding an unexpected tone to your career environment—anything goes! Get ready to embrace unfolding developments and new responsibilities. Special requests may come from bosses or parents.

The final Solar Eclipse of 2021 takes place on December 4 in Sagittarius and ties in with activities related to the May 26th eclipse, once again occurring in your solar fifth house of children, teaching, sports, the arts, romance, and entrepreneurial endeavors. Maybe at this time you'll be considering investing in a business or partnership to add income or expand your creative interests. If your love life is blossoming, you may be announcing plans to marry or buy a home to share with your loved one. Activities involving children claim a significant amount of your time. Cherish the moments—you could look back on this period as one of your most memorable.

Leo | January

Overall Theme

New Year's resolutions could pay off beautifully if you take the lead in implementing plans. The early days of the year could find you in love if you're single or focused on surprising your significant other with future plans for sharing romantic time. You'll have to deal with a few hurdles at your workplace, although solutions are attainable if you take the time to consider more than one option. The New Moon on January 13 in your solar sixth house of daily routines and colleagues gives you a chance to look at new approaches.

Relationships

Romance has a hold on your heart and soul. Cherish those you love and take steps to validate your feelings. Avoid tension on the 8th and 14th and think through differences that crop up and affect moods. Work connections expand and lead to masterful teamwork, especially around the 13th. Stay away from heated discussions on January 21, when differences of opinion lead to a stalemate.

Success and Money

Review your budget and make plans to pay off credit cards that you used for holiday expenses. You can ask for a raise on the 5th or spend money you've set aside for special purchases. You hear good news about projects, performance, and goals on the 22nd and may be asked to present a status report or deliver a plan of work.

Pitfalls and Potential Problems

Be aware that Uranus moves in direct motion on January 14 and could stimulate unexpected news regarding funds availability in your workplace, or the mail may bring an unanticipated bill for services you received early last year. Keep professional matters on an even keel on January 21 and 28, and be sure plans for the next month are in order in preparation for Mercury turning retrograde on January 30.

Rewarding Days

2, 5, 13, 22

Challenging Days

8, 14, 21, 28

Leo | February

Overall Theme

Harmony is in the air as you scramble to take a good look at contracts and review terms of agreements. Pore over the pros and cons of details. It's a good idea to give some thought to promises you made to others and to select the most opportune time to act on them. Although tension cramps your style at the workplace for part of the month, you're seldom at a loss for solutions and feel motivated to initiate positive outcomes.

Relationships

You and a loved one may take a short vacation early in the month. What a nice opportunity to share closeness and strengthen love. Relationships with colleagues are strong and inspiring on the 9th, a good day for holding meetings or attending idea-generating seminars. Disagreements crop up at home base on the 4th, when moodiness or hurt feelings are on display. If you're away on a trip, find a way to neutralize the tension so you can enjoy private time.

Success and Money

Collaborative efforts pay off around the time of the New Moon on the 11th, allowing you to savor compliments that acknowledge the successful interaction of the group. Involvement with legal and medical practitioners identifies solutions and puts you at ease about ongoing concerns. Table action at work on the 18th and 19th, when procedural nightmares delay implementation of plans. Sign contracts early next month rather than rush the process.

Pitfalls and Potential Problems

When you know you've done a good job and feel you've carefully prepared your work or set personal plans in motion, the last thing you want to do is wait to implement them. That, however, is what you must do, especially with Mercury retrograde until the 20th. Don't take money risks on big-ticket items on February 27.

Rewarding Days

2, 6, 9, 11

Challenging Days

4, 18, 19, 27

Leo | March

Overall Theme

March promises to be a productive month. Waiting for the right cycle to emerge becomes an annoyance of the past. You could go into action mode as early as the 2nd and wrap up the month feeling good about yourself, even allowing time for nurturing and recreation. Dreams and intuitive insight blossom. You remember enough to find meaning in dream symbols. Be sure to write them down in your journal.

Relationships

Dates, debates, and educational opportunities have successful outcomes the first ten days of the month. Bond with siblings and neighbors on the 2nd and your significant other on the 8th. Take advantage of the strong momentum with your workmates on the 9th, and schedule working lunches or water-cooler meetings to break strict routines. Celebrate with loved ones on the 13th and make plans for using extra cash that comes your way.

Success and Money

Promoting a strong business ethic and accomplishment record stimulates support from authority figures and staff alike. Discuss accomplishment incentives and determine what drives the motivation of team members. Don't spend or sign documents or contracts on the 28th; better dates are March 2 and 9.

Pitfalls and Potential Problems

Matters at home base are prickly; the green-eyed monster may show up on the 4th, so take it easy when expressing opinions. You could hear of resignations or turmoil in the ranks of officers in organizations or groups. Steer clear of the politics related to the issue on the 19th. Children or romantic interests are out of kilter on the 5th, and blunt statements put a sour note on communication. Lie low at the Full Moon on March 28, letting the sensitivity that surfaces dissolve.

Rewarding Days

2, 9, 13, 22

Challenging Days

4, 5, 19, 28

Leo | April

Overall Theme

As the earth comes back to life in the early days of spring, you come alive with the passion to tackle your bucket list and move pet projects along. Although your ambitions are noble, you remain accountable to authorities who control your paycheck, allowing little time for a sabbatical. April is about choices. Consider yours carefully. Keep your eye on Pluto turning retrograde in Capricorn on the 27th.

Relationships

Some of your best days for enjoying the company of lovers and friends are the 2nd and 3rd. A vacation with loved ones is possible around the New Moon on the 11th, although you'll probably take off over the weekend before it occurs. Friends are eager to reunite, with lively exchanges, introductions to dating prospects if you're eligible, and sponsorship in professional organizations. Siblings ask for advice, money, or help with home projects. A parent could be in a bad mood on the 28th, so don't personalize the message.

Success and Money

Enjoy every moment of your getaway before the 13th of the month. Just don't take your wallet out for frivolous purchases or overly expensive meals that may not meet your standards. Bask in the sunshine of approval from your boss for exceeding performance expectations. Stay away from unwinnable arguments in the workplace on the 15th, and ask for feedback on issues where the team opinion is divided.

Pitfalls and Potential Problems

Organizational matters fall apart on the 5th, challenging you to regroup and take unplanned time to make things right. Sort through problems or messes. With Pluto in your solar sixth house in Capricorn, identify places where you're stuck at work. Guard against overeating or drinking to avoid stomach difficulties.

Rewarding Days

2, 12, 17, 26

Challenging Days

5, 9, 15, 28

Leo | May

Overall Theme

You may have noticed that Mercury retrograde occurs in air signs this year, affecting the way you convey your message and how it's received. Both Saturn in Aquarius and Mercury in Gemini turn retrograde this month, alerting you to take extra precautions when handling sensitive information and critical matters. Expect delays in executing plans. Let intent and motivation guide you in taking a closer look at documents. Recheck numbers to cut down on errors.

Relationships

The year's first Lunar Eclipse takes place in Sagittarius in your solar fifth house on the 26th, affecting matters connected with children, entertainment, risk-taking, romance, and vacations. Use discretion in conversations with close connections to avoid hurt feelings. Shouting matches may get out of control, and mitigating hard feelings comes at a price. Travel with loved ones before the 20th. Enjoy intimate moments on the 1st and 7th.

Success and Money

Business matters seem to fall smoothly into place on the 1st and 11th, yielding surprising outcomes. Focused work pays dividends and reflects masterful leadership. If you're in a leadership position, use the 19th to make decisions about promotions for staff or to announce details about expansion of work. Talk to your financial advisor between the 17th and 20th to make investment modifications.

Pitfalls and Potential Problems

You may clash with your partner on the 4th or 5th over issues related to children and spending priorities. The planetary weather at the beginning of the month blindsides you to the depth of problems that have been percolating but have not yet been addressed. Set aside time to discuss solutions, particularly on the 7th.

Rewarding Days

1, 7, 11, 19

Challenging Days

4, 5, 17, 26

Leo | June

Overall Theme

June is another month with considerable planetary activity that affects schedules, leisure time, and problem solving. These conditions try your patience. Hang loose with timetables so you can more fully understand barriers to progress and renegotiate plans. Although Mercury in Gemini turns direct on the 22nd, Jupiter in Pisces goes retrograde on the 20th, as does Neptune in Pisces on the 25th. The first Solar Eclipse of 2021 occurs in Gemini on June 10.

Relationships

Give love and family relationships a chance on June 1 and 3, when communication is harmonious and parties are receptive to deep discussions that involve sharing inner thoughts and discussing values. Friendships are on deck on the 10th and could involve a reunion of members of a longtime group. You'll hear from in-laws on the 29th or make plans for a visit. Details of family vacations firm up by month's end.

Success and Money

Allocating resources to pay down debt as well as increase the balance in savings accounts is a topic of discussion for you and your partner. College funding options are on the table on the 6th, yet it's too early to make decisions due to a lack of agreement on the optimal approach. Do your homework to make sure your money goes as far as you'd like. Don't sign any papers until you understand the impact of personal responsibility.

Pitfalls and Potential Problems

Avoid the Monday morning blues on the 7th by reviewing work projects carefully before responding to a request for a report. Mistakes can be costly if quality control is lacking. Check financial records on the 18th, including purchase agreements or the fine print in other transactions. Deal with the sensitivity of children or a love interest on the 24th.

Rewarding Days

1, 3, 10, 29

Challenging Days

6, 7, 18, 24

Leo | July

Overall Theme

With summer in full bloom, many of you will be traveling away from home this week starting around the 2nd. Spend time reflecting on family members located in distant places and schedule a visit. Also look at aspects of your life where you desire freedom from emotional scars. Those aha moments may set you free.

Relationships

Diverse relationships receive attention this month, starting with in-laws or family who live in distant locations. Renewal of bonds is important in the form of visits, family reunions, holiday barbecues, or shared vacations. Plan visits with friends that include celebrations, picnics, or trips to parks or historic sites on July 7–11. Save July 21 for romantic interludes or a one-on-one outing with a child. It's possible you will be visiting a party confined to a hospital or rehab center.

Success and Money

The most enjoyable use of funds this month is on recreation and leisure-time activities. Having all travel arrangements in order and reservations confirmed adds to the pleasure of setting off on an adventure with family and friends. Take advantage of discounts and coupons on your travels to get more bang for your buck.

Pitfalls and Potential Problems

During this busy month, you interact with a variety of individuals from all walks of life. Dustups are bound to occur. Vulnerable dates are the 4th, when the Moon clashes with several planets, affecting workplace dynamics. Don't leave without a truce. Another edgy date is the 19th, when home base harmony is in jeopardy and feelings are raw and unpredictable.

Rewarding Days

2, 7, 20, 21

Challenging Days

4, 19, 25, 27

Leo | August

Overall Theme

Deep discussions fill your world this month, beginning with your parents or grandparents. On the 4th, friends seek you out for counsel or ask you to lend an ear over dinner to comment on pressing issues. Use your finest Leo diplomacy, sharing your time and your magnanimous heart. A person in your circle may need encouragement to schedule a surgery.

Relationships

You'll enjoy successful encounters with associates and members of professional organizations as well as friends. Attending meet-and-greet functions expands your contacts and motivates you to take a more active role in an enterprise. Family relationships are pleasant and loving on the 16th, and cordial connections at a distance may include an offer to relocate or change jobs.

Success and Money

Realtors may be contacting you with out-of-the-blue offers for your home. If this is something that interests you, be sure to check market values to get the best price. Talk to more than one company if you decide to sell. A visiting authority figure associated with your company may seek you out based on your noteworthy contributions and request a private meeting. This interaction may lead to a promotion or job offer.

Pitfalls and Potential Problems

Keep a low profile at work on the 1st, when you get wind of tension and turmoil in the ranks. You may have to listen to some volatile conversations, but you're under no obligation to take part unless you're the one in charge. Watch spending on the 10th, when bargains you encounter may have strings attached. Tension with your partner is possible on the Full Moon of August 22. Explore facts first to avoid arguments.

Rewarding Days

4, 6, 16, 25

Challenging Days

1, 8, 10, 22

Leo | September

Overall Theme

Some of the most positive vibes this month come from your interaction with air-sign energy in the form of people or transiting planets. You're ready to tackle an exciting new venture. The Aquarius Moon this month makes favorable aspects to Mercury and Jupiter and brings momentum and the green light to your interests.

Relationships

Friends and neighbors make life enjoyable for you on the 1st and 9th with their positive proposals, invitations, and suggestions for building rapport. Cousins and siblings join the party on the 10th, with frequent calls, text messages, and questions about availability for gatherings. Not to be outdone, your significant other gives your psyche a big boost by showing a tender, nurturing side that seals the bonds of love.

Success and Money

Take the time to review the terms of contracts, sales, and agreements on the 9th and 10th and you will bask in the fruits of your labor financially and emotionally. Depending on conditions elsewhere in your birth chart, these are also perfect dates to apply for a mortgage or home equity loan or to purchase a vehicle.

Pitfalls and Potential Problems

Analyze your financial picture before you buy any expensive items or sign contracts. Avoid September 27, when Mercury turns retrograde in Libra and firm commitments on price could dissolve overnight. Avoid money or emotional arguments on the 2nd. Put your wallet away on the 6th, when planetary aspects complicate transactions; the 9th is much better for purchases.

Rewarding Days

1, 9, 10, 18

Challenging Days

2, 6, 11, 27

Leo | October

Overall Theme

The New Moon in Libra on the 6th drives activity this month in your solar third house. Mercury goes direct here on the 18th. Communication and various forms of social media grab your attention. Looks like you could be making sure security measures are up to date. You may be buying and installing new electronic equipment and upgrading phones to keep up with trending improvements. You could begin a class or teach one locally on a popular topic.

Relationships

Rocky relationships receive attention and time to discuss grievances. You are motivated to do so now and experience relief when you clear the air and release the pain. Partnerships grow, especially when Jupiter goes direct in your solar seventh house of partnerships on the 18th. Your social life picks up on the 11th and 25th. Select entertainment venues that you enjoy and want to share with special people.

Success and Money

Paperwork for bonuses is in the works in acknowledgment of a job well done. Plans to travel fall into place and come with discounts and desirable perks. A workplace fiscal audit reveals extra cash for equipment, awards, and training. Prospects for successful outcomes on deliverables look promising. You may have to spend additional time to complete reports when a deluge of input arrives at the end of a deadline.

Pitfalls and Potential Problems

Planning glitches come to light on the 1st, and you may have to go back to the drawing board to identify solutions and a way to redistribute work. You may feel worn out or under the weather around the 13th. A mental health day is in order. Curb spending on the 17th, and avoid travel on the 20th.

Rewarding Days

6, 11, 25, 30

Challenging Days

1, 13, 17, 20

Leo | November

Overall Theme

Major activity centers around home base this month, with the emphasis on family gatherings, visits, and phone calls. This month offers an opportunity to shine in the events department, with the New Moon in Scorpio on the 4th beaming proudly in your solar fourth house, welcoming visitors to your home. Schedule doctor visits before the 19th so you can get any yearly tests or checkups out of the way ahead of the holiday season.

Relationships

Contacts seem unusually enthusiastic and full of holiday spirit. The astrological weather on November 8 seems to release a fighting spirit for causes, pet projects, and campaigns to address food shortages. Consider volunteering in a soup kitchen or bringing food to a shelter. Spread cheer among coworkers and acknowledge love and devotion to family.

Success and Money

One of your major successes this month is tackling your to-do list. Most likely you have more than one—a personal list and another for work-related reminders. You don't want any unfinished business playing out through the end of the year. Financial reports show savings increases and improvements in investments and retirement funds. Shop for gifts or order them before the 19th to find the best selections.

Pitfalls and Potential Problems

Watch financial transactions around the 1st if you're shopping or ordering online. Competitiveness or jealousy emerges at home base on the 5th and creates angst until somebody gives in and domestic peace returns. Differences of opinion crop up on the 11th related to collaborative work or proposed plans with partners. Testy circumstances could prevent completion of a planned agenda at work on the 19th, the date of the final Lunar Eclipse of 2021.

Rewarding Days

4, 8, 13, 25

Challenging Days

1, 5, 11, 19

Leo | December

Overall Theme

If anyone knows the meaning of exuberance, it's a magnanimous Leo who is ready for excitement and eager to spread goodwill toward loved ones. With an eye on wrapping up loose ends and encouraging others to do the same, you seem to generate enthusiasm wherever you go. You revel in the holiday spirit and recall the successes of the waning year, eager to build on momentum, express gratitude, and carry a positive outlook into 2022.

Relationships

Several days this month focus on meaningful connections. You show appreciation for siblings, cousins, neighbors, and your community early in the month on December 1–3. Attention shifts to lovers, children, and playmates on the 4th, when several social invitations are on the calendar. Romance is a bright and shining star on the 11th, when chemistry and rapport reach new heights. By the time you're ready to welcome in the new year, your home is the place to celebrate with a festive bash and offer a heartfelt toast for a better world.

Success and Money

Joyful interactions lift the spirits of your work and personal contacts. You feel very content to have found the perfect gifts for loved ones and other special people in your life. A lottery or raffle ticket could bring an unexpected windfall on the 4th. Meanwhile, you get good news from your tax accountant about owing less. Some Leos find that a bonus hits their checking account ahead of the holiday bills.

Pitfalls and Potential Problems

Cranky, tired people are in the mix of contacts you encounter on the 2nd, and your best move is to listen to their complaints and say little. You could experience disappointing social events on the 18th, when a mix-up occurs over the timing or location of a get-together.

Rewarding Days

1, 4, 11, 30

Challenging Days

2, 14, 18, 23

Leo Action Table

These dates reflect the best—but not the only—times for success and ease in these activities, according to your Sun sign.

	JAN	FEB	MAR	APR	MAY	JUN	JUL	AUG	SEP	OCT	NOV	DEC
Move			2		1			25		6		
Romance		6		17			21		10		13	
Seek counseling/ coaching			13			3			9			1
Ask for a raise	22				11			4				
Vacation		2		12		29				11		
Get a loan	5				8		10				8	30

Virgo

The Virgin
August 22 to September 22

♍

Element: Earth

Quality: Mutable

Polarity: Yin/feminine

Planetary Ruler: Mercury

Meditation: I can allow
time for myself

Gemstone: Sapphire

Power Stones: Peridot,
amazonite, rhodochrosite

Key Phrase: I analyze

Glyph: Greek symbol
for containment

Anatomy: Abdomen,
gallbladder, intestines

Colors: Taupe, gray, navy blue

Animals: Domesticated animals

Myths/Legends: Demeter,
Astraea, Hygeia

House: Sixth

Opposite Sign: Pisces

Flower: Pansy

Keyword: Discriminating

The Virgo Personality

Strengths, Talents, and the Creative Spark

With a Sun sign that owns the universal sixth house of work, daily environments and routines, health consciousness and care, medical procedures, specific medications and alternative medicine, vitamins, fitness exercises, body workers, nutrition, herbs and spices, pets the size of dogs or smaller, assimilation of facts and information, and efficiency of output, you could write the book on organization. The ruler of your sign is Mercury, the driver of your mental state that often draws you to employment in communication-oriented careers, think tanks, research fields, libraries, diverse health fields, body massage, publications (editing, writing, journalism, etc.), or administrative support roles.

Virgo is the second of the three earth signs. Yours is one of the most analytical signs and shares the rulership of Mercury with Gemini. You have a talent for noticing weak links that need attention and making them a restructuring priority, much like your compatible earth-sign members, Taurus and Capricorn. You eagerly take the wheel and focus on fixing troubled areas using systems that keep you on top of your work. Space management and decluttering operations may appeal to your organizing gene. Others among you prefer the healing modalities, nursing and x-ray technician fields, work at a walk-in clinic, or the specialty of veterinary medicine. Whether your comfort zone lies in cooking light meals or preparing rich dishes, you never lose sight of the nutritional value of food. A fine career choice might be the owner of a restaurant, a deli, a vegan café, or even a catering business.

Career options are quite extensive, and demand for your talent usually grabs the attention of recruiters or headhunters. Some of you have considerable accounting and bookkeeping skills, while other Virgos enjoy the role of inspector, auditor, poll taker, or questionnaire designer. Since you're good with numbers and adept at communicating, you may sometimes be designated the budget officer in a small work environment in addition to your existing duties.

Intimacy and Personal Relationships

You may not be the mushy and gushy type, but your love runs true and so does your support for those you adore. It's absolutely essential that you communicate frequently with your partner about daily activities.

You don't automatically think about who does the lion's share of chores; you just pitch in and run with it, preferring to value the teamwork. Your door is almost always open to your family, and it's not unusual to find you babysitting relatives or having company for the weekend. You will gladly take the lead in planning vacation time so the entire family has a chance to bond and enjoy the fun of maintaining long-held traditions and establishing new ones. Many Virgos treat pets like family and often keep more than one. Getting along with others is an important part of workplace dynamics that includes colleagues, customers, cooperators, and collaborators. Coworkers often morph into close friends. If you're the office manager, one of your roles might be disciplining employees or making such recommendations to your boss. You prefer a congenial work environment.

Values and Resources

Your sign understands planning processes and thrives on using them for daily balance. You are never far from your calendar and note dates of proposed meetings, appointments, and special events as soon as you learn of them. When entertaining, you favor requesting shared dishes at gatherings, so meal preparation tasks are spread around and guests have plenty of opportunities to bond, play games, and enjoy the company. You value steadiness and security, preferring to rely on predictable outcomes related to the people in your life and the work performance arena. Although you may find employment in large organizations, corporations, and government agencies, many of you prefer to work in small groups or companies with very few employees. You enjoy reading material, get considerable useful information from subscriptions, and favor electronic readers to cut down on clutter.

Blind Spots and Blockages

You can be ultra-picky about certain life conditions and just won't budge, an attitude that gives you the reputation of being a nag. Leaving conversations unfinished is not to your liking, nor is leaving loose ends on assignments or not designating a responsible party. Although you don't always show it, you are a worrier and internalize stress rather than talk about it. That habit takes its toll on your bowels, a part of the body affiliated with your sign. Digestion problems, including ulcers, may trouble you, while some Virgos are hypochondriacs or germophobes or pop vitamins excessively. While your sign is affiliated with the preference for an orderly environment, some of you have no visible interest in domestic chores like cleaning bathrooms or laundering clothes. Despite the exhaustion you feel from setting milestones in work accomplishment, you won't hire household help to give you a break so you can relax with much deserved downtime or ditch undesirable chores. You consider that expense a waste of your hard-earned cash.

Goals and Success

You prefer a work environment that gives you considerable autonomy, without bosses looking over your shoulder or prodding you to work faster. Passion and enjoyment of your work are all you need to become a dedicated employee, paying conscientious attention to details and making sure the inner machinery runs smoothly. Keeping your cool and settling arguments without a shouting match makes you a valuable asset in minimizing home and workplace stress. The patience and understanding of health setbacks you experience can lead you to a caregiver role at interim points in your life. People who know you see you as an inspiration, a giving person who pays thoughtful attention to loved ones' needs without looking for compliments or wanting some of the credit for the successful outcome.

Virgo Keywords for 2021
Reliability, reserve, resourcefulness

The Year Ahead for Virgo

Although none of the outer planets are in your Sun sign as 2021 dawns, you've just completed a year when mutable-sign eclipses in Sagittarius and Gemini began to present challenges in two action houses, the solar fourth house of home and the solar tenth house of career. In case you were wondering why the floodgates opened in these houses last year, revealing unanticipated shifts in direction and surprising information about key players linked to these houses, stay alert. They'll be back for more excitement this year, too. In a third high-action house, the solar seventh house of personal and professional partners, dreamy Neptune in Pisces continues to spread a mystical aura over relationship matters. Fantasy-loving Neptune has been in an opposition aspect to your Sun for a number of years. She wants to see you in a pair of rose-colored glasses and hopes you'll wear them so you don't see too many flaws in your partner and let up on the nagging.

Additional outer planetary players are Jupiter and Saturn in Aquarius moving through their tenures in your solar sixth house of health, daily routines, work structure, fitness, nutrition, kitchen facilities, and pets. Whenever Jupiter shows up, you're going to have a chance to heal physically and often mentally from conditions that may be hard to pinpoint. Consider this transit an opportunity to explore the expertise of the medical field while you take better care of yourself and decide on solutions to restore you to an optimal state of good health. Just so you don't get complacent, Saturn in Aquarius arrived in late December to spend 2½ years in this house confronting you with workplace, scheduling, and health challenges that tax your reserve and help open your eyes to what needs your attention. In 2021 Pluto remains in your solar fifth house, making a positive, reassuring aspect to late-born Virgos ready to cut loose from restrictions and take on a new adventure.

Jupiter

With Jupiter in Aquarius traveling through your solar sixth house through December 28, you have opportunities to expand your work contacts and broaden the effectiveness and reliability of performance. Groups demonstrate commitment and show cohesiveness in meeting targets. As new members join the staff, responsibilities shift, giving you the chance to lighten your heavy load and benefit from astute management decisions. Reorganization projects might be on the agenda, calling for your analysis of the workload and solutions for increasing efficiency. Jupiter travels at a rapid pace and moves back into Pisces in May for a brief stay. It turns retrograde on June 20 and moves back into Aquarius on July 28 before going direct again on October 18. During this retrograde period, you may seek the advice of physicians. Since Saturn in Aquarius is also traveling through your solar sixth house, you may address medical issues by seeking referrals or listening to new approaches for treating chronic illness or injuries. Jupiter may also benefit you in adopting or buying a pet, upgrading your kitchen and/or replacing cookware, or finding a more compatible fitness routine to increase physical energy.

Saturn

While in Aquarius, Saturn makes an inconjunct aspect to your Sun in your solar sixth house, a condition known to generate uncomfortable tension. Saturn has the reputation of being a stern taskmaster and expecting continuous performance and sometimes perfection at any cost. Jupiter's presence in this house through the end of the year will lighten the load, even though you'll be taking a hard look at the sources of problems in work routines, friction among coworkers, unmet workloads, and health matters that possibly come up as a result of the unsettled conditions. If you examine these facets of work, you'll be using Saturn's resourcefulness astutely. Just like Virgo, Aquarius is one of the most analytical signs and focuses intently on an issue. This Saturn transit puts pressure on accomplishment, which may lead to workaholic tendencies or making unrealistic demands on others involved in the work. Meet the situation head-on by learning to value your assets and those of others, praising quality work, and reviewing the timetable and making adjustments to deadlines to reflect reasonable prep time that results in quality work. This year, Virgos born between August 23 and September 6 feel the greatest impact from Saturn's transit. Cherish the boost of solid ambition you'll receive from this planet.

Uranus

Quirky, chaotic Uranus in Taurus, although in a sign friendly to yours (Taurus), is careening through your solar ninth house of the higher mind, educational advancement, foreign cultures, publishing, philosophy, religion, in-laws, and long-distance travel until 2026. Flashbulbs go off when Uranus lands here—sudden illumination! Virgos born between August 28 and September 7 experience the most activity at various times, driven by the location of Uranus and affiliated planets in the birth chart. You may do an about-face in your attitude toward religion, a political stand, or a relocation decision. Since you tend to be skeptical, information that comes forth will have to be based in solid fact to get you to budge, yet it feels less risky to you to do so this year. Uranus in the ninth house could lead you to study a new language, accept an interim assignment in another location, go back to school to elevate career prospects, or participate in a cultural exchange program. You could plan a destination wedding and marry in another country, suddenly decide to retire, take the trip of a lifetime to reward yourself for years of hard work, go on a safari adventure to stretch outside your comfort zone, or take a sabbatical to a remote location to research material for a book.

Neptune

Back in April 2011, Neptune in Pisces made a preliminary appearance in your solar seventh house of personal and business partners, roommates, the public, advisors, consultants, cooperators, and individuals in the medical and legal professions. In 2021 Neptune is still making an opposition aspect to your Sun sign, especially if you were born between September 9 and 17, and it calls for you to dissolve boundaries that attract negative energy and create confusion. Shake it off! Live in the reality of knowing that when you recognize strange behavior, it's okay to call it what it is and move away. Neptune transiting here brings you many admirers, creating an opportunity to loosen up and let others into your life. Choose those who display integrity. If you're single, don't feel obligated to date all who ask you just because they suggest it. Instead, put a little romance in your life by taking on those aspects of Neptunian energy that reflect the dreamy, partnership-oriented side of the planet. Those Virgos already in a partnership enjoy spiritually evolved connections with a clear vision for the future. This transit helps you identify areas that need clarification in your relationship after bouts of confusion or misunderstanding.

Pluto

Based on the activity you've experienced since 2008 in your solar fifth house of social and romantic life, sports, children, competition, speculation, risk-taking, outdoor activity, vacation destinations, and dating, you are identifying ways to eliminate old habits and increase your personal power in these areas. Pluto in Capricorn is making a positive trine aspect to your Sun and encourages you to discover ways to have more fun. As you settle into new routines, your challenge is to work more enjoyment into your agenda. The fifth house is all about creativity and playtime, yet your responsibilities may have escalated after you dealt with transiting Saturn in Capricorn here over the last 2½ years. Break the mold and make meaningful and efficient changes to free up quality time. The fifth house covers a lot of territory. You could lighten the workload by scoping out qualifications of new hires to make sure the fit is perfect and to bring out the best in your team. If you're single and getting serious in the love department, you may get engaged, erasing any fear of commitment. Also, examine investments, either the speculative type or the one you make to purchase a new home—ask the right questions. Be sure to build solid relationships with children and loved ones, putting you on solid ground with your life plan and balancing choices for a better future. Virgos born between September 16 and 20 feel the strongest vibes from this Pluto transit in 2021.

How Will This Year's Eclipses Affect You?

In 2021, a total of four eclipses occur. There will be two Lunar Eclipses and two Solar Eclipses, creating intense periods that begin to manifest a few months before their actual dates. Eclipses unfold in cycles involving all twelve signs of the zodiac, and usually occur in pairs about two weeks apart. Think of eclipses as opportunities to release old patterns and conditions that have outlived their usefulness. Have no fear of them, since they can bring you unexpected surprises and windfalls. The closer an eclipse is to a degree or point in your chart, the greater its importance in your life. Those of you born with a planet at the same degree as an eclipse are likely to see a high level of activity in the house where the eclipse occurs.

Virgo, get ready, because two eclipses take place in your solar fourth house of home, foundation, base of operations, family, domestic life, real estate, gardens, and culinary expertise. The first one is a Lunar Eclipse in Sagittarius on May 26. It will most affect those born between August 27 and 29, highlighting ongoing situations at home base. One facet has you examining current routines and how family members participate in or help to run the household, who pays the bills, who does the cooking, and how you manage childcare. Other matters could involve individuals moving in or out of the home or projects involving home maintenance, remodeling, landscaping, or decorating. Real estate sales or purchases might be on your agenda if you need a larger home or are downsizing. In some cases, older or ill family members may need care, and this eclipse points to the need to seek appropriate medical care or accommodations.

On December 4, the last Solar Eclipse of the year takes place in this same house in Sagittarius and may build on or finalize activities related to the fourth house that you initiated in May. Its impact lasts for the next six months. Those Virgos born between September 4 and 6 feel the greatest shift.

The year's first Solar Eclipse takes place on June 10 in Gemini in your solar tenth house of career, ambition, leadership, and attitude toward authority figures. This eclipse could shake things up in your employment arena or with the benefits package you're receiving as a retiree. Some of you welcome a new boss, while others rue the management change and look for ways to cope. You might receive a promotion or opt to apply to another company to showcase your talent, especially if you've been experiencing tension or unresolved conflict over how you spend your valuable time. Reserve your energy for engaging new connections. Don't look for problems, but do tackle them if they come up. Note that key career contacts may leave or go on a sabbatical, giving you food for thought.

The last Lunar Eclipse of the year occurs on November 19 in Taurus in your solar ninth house of the higher mind, educational advancement, foreign cultures, publishing, philosophy, religion, in-laws, and long-distance travel. With transiting Uranus in Taurus already traveling through this house, an eclipse here should add life to matters related to these themes. This eclipse makes a positive trine to your Virgo Sun. Use your resourcefulness to experience new adventures.

Virgo | January

Overall Theme

Take a deep breath. You'll start the year catching up on your sleep when the hectic holiday pace subsides. First you settle into new routines by spending a few quiet days to review your agenda and develop plans for the year ahead. Anticipation springs from within as you reflect on the quality relationships you'd like to have with family, intimate connections, and workplace authorities. Feelings of gratitude emerge as you acknowledge all that you have and the people you cherish.

Relationships

Spend quality time with family on the 10th discussing shifting responsibilities, catching up on news, sharing details of planned household projects, and addressing areas where you'd like to see improvement. Ask for input and feedback. Enjoy a social event or date with your significant other on the 12th and open up about your vulnerabilities. Discuss the value of date nights and events you'd like to put on the calendar in 2021.

Success and Money

Business and career matters take center stage around the 24th, when excellent communication exchanges set a positive tone for the success of established goals and encourage team participation. Report contents pave the way for solid financial dealings and ensure the availability of resources to fund projects.

Pitfalls and Potential Problems

Energy could be low on the 1st, so lie low and rest. Unresolved family matters, even conflicts that may have been tabled for discussion, come up on the 11th. Be objective and avoid confusion by giving weight to diverse opinions. Wait a day to agree on a decision. Don't make major purchases on the 28th or on the 30th, when Mercury goes retrograde.

Rewarding Days

2, 10, 12, 24

Challenging Days

1, 11, 21, 28

Virgo | February

Overall Theme

Relationships with intimate and business partners take center stage this month. You'll not only schedule personal time with your significant other but also assess the status of joint funds and discuss options for purchasing items that have been on your mutual wish list. Gatherings with workplace associates yield productive discussions and checkpoints for critical timelines.

Relationships

Romance is in the air, inspiring you to schedule an early celebration of Valentine's Day or surprise a partner with tickets to a special event. Expressions of love from dear ones kindle your spirit and motivate you to purchase gifts or flowers to show your feelings. The 9th promises rapport and is the perfect day for socializing and splurging on a date. Schedule work meetings on the 11th or 21st. If you're invited to an after-hours work-related event, be sure to attend to show support.

Success and Money

Accolades come your way for performance excellence later in the month. One of the benefits might be extra cash in your paycheck. Management may initiate a competitive measure to motivate the team that meets with your approval and gets the wheels turning. Wait until Mercury goes direct on the 20th to move forward with contracts.

Pitfalls and Potential Problems

Avoid sulking or pulling back your energy on the 1st. The previous weekend may have been taxing, resulting in not enough sleep. Communication shows strain and could be confusing on the 5th. Arguments surface on the 16th when bossy contacts take a "my way or the highway" position, and the standoff continues through the 18th. Financial disagreements could be at the core of the friction.

Rewarding Days

2, 9, 11, 21

Challenging Days

1, 5, 16, 18

Virgo | March

Overall Theme

Your financial health is a major factor this month. The need for household improvements crops up unexpectedly. Keep your checkbook handy and be on the lookout for sale announcements that match your purchasing goals. If you've been able to keep your credit cards free of excess debt this month, buy the item and look at options to pay off debt quickly.

Relationships

Spouses, friends, children, or romantic interests compete for your time. The calendar fills up and you have decisions to make about what you can afford in terms of time and money. With the Sun in your opposite sign right now, some invitations come from sources that don't interest you, suggesting that you apply filters immediately and decline. Some of your best days for interacting with others are the 13th for family fun and the 5th and 27th for time with friends and lovers.

Success and Money

Be sure to check credit scores before securing a personal or auto loan. Check credit card offers for those that will give you an interest-free period of at least a year to pay back your debt on household purchases. Shop for competitive rates on the 2nd and 27th. Enjoy sports and entertainment using your resourcefulness for procuring discount fares and passes to favorite venues. Join a company team or neighborhood league if you like being an active participant in sports.

Pitfalls and Potential Problems

For one reason or another, your debt load climbs this month due to unplanned circumstances. You and your spouse may be at odds over the spending cap on replacement items for your home. Have all your options ready when it's time to make the decision. Avoid making major purchases on the 4th, 6th, and 28th.

Rewarding Days

2, 5, 13, 27

Challenging Days

4, 6, 19, 28

Virgo | April

Overall Theme

Just as you think you're getting somewhere with a child or a love relationship, transiting Pluto in Capricorn goes retrograde in your solar fifth house and puts you in a holding pattern until October 6. Treat this slowdown as an opportunity to study the source of the block in communication with your child or the reluctance on the part of your romantic interest to commit to a more permanent relationship. Draw strength from your abundant patience and take baby steps in your pursuit of quality communication.

Relationships

You start the month feeling successful from teaching moments that give you insight into how smoothly the minds of your close associates work. Hints of breakthroughs and better rapport are just the charge you need to inspire you to do more to build momentum. Work connections are generally upbeat and congenial though impersonal, providing solid evidence of goal progress.

Success and Money

The New Moon on the 11th in your solar eighth house sheds light on the plus side of your financial picture. Continue with your plan to pay down debt and implement pending strategies. You get good news on the 23rd and view your portfolio of assets with optimism for the future. Teamwork seems flawless on the 7th and conversation flows effortlessly.

Pitfalls and Potential Problems

Moodiness prevails in your household on the 3rd; reasons are vague, but you won't get anywhere if you argue prematurely. A child could be unusually stubborn on the 5th and reluctant to share details, possibly due to a fear of failure or low self-esteem. Don't ask for a raise or request a private meeting with authority figures on the 17th.

Rewarding Days

1, 7, 11, 23

Challenging Days

3, 5, 17, 28

Virgo | May

Overall Theme

Spontaneity drives the energy of this spring month, which has you exploring new realms for speculative enterprises during a weekend outing on the 1st. By going off the beaten path, you discover an opportunity worth pursuing that has the potential to open doors and tempt you with a promising career option.

Relationships

Spend some enjoyable leisure time with friends, children, and lovers during the first twelve days of the month. Encouraging words build confidence that has been lacking in others. Conversations leave a lasting impression. Set up a date night with your partner on the 7th. It will make you glad that you took time to unwind before tackling pressing household chores over the weekend.

Success and Money

Those of you who work on commission in sales get good news on the 13th when greater returns than anticipated come through—just what your wallet needed. Bosses spend reserve cash on upgrades in workplace amenities and could also modify color schemes or add artwork to the decor.

Pitfalls and Potential Problems

If you're thinking of starting your own business after your discoveries earlier this month, spend time doing more research on your business idea. Whatever plans you have in the pipeline will have to wait. The year's first Lunar Eclipse occurs in Sagittarius on the 26th in your solar fourth house of home. Then Mercury turns retrograde on the 29th in your solar tenth house of career and pushes the pause button on any major activity for the next three weeks.

Rewarding Days

1, 7, 13, 23

Challenging Days

5, 12, 20, 27

Virgo | June

Overall Theme

Vacation plans are right around the corner. You may have run into some timing issues this month, with your Sun making hard aspects to both Venus and retrograde Mercury. Adding to the inconvenience, you may have had to juggle travel arrangements or make a lodging change. Foreign travel may be part of your plans. Be sure to check paperwork, verify changes, and pack your passport.

Relationships

Camaraderie flows with friends during the first half of the month. Reunions stir up fond memories and stimulate an interest in scheduling more frequent get-togethers. You could be asked to coordinate a gathering. Don't overthink the task; just make a to-do list and watch the pieces fall into place. A professional group's mission makes an impression on you. After learning more about emerging goals, you find agreement and rapport with leadership figures. Close relationships get a boost in anticipation of exciting vacation plans.

Success and Money

A Solar Eclipse in Gemini on June 10 falls in your solar tenth house of ambition and career, signaling opportunities for winning your boss's approval and moving up the ladder as a coveted position opens. Be sure to update your resume and get in the running. Thanks to your budgeting expertise, you have vacation expenses fully covered, even if unplanned events disrupt part of the schedule.

Pitfalls and Potential Problems

Although Mercury goes direct on June 22 when it ushers in the summer solstice, you're better off resuming plans after the 27th. A Full Moon in Capricorn on the 24th may leave you exhausted. Neptune goes retrograde on June 25 and most affects those who were born between September 15 and 17. Don't give away any secrets at the workplace on the 9th.

Rewarding Days

3, 7, 13, 23

Challenging Days

6, 9, 10, 24

Virgo | July

Overall Theme

The Moon is in Aries and your solar eighth house of joint assets and mortgages on July 1, making harmonious aspects to a number of planets. What a great day to apply for a loan if you're serious about shopping for a home or vehicle or consolidating debt. Later in the month, your domestic scene focuses attention on searching for the truth behind confusing matters that originated between July 4 and 12. You and your spouse may argue over details until facts are disclosed.

Relationships

Interactions with others have been both blissful and blistering this month on the home scene, at the workplace, and with medical practitioners. With the exception of July 4, positive communication flows for the first ten days of the month, and understanding seems a given. A loving vibe on the 21st gives home base a big boost and clears the air of leftover angst.

Success and Money

One of the most productive days on the work scene is July 7, when goal alignment inspires colleagues and ideas flow. Funding news is positive on a personal level on the 2nd and in the work sector on the 9th. A contract may be renewed for a longer term. Salary ranges expand and motivate the desire to compete for more responsibility and a leadership role.

Pitfalls and Potential Problems

With this month's activity in your solar seventh house of partners, you're motivated to get to the bottom of relationship blocks. Bypass heated discussions at the Full Moon on July 23 in your solar sixth house of health. You'll discover that you still have fences to mend with your significant other on the 27th, when another piece of the puzzle comes to light.

Rewarding Days

2, 7, 9, 21

Challenging Days

4, 12, 15, 27

Virgo | August

Overall Theme

For those of you engaged in legal battles, the month starts out with news about supplying information needed for a settlement and considering the option of going to court. Virgos under the care of one or more medical practitioners will be scheduling diagnostic tests or weighing the effects of medication on health conditions. Who needs this in August when it would be so much more satisfying to play at the beach?

Relationships

Close friends contact you wanting to engage in fun and games around the 6th. Spend a blissful weekend leaving worries behind and say yes without making excuses about unfinished business. The next ten days work well for a relaxing visit to a lake, a mountain retreat, or a park adventure with your family. Build in some bonding time with your children to include sports or entertainment venues.

Success and Money

You've got the game and now the name for getting the work accomplished at a high quality level. Authority figures show appreciation and heap praise on you on the 3rd, which should be a relief to you since you have much deserved vacation plans on the horizon. Uranus goes retrograde on August 19 in your solar ninth house, a day to avoid surgery or non-emergency medical procedures.

Pitfalls and Potential Problems

Avoid the temptation to bring work with you when you go on vacation. If the 9th is your first day of downtime, you could feel a bit under the weather after the hectic pace you kept prior to your vacation. You might possibly have scheduled a doctor appointment on this day before taking time off. The 17th is a day to check household systems or look for signs of infestation or leaks when you return home.

Rewarding Days

3, 6, 19, 24

Challenging Days

1, 9, 17, 28

Virgo | September

Overall Theme

The focus this month is on you, starting with your definition of a new beginning since the New Moon falls in your solar first house on September 6. Review your list of action items for those that reflect personal goals and your preferred order of accomplishment. You have work to do in making inroads and incorporating adventure into your desire for change. Bag rigidity—enjoyment is the operative word. You get the green light to attend a seminar or enroll in local classes.

Relationships

Look closely at the relationship you have with yourself for clues about the health of your relationships with others. Communication with cousins, siblings, and neighbors is more frequent than usual this month and includes invitations for dinners, parties, and sporting events. Contact someone you've been meaning to call but haven't talked to in a long time. Your thoughtfulness means a lot more to this individual than you may know.

Success and Money

You're at the right place at the right time to snap up bargains in household goods and clothing on the 9th. You'll meet planned deadlines successfully if you turn in reports and give your boss a personal overview between the 12th and 20th. The company head agrees to pick up the tab for a course for you or customized team training.

Pitfalls and Potential Problems

Don't schedule important meetings on the 1st, and avoid tense communication with authority figures on that date. You'll encounter overly emotional attendees at professional gatherings on the 3rd; very little progress will be made on agenda items. It's time for Mercury to turn retrograde again in Libra on the 27th. This shift is likely to interfere with your plans for late-month local travel and planned events.

Rewarding Days

6, 9, 12, 28

Challenging Days

1, 3, 14, 27

Virgo | October

Overall Theme

This month is among the busiest of the year, with several shifts in planetary direction. Finances receive the lion's share of attention, affecting spending. The focus of activity revolves around restoring balance and completing tasks. You'll be relieved to learn that you can go forward with projects, sign important papers, and set up appointments once Mercury goes direct on October 18.

Relationships

Deep discussions take place on the 6th, the date of the Libra New Moon, involving family decisions and investments in home improvements or furniture. Doing your homework, researching vendors, and talking with contractors yields valuable information and allows you to build rapport with businesses that are likely to win your approval for doing the work. Emotions peak on the 20th, the Full Moon, when intimacy is highly charged. Share your dreams with your loved one.

Success and Money

Comparison shopping demonstrates your resourcefulness. Be on top of your game on the 7th to negotiate successful contracts and purchases. Grab the chance that comes your way to take the lead in a work setting when your boss asks you to deliver a status report on the 25th. Make sure presentation materials reflect key points. This opportunity could be a test for a move up in the organization.

Pitfalls and Potential Problems

You could use a day to lie low and give some thought to strategy for upcoming assignments. A good day to retire to your personal space is October 3rd. You'll hear news about neighborhood disruptions, possibly construction or repairs, around the 8th. Stay away from holding major events or meetings on the 22nd, when the harsh planetary lineup puts a cap on productive outcomes.

Rewarding Days

6, 7, 20, 25

Challenging Days

3, 8, 22, 27

Virgo | November

Overall Theme

With only two planets in retrograde motion this month, you would think the time is ripe to hit the ground running with ideas and passion for furthering cherished plans, especially those you make with loved ones. Timing is everything, though. It's a no go on the 1st, when opposition blindsides you, and on the 4th. The 3rd gives you a glimmer of hope and boosts your economic worth and spending power.

Relationships

Children, friends, and romantic partners are the center of your world this month, and you spend quality time making them feel cherished. An element of surprise on the 9th keeps those in your circle entertained and grateful for the kind gesture of love. Early shopping for a partner's holiday gift gives you abundant ideas for fulfilling a wish list. Relatives at a distance finalize plans for holiday visits.

Success and Money

On the 3rd you may discover that you're going to receive a bonus, or a dividend check arrives. It's also a good day for shopping or making comparisons on a new vehicle purchase that's in the works. The 20th is perfect for planning outings for visiting relatives or hosting meals to introduce them to dear friends. You and your partner are determined to get the most for your money and agree to study product reviews to become familiar with the purchase options.

Pitfalls and Potential Problems

Saturn opposing the Moon on Thanksgiving can be a downer for sustaining cheer at holiday gatherings. More than one visitor may be feeling the blues. Find some games that guests can play to break the ice and lift the mood.

Rewarding Days
3, 9, 13, 20

Challenging Days
1, 4, 18, 31

Virgo | December

Overall Theme

What an ideal time to reflect on relationships and renew the bonds you have with friends and family. This time of year is the season of celebration, giving you a chance to show appreciation for the special people in your life. The final Solar Eclipse of the year occurs on December 4 in Sagittarius and your solar fourth house, highlighting activity at home base. An eclipse located here sparks the incentive to host travelers and entertain others with special dinners and parties.

Relationships

After months of trying to interpret confusing signals in your solar seventh house of one-on-one relationships, Neptune finally goes direct on December 1, opening the door to clearer communication and easy bonding with your partner. After the exhausting waiting period you just experienced, you welcome the shift in attitude. The 4th, 5th, and 7th are ideal for discussing plans, enjoying holiday events, sharing fears about limitations, and setting goals to strengthen commitment.

Success and Money

With considerable attention on your tenth house of career this year, you have a reason to be joyful thanks to financial windfalls or job advancements that have come your way. Despite setbacks, you've been able to achieve your goals and develop new ones for the future. Money prospects for you and your partner are optimistic in the year ahead.

Pitfalls and Potential Problems

The intensity of the Solar Eclipse on December 4 calls attention to those who live in your home and the possibility of someone moving in or out based on other conditions in your birth chart. Be sure to discuss details with affected parties and identify any anger issues if the relocation plans come up without warning. Those of you born between September 3 and 5 experience the greatest impact from this eclipse.

Rewarding Days

4, 5, 7, 30

Challenging Days

2, 11, 18, 31

Virgo Action Table

These dates reflect the best—but not the only—times for success and ease in these activities, according to your Sun sign.

	JAN	FEB	MAR	APR	MAY	JUN	JUL	AUG	SEP	OCT	NOV	DEC
Move		9			1			19			9	
Romance	12			7			2			20		
Seek counseling/ coaching			13			3						30
Ask for a raise	24				23			3	28		3	
Vacation			8			7			12			5
Get a loan		2		11			9			6		

Libra

The Scales
September 22 to October 23

Element: Air

Glyph: Scales of justice, setting sun

Quality: Cardinal

Anatomy: Kidneys, lower back, appendix

Polarity: Yang/masculine

Colors: Blue, pink

Planetary Ruler: Venus

Animals: Brightly plumed birds

Meditation: I balance conflicting desires

Myths/Legends: Venus, Cinderella, Hera

Gemstone: Opal

House: Seventh

Power Stones: Tourmaline, kunzite, blue lace agate

Opposite Sign: Aries

Flower: Rose

Key Phrase: I balance

Keyword: Harmony

The Libra Personality

Strengths, Talents, and the Creative Spark

You grace the earth with your presence in search of balance using your intellect and curious mind. With Venus as your sign ruler, you are on the lookout for opportunities to put your social and diplomatic skills to work in both your personal and your business environment. You look for avenues to reach a compromise when important matters such as project paths, political or theological ideology, or collaborative ventures are at a stalemate. Those of you with an interest in law or fair management practices are easily drawn to the fields of arbitration, dispute resolution, or mediation, where your finely honed communication savvy gets a workout. At times you may use the phrase "it just isn't fair" when you run across situations that indicate behavior or actions that seem slanted in a less than optimal direction. The legal profession may have considerable appeal for you, although not necessarily the specialty of criminal law. Family law, divorce, accidents, and estate management are subjects that draw your interest to provide an array of options for handling these sensitive issues. Your caring nature might draw you to the medical field, as long as it doesn't involve stomach-turning, bloody confrontations in the emergency room or work in an operating room. Some Libras work in medical practices as a member of the support team and take care of medical claims, schedule appointments, or counsel patients. With your gracious good manners, you make an excellent front office receptionist for companies, groups, or teams, and excel at organizing social events and fundraisers.

Creativity is one of your strongest attributes, which you apply to your love of artistic pursuits that often require dedicated use of your hands. The range of career options may include choices in the beauty industry, such as cosmetologist, dermatologist, hair stylist, or color specialist, or in body work, including massage, reiki, or pilates. You have a flair for sales and gravitate toward firms that sell affiliated products. You're also adept at demonstrating highly effective makeovers and use of techniques that improve the appearance of your clients.

Intimacy and Personal Relationships

Since Libra is the second air sign in the zodiac, the seventh house of partners is your domain. You could probably fill a book with all you know about relationships—the good, the bad, and the ugly. It's not unusual for you to have more than one marriage in your bio, and you internalize everything you learn about what worked and what went wrong. You don't like being alone, and once you heal from the scars of a broken relationship, you are back on the circuit in search of the perfect partner. You are loyal to partners and stay the course unless conditions are severely uncomfortable. Sometimes you develop a blind spot about a partner and may not realize that you're not seeing the big picture. Since relationships are a huge life lesson for you, you may be drawn to a rewarding career in consulting, coaching, psychology, or teaching.

Values and Resources

Everything about the cooperative nature of the seventh house appeals to you. Although this house resonates strongly with peace and harmony, it is just as strongly affiliated with clashes, conflict, and disagreements with partners. You suffer dearly if an intimate relationship is out of whack due to misunderstandings or if a work partnership forces you to cope with a stressful daily environment. Most likely you will complain out loud or emit an aura that says you're miffed. Your body language speaks loudly, and those around you get the message. Then you'll put all your efforts into looking for a new perspective and a viable solution to ease the tension. Voilà! Go straight to your talent for resolving personnel issues for inspiration. Schedule time to talk it out, whether it's a personal or a professional communication breakdown. You're proud of keeping journals and records of life events. Some of you write memoirs or claim the role of family historian.

Blind Spots and Blockages

One of the chief criticisms leveled against you is that you're wishy-washy. Those with whom you come in contact often don't know where you stand on an issue. Your defense mechanism is to say that you don't want to get in the middle of things or take a position. By exhibiting passive-aggressive behavior, you may come across as being disloyal to those you love who could really use your support. Be sure to solve relationship problems to avoid festering feelings. If you ask more questions, you might actually see things very differently. Think of ways to be fair to others by listening carefully to what they have to say instead of appearing overly eager to voice your opinion. Although you cherish family and have many friends and associates, you can be almost clannish in only hanging out with certain family members and excluding others to the point of exhibiting favoritism, a charge you often deny. Sometimes you have trouble making up your mind when confronted with options. Work on creative avoidance, indecisiveness, or procrastination. Do your deliberating privately and come to the table prepared.

Goals and Success

Be sure you have your sounding board lined up so you can bounce creative ideas off your partner or confidant when you're in goal-setting mode. Ask for comments, but don't expect others to make decisions for you or to share the blame if what you choose doesn't work out. Lean on your fantastic personal communication skills to set the tone for ongoing success. When it comes to keeping up with electronic technology, two types of Libras exist—the ones who easily navigate the internet and enjoy the accessibility of leading-edge information sources and rapid response times, and the ones who avoid most types of web communication and have to force themselves to read and respond to email or social media outside of what the workplace demands. If you're the latter version, take a course or read up on how to safely navigate the field. Your connections will benefit from your knowledge and availability to stay on top of the work. Set goals for providing courteous and thoughtful service to your contacts. Honor the integrity of your relationships and let your cooperative spirit soar in 2021.

Libra Keywords for 2021
Clarification, compromise, cooperation

The Year Ahead for Libra

You learned how to spell "relief" in 2020 when eclipses in cardinal signs Cancer and Capricorn finally moved out of the strike zone that challenged both your job and your household security since July 2018. Events at home base have been particularly taxing, with a full house of planetary company. Since 2008, Pluto in Capricorn has been applying pressure on you to change practices that no longer serve your needs and the way you interact with others in your home. Since December 2017, Saturn in Capricorn has been in your fourth house too, demanding that you take a stand while making family members hot under the collar when you blow them off and won't discuss sensitive issues. Jupiter in Capricorn has been a bright spot over the past year, aiding domestic tranquility and increasing property values and net worth as long as you don't spend all the profits on fun and games. Any home improvements you're planning reflect the goals of you and your partner. You may be waiting for someone to move out to accommodate your decorating vision, or perhaps you're remodeling to make room for a new family member, a tenant, or a relative who is ill or downsizing and needs a new home.

Events that revolve around your career decisions are drivers of your next steps. Eclipses in your solar third and ninth houses influence the energy patterns in 2021. Perhaps you're thinking of selling your home and moving as a result of a job change or a transfer to a distant location. Certain Libras pursue an advanced degree and take a sabbatical from work to expedite obtaining the credentials, while others engage in pleasure travel to fulfill a bucket list quest or get acquainted with relatives in distant locations or countries. Relatives near and far could be in touch much more frequently than usual. Don't rule out hosting reunions and having company coming and going. Count on your gifts of cooperation and communication to unite family, develop harmonious relationships with neighbors, and bring people together to share joy. You have the power to create happy times as you celebrate life.

Jupiter

Throughout most of 2021, Jupiter in air sign Aquarius is in positive aspect to your Sun, taking up residence in your solar fifth house of recreation, vacation, sports, children, entertainment, romance, creativity, risk-taking, and entrepreneurial ventures. You enjoy going places with partners and prefer to travel with them rather than go sightseeing alone. New adventures appeal to you since you're very fond of travel and amusement. You may be planning for a unique trip or two this year well in advance and scope out sights you've never visited before, collecting books and brochures. Comedy and show business venues are other interests, even a Broadway show or a popular play. Single Libras attract new love interests and change routines to include matters of interest to those you are dating. Clarify plans with children and schedule exclusive time with them to bond and enjoy their interests, including sports, fitness venues, parks, and scouting. Jupiter has the company of Saturn in Aquarius in this enterprising fifth house for most of the year. Get moving and enjoy a socially balanced year brimming with fun and relaxation.

Saturn

At the start of 2021, Saturn is in the first degree of Aquarius in the company of transiting Jupiter in your solar fifth house of children, creativity, entertainment, gambling and other risk-taking ventures, recreation, romance, sports, and coaching or teaching. Opportunities abound for you to work out tension through recreational pursuits and a well-tailored fitness program. If you're concerned about a child, it's time to look into details and search for answers and a solution to point your child's welfare in the right direction. Conferences with teachers and doctors may be in order. For some Libras, romantic interests may need attention if you sense your partner is pulling away. Do an inventory on goals, feelings, and the flow of communication. How solid is the cooperation between the two of you? Depending on aspects in your birth chart, you may have to make alternate plans for vacations or high-end entertainment goals this year. Jupiter in Aquarius gives you a boost and lessens the impact—relief! Be sure to question inconsistent information regarding social outings as well as investment options. Sign nothing until you've read all details. Timing is everything. Those of you born between September 24 and October 7 feel the deepest impact from Saturn's transit. Be sure to schedule health checkups and maintain a diet rich in nutrients and energy-boosting foods.

Uranus

The year begins with Uranus in Taurus retrograde in your solar eighth house of birth, sex, death, taxes, regeneration, other people's money, joint income, mortgage and investment holdings, psychological depth, mysteries, money you owe, and what type of repayment plan you are considering. Look at all the possibilities for stirring up the unexpected, since this is just the tip of the iceberg! Give yourself credit, though, because you're capable of planning well for unanticipated change and rolling with the punches. Rely on your adept negotiating skills and solution-oriented mindset to act on emerging developments. Share insights and bond closely with your intimate partner. Uranus is a high-impact planet, and an eighth-house transit of this chaotic planet calls for careful attention to financial details, such as developing a budget and sticking to it; crafting a will; settling legal matters, including estates, lawsuits, or mortgage financing; and understanding flexibility if you or a partner lose your income source due to downsizing, sale of a company, or relocation. Those in your circle may be affected by accidents, injuries, or the need for surgery. Play it safe and look over legal documents, insurance policies, and retirement benefits.

Neptune

Here you are with another year of Neptune in Pisces in your solar sixth house, where it has been in residence since April 2011. In this house, you come in contact with those in your daily environment, work, or home, and see firsthand the level of organization that exists to accomplish goals, complete tasks, work cooperatively with team members, and monitor systems critical to keeping deadlines. Neptune here monitors your health, medications you take, nutrition, and the welfare of your pets. Don't be alarmed if you develop allergies to foods or medications or materials in your environment. This scenario is reflective of Neptune in harsh aspect to key planets. Don't become a germophobe, which is sometimes a side effect of developing an overblown fear of something awful happening. Instead, focus on a clear image of good health, serenity, and prosperity. Write positive affirmations and internalize the balanced message that becomes part of your self-talk. Stay alert to confusing messages and inconsistent behavior in the work arena or at home. Act rather than react to the core issue after you study the details. Throwing a blanket of fog over issues is part of Neptune's modus operandi, creating doubt and delaying progress. It's up to you to walk through the illusion, albeit slowly, and come up for air clearheaded and pleased with your progress. In 2021, Neptune most affects you if you were born between October 11 and 16.

Pluto

Pluto in Capricorn is no stranger to your solar fourth house of family, home base, people who live with you, your physical home and decor, landscaping, real estate ventures, and end-of-life matters. Pluto has been here since 2008, making some slow but very deep progress toward encouraging you to change your ideas about people and the management of conditions where you feel stuck. The shift has to come from within; otherwise it remains an emotional irritant that is both frustrating and depressing, especially if you're blocking the truth and settling for "someday I'll do something about it." Based on the high degree of eclipse energy and the presence of Jupiter and Saturn in Capricorn in this house over the past few years, certain Libras have begun to meet the challenge by shifting plans and goals to pave the way to a better, less stressful life. Any number of scenarios may be driving your path, including retirement, ill parents, children leaving the home, taking on roommates, grandchildren spending considerable time in your home, the desire for a larger or smaller residence, or a remodeling plan to suit your desire to age in place.

Pluto lingers here in your solar fourth house until March 2023, when it makes a brief appearance in Aquarius before sliding back into Capricorn in mid-June, a teaser appearance at best. In 2021, those of you born between October 16 and 20 feel the most significant impact. Consult professional specialists to gain insight into possible solutions and you'll be able to eliminate the baggage that affects your mobility. Toast the new year with joyful optimism.

How Will This Year's Eclipses Affect You?

In 2021, a total of four eclipses occur. There will be two Lunar Eclipses and two Solar Eclipses, creating intense periods that begin to manifest a few months before their actual dates. Eclipses unfold in cycles involving all twelve signs of the zodiac, and usually occur in pairs about two weeks apart. Think of eclipses as opportunities to release old patterns and conditions that have outlived their usefulness. Have no fear of them, since they can bring you unexpected surprises and windfalls. The closer an eclipse is to a degree or point in your chart, the greater its importance in your life. Those of you born with a planet at the same degree as an eclipse are likely to see a high level of activity in the house where the eclipse occurs.

The first eclipse in 2021 is a Lunar Eclipse in Sagittarius on May 26 in your solar third house of communication, community matters, contracts, education, electronic equipment, mental outlook, relatives such as siblings and cousins, neighbors, and transportation (vehicles and conditions). This eclipse most affects you if you were born between September 27 and 29. You could take on writing or speaking assignments, become involved in contract negotiations for professional or personal projects, communicate more intensely with family members, or become involved in neighborhood issues or serve on committees. You'll need reliable transportation, especially if increased travel has you covering local neighborhoods at a stepped-up pace. Your healthy mindset plays a big role in the outcome of events.

On December 4, the last Solar Eclipse of the year takes place in this same solar third house in Sagittarius and may build on or finalize activities related to this location that you initiated in May. Its impact lasts for the next six months. Those of you born between October 4 and 6 experience increased activity in matters connected to this house. Be ready to compromise on terms, dates, or monetary compensation.

The year's first Solar Eclipse takes place on June 10 in Gemini and your solar ninth house of long-distance travel, higher education, relocation, journalism or writing fields, foreign cultures and nations, in-laws, philosophy, and religion. You're most affected if born between October 11 and 13. Those of you interested in moving up the career ladder may enroll in a degree or certificate program to develop the ideal qualifications for a successful transition. Others relish the dream of exotic travel and plan for a trip to a distant location. Some Libras accept work details to another location to gain favored work experience. Those of you with in-laws living at a distance may hear unexpected news about them or learn they will be visiting you for a long period of time.

The last Lunar Eclipse of the year occurs on November 19 in Taurus and your solar eighth house of birth, sex, death, taxes, regeneration, other people's money, joint income, mortgage and investment holdings, psychological depth, mysteries, money you owe, and estates. Those of you born between October 19 and 21 see the most action and could experience an unexpected windfall as the result of a win of some type, a large bonus, an indirect benefit from your partner's pay raise, or an inheritance. You could be looking at refinancing your home, taking out a home equity loan to remodel key rooms, or upgrading to get your home ready for a sale if relocation is on your agenda. Keep an eye on your savings and investments and diversify your portfolio. This year could be perfect for balancing your budget, increasing your holdings, and managing wealth.

Libra | January

Overall Theme

You begin the year with the understanding that clarification of your commitments and messages is in order. Those in your circle are ready to hear the truth and want to know more about your thoughts and feelings. With Pluto being the remaining occupant of your solar fourth house (after the eclipses plus Jupiter and Saturn in Capricorn left late in 2020), you don't have to keep those secrets locked away any longer. Get rid of any resentments and let go of the angst and the baggage.

Relationships

Fill your social calendar on the 3rd, 6th, and 14th with post-holiday events and obligations. The first half of the month works well for bonding and healing hurt feelings. Date or party night is likely on the 14th and could be tied to a work-related function. Avoid heated discussions with loved ones on the 19th, when egos are fragile.

Success and Money

With Uranus in Taurus moving direct in your solar eighth house on the 14th, you and your partner bond over joint financial matters and work on plans to make your money go a lot further. Review your savings and your debt load. Make smart decisions regarding allocation of holdings and redistribute funds that meet current needs if your plan is inadequate. Target debt repayment. Spend holiday gift money on the 6th, and be sure to buy something for yourself, a long-cherished item.

Pitfalls and Potential Problems

Nothing ever gets solved by sulking; you could be in the company of someone on the 1st who is doing just that. Be encouraging and upbeat to defuse negative energy. Be sure you don't grab the bait and act surly. Stay away from group arguments on the 28th. Mercury goes retrograde on the 30th in Aquarius in your fifth house. Table risk-taking ventures.

Rewarding Days

3, 4, 6, 14

Challenging Days

1, 7, 19, 28

Libra | February

Overall Theme

You're feeling more upbeat than usual now. Why not plan a trip this month, maybe a winter getaway or a pre-Valentine vacation with your significant other? This respite should chase away the phantoms of overwork that have eaten into your downtime for the last six months. If travel isn't an option, then there's no place like home when you're up for entertaining. Since you like to party, show off your new décor, dazzle visitors with fantastic food, and get them involved in fun and games, now is a good time to host the perfect bash to chase away the winter blues.

Relationships

The dreamy Pisces Moon around Valentine's Day has the company of romantic Neptune, just what you desire to spend some alone time with your sweetheart. Midweek celebrations bring opportunities to see old · friends or celebrate a birthday in a unique location. Neighbors may be moody on the 7th or at odds over boundaries. Limit comments until you have more information.

Success and Money

You start the month feeling pumped about the extra cash in your wallet and receiving payment for work that set a precedent in meeting goals. Share with others and enjoy social connections. Sports venues prove enjoyable. Family matters are favored on the 9th, when you host a gathering and hear unexpected good news.

Pitfalls and Potential Problems

Communication may be a bit erratic until after Mercury goes direct on the 20th. The 4th is a day to table negotiating on purchases. It could be expensive in more ways than one if agreement is not possible or if someone confronts you with too many conditions to conclude a transaction. Sleep in on the 27th, the Full Moon, after an exhausting end to a week that had you deciphering messages from a distance.

Rewarding Days

2, 9, 11, 16

Challenging Days

4, 7, 22, 28

Libra | March

Overall Theme

March is a perfect month for you to shower a little personal attention on yourself—the spa, a manicure, a new hairstyle, wardrobe enhancement, and playtime. In case energy has been flagging, take the time to schedule a doctor visit and make appointments for routine prevention tests. Dietary changes work wonders for your vitality and skin tone.

Relationships

Workmates play a starring role this month in important areas of collaboration and division of labor to move projects forward. Note where you observe the most harmonious approach to problem-solving and engage those who demonstrate tact in working out details and show a willingness to compromise. Loving relationships dominate at home base the weekend of the 13th and 14th. Take advantage of smooth sailing in sensitive areas through the 22nd, with the exception of the 18th, when tension surfaces.

Success and Money

Business enterprises thrive this month and show how the power of open discussions and inclusiveness improves teamwork and commitment to meeting deadlines. Realistic attitudes toward budget limitations clarify the scope of spending in both professional and family environments. Set goals that complement present conditions as well as objectives that work better in the latter part of the year. Plant the seeds of optimism.

Pitfalls and Potential Problems

Keep an eye on spending on the 4th, when the bargains are marginal and better selection is just around the corner if you're patient. Contacts at a distance are peevish on the 19th and want to argue over small stuff. Take the high road and set a time to talk the following week.

Rewarding Days

2, 13, 22, 28

Challenging Days

4, 18, 19, 29

Libra | April

Overall Theme

The 1st of the month shows planets in late degrees in harmonious aspect in your solar second house of income and resources. If you've been waiting patiently to purchase a big-ticket item, including a vehicle, this could be an ideal day to find appealing selections in the available inventory. Check details and ask lots of questions, including ones that cover flexibility in price. Signing a contract may work better on the 10th, the day before the New Moon in Aries.

Relationships

Romance is in the air on the 7th and may include a night or a few days of entertainment, an early spring break, or a mini vacation. Single Libras seek out the company of compatible individuals, while those with partners may share a surprise with resident family members on the 5th. Shower your spouse with attention on the 11th.

Success and Money

Load up on self-confidence to take advantage of compatible aspects that strengthen bonds of friendship. Timing is everything when you use your bargaining skills to land the perfect deal for purchasing personal goods and make note of the best days to sign contracts. Use the 23rd to chill and review paperwork related to new acquisitions. Enjoy the flow of positive communication and dance to the music of success.

Pitfalls and Potential Problems

Avoid signing contracts on the 3rd—don't allow anyone to rush you or put a limit on how long an offer is viable. Read the fine print. When the salesperson stops badgering, a family member may begin putting pressure on you around the 5th. Don't agree to anything you don't like. Avoid arguments at work on the 19th, when you may have to deal with emotional outbursts, stubborn positions, and an unappealing delivery style.

Rewarding Days

1, 7, 11, 23

Challenging Days

3, 5, 19, 27

Libra | May

Overall Theme

Keep your eye on planetary activity this month, with erratic shifts that affect your plans and responsibilities. Saturn gears up for its annual trip into retrograde motion on May 23 and Mercury gets ready to turn retrograde again on May 29. Note that all three Mercury retrogrades this year are in air signs, with a strong emphasis on messages and how you relate to others. On May 26, the first Lunar Eclipse of 2021 occurs in Sagittarius and most affects Libras born between September 27 and 29.

Relationships

Embrace activity at home base on the 2nd, when family members cherish a day of communicating, sharing experiences, and playing games. You could be hosting other family members on this date. Caregivers and medical personnel figure prominently on the 7th, when you seek advice or consult with them about health concerns for you or another relative. You get the green light for a proposed initiative from your boss around the 17th and start to work on plans immediately.

Success and Money

Respect for your professional contributions tops the list of this month's accomplishments. Bonding with family members and entertaining in your home show your flair for making others feel loved and welcome. Enjoy the camaraderie. For entrepreneurial types, work contracts may be renewed or extended.

Pitfalls and Potential Problems

Avoid travel on May 26, the day of the Lunar Eclipse, especially a long-distance trip. Friction with partners occurs on the 8th if an old issue surfaces again. Don't try to solve it until after the 11th, another day when the argument may include financial disagreements that are more complex than usual. Watch that credit card spending!

Rewarding Days

2, 7, 14, 17

Challenging Days

8, 11, 19, 26

Libra | June

Overall Theme

Erratic energy is in the air with two planets turning retrograde, Jupiter on June 20 and Neptune on June 25, while Mercury moves direct on June 22. The year's first Solar Eclipse on June 10 highlights your solar ninth house of long-distance travel, legal and medical dealings, publishing, higher education, philosophy, and people at a distance. Take your pick—you are likely to have dealings in two or more of these subject areas.

Relationships

Count on in-laws and other relatives who live in distant locations to pop back into your life. Some have messages about life status and others want to arrange visits or invite you to a celebration. Friends and lovers take center stage for some of you as you respond to an accelerated social calendar and decide what is possible to accomplish. You could have double bookings or deal with work conflicts. People at your workplace perform energetically to make ambitious deadlines and bring in deliverables well in advance of vacation time.

Success and Money

Your team and those you mentor receive high praise for accomplishments, including cost savings initiatives, potential new contracts, and coveted assignments. Those of you in leadership positions set the tone of future performances by acknowledging accomplishments and rewarding employees. Plan a ceremony or small party to mark milestone achievements. Goodwill builds rapport and trust.

Pitfalls and Potential Problems

You may be ready to cut and run to recharge your batteries. Begin travel after June 25 for smoother interactions. Partners show impatience on the 4th, and it will take a calm attitude to ride out the storm. Between the 13th and 19th, resolve blocks to progress in the workplace.

Rewarding Days

1, 3, 10, 15

Challenging Days

4, 13, 19, 24

Libra | July

Overall Theme

On the 4th of July holiday, the Moon in Taurus joins Uranus in your solar eighth house, ripping open old sores related to partnership assets and leading to some intense discussions, especially if you were born around October 6–8. Past behavior comes to light and puts a damper on next month's vacation plans. You have some explaining to do and solutions to apply to resolve misunderstandings related to financial management.

Relationships

The month starts out well but soon wanders into a sea of distrust over issues connected to escalating expenses with you and your partner. The New Moon on the 9th brings successful outcomes to workplace matters and spontaneous celebrations with team members,. You could play a major role with members of a professional organization on the 12th when you deliver a keynote speech or make a presentation to introduce others to a new undertaking that calls for their participation.

Success and Money

Get to the bottom of why the budget took off on a runaway train earlier in the month. Some type of corner cutting may have backfired. This setback may affect vacation plans. Your spouse has other ideas for recreation that sound inviting and are a departure from your usual leisure fare. By the 25th you discover a partner's proposal has additional expenses that escalate costs, so it's back to the drawing board.

Pitfalls and Potential Problems

Nurse hurt feelings on the 5th in the aftermath of budget disclosures. It may be too soon to get anywhere, but think of a compromise to mitigate anger. A child may be out of sorts on the 25th, and a partner may object to plans that carry too much risk. Next month shows more promise for emerging plans.

Rewarding Days

2, 9, 12, 23

Challenging Days

5, 16, 25, 30

Libra | August

Overall Theme

You start the month working out details of your personal financial circumstances in preparation for some time off and fun with the family. Then it's possible that travelers from a distance who are scheduled to visit will cancel due to unforeseen circumstances. It will all work out for the best since you run into some work issues that need final tweaking and approval before you can leave for vacation. Go with the flow.

Relationships

Harmony, insight, and refreshing solutions enhance workplace dynamics, and a strong show of teamwork gets the job done. Authority figures are effusive with praise and acknowledge a job well done. Be patient because the money is coming. If you belong to clubs, groups, or professional organizations, you may be asked to take a leading role.

Success and Money

Although you have to move a few rocks in the road financially early in the month, you manage to orient your money in the right direction and consolidate debt. Work accomplishments are recognized and performance visibility gives you a leg up in the competition for future assignments. Your generosity toward team members reflects your considerate attitude toward colleagues.

Pitfalls and Potential Problems

Stay mindful of limits you've placed on spending to sustain your debt reduction goals. Be sure to set up an emergency fund if you don't already have one. Uranus is bouncing around in your solar eighth house and goes retrograde on August 19 in Taurus. It most affects you with a stressful aspect if you were born between October 6 and 8.

Rewarding Days

6, 9, 11

Challenging Days

1, 3, 16

Libra | September

Overall Theme

Enjoy long-distance travel through the 7th of the month, and give your-self a day to sleep in or relax when you return. The momentum is going to change while you're away on vacation, and you may hear about it via a text message from a coworker. Don't let the news keep you from your plans or prompt you to cut your vacation short. Stuff happens! By the time you return, the bump in the road will be under repair and you can merge into problem-solving mode on the 9th, a day when your mind is sharp and solutions flow.

Relationships

You have the magic touch with relatives who live at a distance or people from other cultures. Meetings with friends or groups have successful outcomes when participation is welcome and flows smoothly. You and a partner may not be in sync on the 23rd, especially if you're distracted during a discussion. Unusual displays of commitment surface around September 21 related to work or people you see on a daily basis.

Success and Money

Victory means you have discovered options to solve unexpected snafus that occur in your home, in a business setting, or among friends. This cycle brings the reward of increased self-confidence in using resources wisely. You are one of the signs that owns mediation skills and is con-stantly inventing better versions of them to keep relationships balanced.

Pitfalls and Potential Problems

Challenging days have taxed your brain. Remain objective and you'll come out ahead. Make your moves before Mercury goes retrograde in Libra on September 27 for the next three weeks. Table major decisions until after October 18. Stay out of organizational politics on the 3rd and 4th, when you may not have all the facts.

Rewarding Days

1, 7, 9, 21

Challenging Days

3, 4, 16, 23

Libra | October

Overall Theme

How fast can you catch your breath? You'll find that many important areas that were on hold suddenly break loose in several departments of your life. The glut of planets that have been retrograde return to direct motion and that means "take action." Pluto is the first to spring loose on October 6, then Saturn goes forward on October 10, followed by both Jupiter and Mercury on October 18. Jump-start the positive momentum that gives the green light to resume plans.

Relationships

Look for invitations to weddings and birthdays this month; attend a school reunion for a milestone anniversary. Siblings and cousins step up the frequency of phone calls and may ask for assistance in planning a family event. Neighbors look for help with community undertakings and holiday parties. Work and organizational relationships thrive under revised operating procedures and shared commitments.

Success and Money

Your homework pays off. Check your credit standing first. Then hit the sales and make desired purchases on October 9 and 10, when the planetary aspects are good for getting the deal you want and paying a fair price for goods and services. Drive a hard bargain for a household item on the 24th, when stepped-up competition for your business inspires you to negotiate.

Pitfalls and Potential Problems

The New Moon in Libra works well for you on the 6th, but wait twenty-four hours before signing a contract after a hard sell on an appliance, remodeling contract, or vehicle. Be wary about language explaining warranties and look at expiration dates carefully. Check contractor references and don't agree to a large down payment on remodeling jobs .

Rewarding Days

6, 9, 10, 26

Challenging Days

1, 3, 13, 20

Libra | November

Overall Theme

You'll be over the Moon with anticipation when extra money comes your way in the form of a bonus, raise, winning ticket, or unexpected gift from a relative around the time of the Scorpio New Moon on the 4th. The month includes its share of drama, with the last Lunar Eclipse of 2021 in Taurus and your solar eighth house of joint funds, debts, and obligations on November 19. Spend what you budgeted, but don't go overboard after working hard all year to pay down your debt.

Relationships

Your family will be glad to see you smiling and whistling a happy tune around the house as you work, sometimes secretly, to plan surprises and trips for everyone. Parents and grandparents get additional attention and invitations for meals, visits, and vacations. Enjoy the bonding time and do what you can to spread cheer. Opportunities to volunteer are welcome in the community at this time.

Success and Money

You have proudly met certain financial goals and succeeded in reducing your debt load. On top of that, your stellar performance has paid off in the form of unexpected income or windfalls from other benefactors. Develop a plan to fund purchases and continue to watch your savings grow.

Pitfalls and Potential Problems

Avoid showing your sourpuss side on the 1st, when you're either ill or out of sorts. If you come home from work feeling moody, chill and spend time resting. Don't make major plans for a couple days. By Wednesday you'll be in better shape. Communication gets testy on the 7th and is a bit strained with a partner on the 16th. Watch your tone of voice or this could be a highly charged shouting match.

Rewarding Days

3, 4, 9, 24

Challenging Days

1, 7, 16, 19

Libra | December

Overall Theme

The month begins with the Moon in your sign calling for harmony and cooperation on all fronts. A sense of benevolence and goodwill settles into the landscape, making you aware of the importance of thoughtful communication and the power of your word. The final Solar Eclipse of the year falls in Sagittarius and your solar third house on December 4, reminding you to contact cherished relatives and neighbors to let them know you value their presence in your life.

Relationships

Most of the month highlights the quality of the rapport you share with your closest contacts, neighbors, and relatives. Loving gestures unite family members on the 7th, generating proud feelings, congratulatory exchanges, and possibly a celebratory meal for achieving milestone accomplishments. Excitement, caring exchanges, love, and spiritual meaning reflect the tone of your at-home holiday celebration on the 25th.

Success and Money

Congratulate yourself on getting through the holiday season debt-free thanks to your solid plan to budget wisely, adhere to spending limits, and shop for early sales to find items for those on your gift list. Valuable insight comes from discussions with close relatives or your significant other, especially from the 4th through the 10th.

Pitfalls and Potential Problems

Watch prices and bait-and-switch sales on the 2nd, when information may be confusing over what you actually get for your money. Seek clarity before purchasing. Libras born late in your sign face emotional upheavals with a partner around the 14th. By the weekend, one of you is feeling ill and may need an appointment with a physician. Table legal appointments until after the first of the year.

Rewarding Days

1, 4, 7, 25

Challenging Days

2, 11, 14, 19

Libra Action Table

These dates reflect the best—but not the only—times for success and ease in these activities, according to your Sun sign.

	JAN	FEB	MAR	APR	MAY	JUN	JUL	AUG	SEP	OCT	NOV	DEC
Move		11			14				1			
Romance	14	16				1					4	
Seek counseling/ coaching			22	11			2		9			7
Ask for a raise					17			6			3	
Vacation	3			7		10				10		4
Get a loan			2				12			6		

Scorpio

The Scorpion
October 23 to November 21

♏

Element: Water

Quality: Fixed

Polarity: Yin/feminine

Planetary Ruler: Pluto (Mars)

Meditation: I let go of the need to control

Gemstone: Topaz

Power Stones: Obsidian, garnet

Key Phrase: I create

Glyph: Scorpion's tail

Anatomy: Reproductive system

Colors: Burgundy, black

Animals: Reptiles, scorpions, birds of prey

Myths/Legends: The Phoenix, Hades and Persephone, Shiva

House: Eighth

Opposite Sign: Taurus

Flower: Chrysanthemum

Keyword: Intensity

The Scorpio Personality

Strengths, Talents, and the Creative Spark

With Pluto as your sign's natural ruler, you have a very passionate spirit, showing fierce determination when the situation calls for it and holding on tight to what you believe and value. Some would call you stubborn since you take a serious approach to managing obligations. You place a high premium on getting to the gist of problems by asking appropriate questions and analyzing the inner depth of your contacts' minds and motives, an asset that gives you a leg up in the fields of criminal law, jury selection for courtroom trials, industrial psychology, and various aspects of police work. Many of you rise to the rank of police commissioner, chief inspector, or district attorney. You leave no stone unturned and demonstrate your performance excellence as a researcher, digging deep for what you need to validate evidence for a case related to a crime scene or a medical or scientific research project. If you like the pathology part of crime scene analysis, the work of a coroner, after attaining a medical degree, may draw your interest. Other viable career options include work as a sex therapist or self-help psychologist.

Mysteries fascinate you, whetting your appetite to get to the bottom of them by identifying related issues and putting clues together. The solar eighth house is your natural domain and shows your preference for reading material related to crimes, psychological dilemmas, romance, sex, and death. If you're a writer, you have the talent to develop exciting stories or books based on true crime or factual life incidents that mesmerize your intended audience with detailed clues to solve the case.

Like the phoenix, you periodically rise up out of the ashes when the going gets tough and bounce back through a powerful rebirth of your psyche. With a regeneration mentality, you can be a master at eradicating what you no longer need in life, such as debts, garbage, partners, pests, addictions, pack rat collections, or annoying bad habits.

Intimacy and Personal Relationships

Secretly you are in search of a soul mate and normally won't get into a relationship until you find the adored one who fits the mold. Why do I say secretly? Probably because you are not one who lets your feelings slip out through your penetrating gaze or your loose (yet loving) lips. You're afraid of the age-old condition called vulnerability and the hurt that comes if you lose your heart to someone who stomps on it. Your goal is to know your partner from the inside out, to share body, mind, and spirit, confide intimately, and ultimately trust your significant other. Only then will you commit for life. You could find yourself the repository of others' secrets, because people from various walks of life gravitate to you for your willingness to listen. Even in the initial stages of bonding, they want to tell you their life story. Other strangers want to do this too—have you noticed? You may succumb to bouts of jealousy, even with a partner who is loyal, in your corner, and dedicated to loving you forever. Remember that your life will change forever if you take the plunge.

Values and Resources

You place a significant premium on having solid investments, a healthy bank account, a partner who honors your mutual goals on spending and saving for a rainy day, and commitments related to real estate purchases. Look out if one of you is a gambler and spends hard-earned cash on the ponies, the slots, or high-stakes games. Intimacy is also sacred to your soul; sometimes it is the source of painful life lessons and drives your choice of a career in psychology or marriage counseling. You understand the correlation between keeping pain bottled up and its effects on your health. As someone who respects medical professionals, you are loyal to those caregivers who have helped you or your family in times of crisis and often form lifelong associations. Surgery is a field dominated by the eighth house, especially the ones related to extractions and elimination. A good number of Scorpios gravitate toward work as lab technicians, dentists or their associates, proctology, transplants, or various aspects of garbage removal or plumbing. Keeping secrets reinforces your quest for power.

Blind Spots and Blockages

While you are very good at eradicating unsavory conditions that hold you back, you can stubbornly hold onto them far longer than necessary. You don't like change for change's sake and will turn a blind eye to the truth until a difficult situation becomes unbearable. Then, look out! The purge is going to erupt like a lightning-struck tower, deterring the unsuspecting from entering your energy field or running interference with your plans. The aftermath can be harsh and unnecessary if you have shocked your friends and loved ones with unknown facts. Learn to share your pain instead of keeping it inside. You're known for being a scorekeeper when things don't go your way, and you compare what others have to what you own, regardless of the difference in circumstances. Those who know you feel you withhold information about yourself and other conditions when sharing would be appropriate. A criticism is that you can be too intense, so find a way to lighten up. Participation in meditation, yoga, or tai chi offers stress relief.

Goals and Success

As the zodiac's second water sign, you inherited the deep insight and intuition affiliated with the water element. You excel in enterprises that allow you to investigate facts and make sense of puzzling information or conditions that inhibit understanding of the big picture. Your penetrating gaze has a way of getting others to tell the truth when you need answers and suspect that you're only getting half the story. The term "suspicious mind" aptly describes your probing nature. You probably get the chills when you have an internal aha moment in pursuit of the truth that leads to asking all the right questions and making the appropriate moves. You have the chops to make an excellent analyst, researcher, or diagnostician. Finding the perfect career or life role leads to ultimate satisfaction. Once you make that connection, you are a role model for embracing gratitude and encouraging others to find their bliss.

Scorpio Keywords for 2021
Intensity, intimacy, introspection

The Year Ahead for Scorpio

Those who know you call you dedicated and determined to stick to your plans while following up on important details. The most intense house in 2020 was your solar seventh house of intimate, personal, and business partners, thanks to the presence of chaotic Uranus in Taurus, your opposite sign, shaking up the status quo and leaving a periodic calling card to remind you to value cooperation and let up on rapid-fire inquisition. Perhaps you found yourself at odds with your partner's ideas and thinking patterns and had trouble earning credibility for your point of view. Your solar third house of communication, education, how your mind works and your mental state, community and neighbors, electronic equipment, sisters, brothers, cousins, and methods of transportation was also a hotbed of activity in 2020, playing host to Jupiter in Capricorn until December 20 and Saturn in Capricorn through December 16. Pluto in Capricorn has also been in the third house since 2008, applying pressure on you to change thinking patterns that put you in a rut and no longer suit your style. Pluto hangs out in this house for a couple more years, reminding you that you have time to make astute decisions that change your life. Eclipses in your solar third and ninth houses have been a fixture for the last few years. The last one in Capricorn occurred on July 5, 2020, and cleared the way for smoother relationships with relatives and better negotiating and buying power for contracted services. Eclipses began to migrate to your solar second and eighth houses in 2020, shifting the emphasis to financial matters and making dramatic appearances in these departments in 2021. This year, expect new directions in how you or your partner earn your income, manage debt, or make adjustments to investments.

Note that the action-oriented solar fourth house of home and family matters will become the center of activity this year, with both transiting Jupiter and Saturn in Aquarius making a strong impact on household conditions and relationships that have been waiting for a release. You have the momentum to develop greater rapport with partners and family members and set meaningful goals to upgrade the quality of your living space. Your solar fifth house of romance, children, and vacations hosts Neptune in Pisces once again (in residence here since April 2011), raising your hope that it is possible to attract spiritual, mystical love while understanding what it means to be loved unconditionally for exactly who you are. Enjoy watching your visions come to life.

Jupiter

As the new year dawns, Jupiter is in air sign Aquarius in challenging aspect to your Sun and claiming space in your solar fourth house of home, family, foundations, domestic matters, relatives who live with you, real estate, home renovation or decorating, and any conditions that may revolve around your parents. Every degree of your sign makes a connection with Jupiter in 2021, shedding light on the feasibility of your plans for improving your home, the cost of doing business with contractors if a large remodeling or landscaping project is in the works, and reaching new understandings with those who live with you. A number of scenarios are possible with this movement, depending on other conditions in your birth chart. When Jupiter travels through your fourth house, it sometimes calls attention to the health of your parents or elderly relatives who may be living with you. You could assist them in locating specialists, setting up appointments or medical tests, or downsizing to a more manageable living space. Someone could live with you for a time or recover from surgery in your home. You could be among those individuals who sell their home when Jupiter transits the fourth house, or you could contract to build the home of your dreams. Children who live with you may move out, leave for college, or get married. Jupiter has the company of Saturn in Aquarius at your base of operations for most of the year. Manage the intensity of decisions with solid logic. Throw a little humor into the mix and take a short vacation for a change of scenery.

Saturn

The year starts out with Saturn at 1 degree of Aquarius in the company of transiting Jupiter in early Aquarius in your solar fourth house of home, foundations, domestic undertakings, family, your parents (often your mother), relatives in residence, redecorating or remodeling projects, landscaping plans, or real estate transactions, including sales, purchases, rentals, and exchanges. Saturn plays a role in adding responsibility or emphasizing limitations on conditions related to your household and the relationship you have with others in residence. With Jupiter active in this house, real estate matters are sure to surface. If you find a home at an auction or at a reduced price, be sure to schedule a title search so you don't make a down payment on a home that is not really available and could actually belong to someone else who is not offering the property for sale. Jupiter in Aquarius could aid you in lessening the impact of harsh circumstances and unnecessary expenses. Ask direct questions and request to see paperwork trails if you're not satisfied with the information available. Those of you born between October 29 and November 6 experience the strongest impact from Saturn's transit this year. Monitor quality control for any projects that are in the works in your home.

Uranus

The environment is jumpy when Uranus comes calling in your opposite sign and settles in your solar seventh house of personal and business partners. This includes the public too, as well as collaborators and those with legal or medical connections. The year begins with Uranus in Taurus retrograde here, giving you the feeling that someone or something is about to affect your love life by landing in it suddenly and exiting just as quickly. Closely examine the bond you share with your partner for clues. By January 14, Uranus turns direct in motion and most affects those of you born between October 28 and November 7 before going retrograde again on August 19 and resuming direct motion in January 2022. Take Uranus seriously. This planet operates at a high level of impact, especially right now if you have planets in Taurus or in one of the other fixed signs (Aquarius, Scorpio, or Leo). A seventh-house transit of this chaotic planet influences the stability of your marriage, a business partnership, or your connection with your significant other. Uranus here has several meanings that could show up as a change in behavior by one or both partners, career setbacks that affect job stability, a midlife crisis, adverse publicity, or taking on a roommate who upsets the routine in your household. Examine disruptive activity and get to the heart of the problem to deal with intense conditions. Enjoy the love that renewed bonding brings your way.

Neptune

With a harmonious water-sign planet like Neptune in Pisces moving through your solar fifth house of children, entertainment, love, romance, sports, teaching, and vacation, you'll discover options for enjoying leisure time and escalating the activity in your social life. The planet of mystique and the higher octave of Venus has been traveling through this house since April 2011, leading the way to adventure on the spiritual plane or to relaxation on the inner plane via a spa getaway, or to acknowledging your love of competition through water sports. Transiting Neptune tends to exude a preference for relaxation. Be sure you don't go overboard with too much of a good thing by escaping from responsibility, ducking work, leaving a well-paying job, or letting maudlin feelings overcome your survival instincts. Those of you born between November 9 and 16 experience the most intensity from this Neptune transit in 2021. Be most attuned to circumstances that occur when the eclipses in Sagittarius and Gemini create a charge in June and December. Watch what you eat if you are traveling and don't know much about the quality and preparation of food. Stay alert to communicated inconsistencies and resolve to deal with the discrepancies you uncover.

Pluto

Since 2008, Pluto has been nesting in your solar third house of mental agility, communication, education, neighborhood, close relatives, contractual obligations, electronics, and transportation modalities. Your mind may not do a complete 180 on how you view life, but you may have noticed that you have relaxed certain opinions that gave you a reputation for being rigid. Have you noticed that others are more receptive and friendlier toward you? Eclipses in Capricorn that stuck to penetrating Pluto or those in Cancer that opposed its place in your mental third house for the last few years are gone. In 2021, only Pluto hangs out here and affects decisions that come up, such as an auto purchase, educational choices, community relations, contact with siblings and cousins, or installation of electronic equipment or upgrades to existing systems. Part with the cash for a new kitchen or replace worn-out furniture. Give yourself an energy lift by unloading what you no longer need. This year, those of you born between November 15 and 20 feel the greatest impact from this Pluto transit, with a rewarding sextile aspect that stimulates your desire to regenerate outdated ideas and methods of communication. Ring in the new year with optimism for a rosy future and a gathering with people you seldom see.

How Will This Year's Eclipses Affect You?

In 2021, a total of four eclipses occur. There will be two Lunar Eclipses and two Solar Eclipses, creating intense periods that begin to manifest a few months before their actual dates. Eclipses unfold in cycles involving all twelve signs of the zodiac, and usually occur in pairs about two weeks apart. Think of eclipses as opportunities to release old patterns and conditions that have outlived their usefulness. Have no fear of them, since they can bring you unexpected surprises and windfalls. The closer an eclipse is to a degree or point in your chart, the greater its importance in your life. Those of you born with a planet at the same degree as an eclipse are likely to see a high level of activity in the house where the eclipse occurs.

Scorpio, get ready, because two eclipses take place this year in your solar second house of assets, income and money you earn, material goods, resources, self-development, and various forms of compensation. The first one is a Lunar Eclipse in Sagittarius on May 26 that relates to your earning power and how you intend to use disposable cash in the coming months. You may be saving to fund a special project or make a big-ticket purchase. You may also have specialized training on the agenda to help you meet professional or personal goals.

The second eclipse in Sagittarius is a Solar Eclipse on December 4 that further elaborates on your monetary plans and speaks to what you're earning and likely bonuses that come your way. You'll be able to congratulate yourself on how well you've managed your expenses and met your goals.

The first Solar Eclipse of the year occurs on June 10 in your solar eighth house of partnership funds, joint assets, holdings and investments, money you owe, and your method of debt reduction. This eclipse is in Gemini and is likely to have you taking inventory of your savings, loans, and retirement funds as well as the status of your will or insurance policies. You'll gain insight into any gaps in financial plans or where any of them could benefit from an overhaul.

The second Lunar Eclipse of the year takes place on November 19 in Taurus and your solar seventh house of partners and calls attention to matters related to your marriage, business relationships, dealings with roommates, cooperative ventures, and the public, including professionals who provide you with advice, counsel, or medical or legal assistance. If you're contemplating an intimate or business partnership, this eclipse may be instrumental in bringing just such an arrangement your way. Transiting Uranus is in this same house in 2021 and tends to attract unexpected people, meetings, or events. Be optimistic and welcome the beneficial conditions that allow you to shine in relationship matters. Take the lead in issuing invitations to newcomers, develop bonds, and cherish your dreams of partnerships that fulfill your goals.

Scorpio | January

Overall Theme

As the new year dawns in 2021, your picture is bright with optimism for attracting an abundance of mental clarity, spiritual insight, and romantic overtures. Your inner knower works overtime to pull you toward awakening buried feelings, seeing others in a new light, and throwing your sharp mind into your work with a new perspective on problem-solving. Introspection gives you a chance to take stock of your mental and emotional processes.

Relationships

Certain relationships have been tentative, compliments of Uranus in Taurus in a long retrograde phase in your solar seventh house of partners. On the 14th, chaotic and unpredictable Uranus goes direct in motion and shifts out of a holding pattern, allowing you to see more clearly what has been stifling the momentum in close relationships. You have work to do to engage in meaningful dialogue and build trust.

Success and Money

The first week of the year reveals a positive direction for career and job matters. Set up time to talk about ongoing goals and what it will take to accelerate the timeline. If you're a manager, discuss hiring new staff to make sure the job gets done with qualified talent. The New Moon on the 13th opens the door for smooth negotiation of contracts. Check with your banker around the 24th if you're looking to refinance a mortgage, consolidate debt, or obtain a car loan.

Pitfalls and Potential Problems

Colleagues or members of groups could be a bit down on the 4th, making the day unfavorable for introducing new objectives. Staffing shortfalls require study and decisions for filling positions. Tension makes a statement on the 21st in partnership matters when a standoff or complete opposition to proposed changes manifests.

Rewarding Days

1, 13, 14, 24

Challenging Days

4, 8, 11, 21

Scorpio | February

Overall Theme

Matters connected to professional undertakings in groups or organizations set the tone for your interests this month. You could be heading up activity in a charitable drive or fundraiser, booking entertainment or setting the location for a gala, or looking at the solvency of your employer's resources in preparation for an audit in the coming months. If you're asked to join a new group, examine the time commitment carefully to make sure it meshes with your schedule.

Relationships

Enjoyment comes from meeting and bonding with kindred spirits and getting to know new people who move into your neighborhood, join committees, or have connections to mutual friends. Romance is right on target for Valentine's Day with the Moon in positive aspect to your Sun. You and your partner celebrate your relationship in a cherished spot and share your feelings of love and happy memories.

Success and Money

You get the most for your money when making vacation plans, booking reservations to celebrate special occasions, purchasing jewelry, or shopping for unique gifts that bring unexpected pleasure to loved ones. Mercury goes direct on the 20th and gives a thumbs-up to organizing ideas for a home project before you actually meet with the contractor. Have your list of questions ready and be sure to ask for references.

Pitfalls and Potential Problems

On the 4th you could be feeling way too intense to concentrate on suggestions for improving the flow of work or the direction of a project. Buy time by asking questions. Audits or project reviews trigger unexpected queries on the 26th and 27th. Be prepared to work on the weekend to locate documentation and work quietly to produce supporting data.

Rewarding Days

1, 2, 11, 14

Challenging Days

4, 7, 26, 27

Scorpio | March

Overall Theme

Scorpios who garden are itchy for the spring thaw to get back to assessing the quality of their soil so they can make the needed amendments and begin growing seedlings for spring and summer crops. You appreciate easy maintenance shrubs and trees and could do without those that have leaves to rake. Use introspection the first few days of the month to go to the drawing board and outline project details and anticipated costs.

Relationships

Aspects look bright and positive for interactions with your siblings, cousins, and other close relatives on the 8th. Expect phone calls and visits. Community activity grabs the attention of neighbors, and they bond over matters connected with road improvements and safety. You may hear of special meetings to address proposals. You and your significant other enjoy downtime and entertainment venues around the 18th.

Success and Money

Lending an ear to help others with financial dilemmas allows you to show your fiscal savvy and point the way to solving a perplexing problem for a relative or a work situation. You'll have the attention of your boss and support of the team on the 24th when you deliver a product that has been in the works for months. Money in the form of bonuses or raises is in the pipeline.

Pitfalls and Potential Problems

Take time to recover from low energy after a bout with a cold or the flu on the 4th. Stay home and let rest be the healing balm. The rest of the month looks hectic. Check bills that come in around the 5th for accuracy and call vendors to correct discrepancies. A social event on the 12th is not what you expected. The sponsor organization deserves feedback, especially if you paid to attend.

Rewarding Days

3, 8, 18, 24

Challenging Days

4, 5, 12, 28

Scorpio | April

Overall Theme

You start the month intensely involved with accounting matters as the tax filing deadline looms. Gather receipts and examine unusual expenses that may not show up in your returns on a regular basis, especially if you have moved or bought property. Make sure any refund is safely deposited directly in your account. Pluto turns retrograde in your solar third house on the 27th right after the Scorpio Full Moon on the 26th, highlighting matters related to stressful communication. Share concerns with a trusted advisor.

Relationships

Through April 8, work and home relationships are generally smooth and the flow of discussion highlights progress in undertakings at your workplace and at home base. Money matters are up for review, especially to decide on how to use extra funds. Interaction with a friend leads to plans for a vacation together, either just the two of you if single or your families if you're married, especially around the 23rd.

Success and Money

Cash flow is excellent and largely driven by financial acumen and careful planning for tax payments and paring down debt. Put bonus money to good use for a household purchase or toward a much deserved getaway with family or friends. Treat a friend to lunch or a movie on the 23rd and make time for a long-overdue chat.

Pitfalls and Potential Problems

You and your spouse may not agree on the bottom line or even when to execute a contract for planned expenses. An argument could develop over the filing date for your tax return if you wait until the 15th; another date for engaging in difficult dialogue regarding spending is the 3rd. Entertainment expenses escalate on the 9th, possibly due to a misunderstanding over what is included in a package deal.

Rewarding Days

1, 2, 7, 23

Challenging Days

3, 9, 15, 27

Scorpio | May

Overall Theme

The New Moon in your opposite sign of Taurus on May 11 in your solar seventh house of business and personal partners generates an aura of optimism for your cherished goals and plans. Take time on the most receptive dates to lay out details about important directions and intentions. Personal relationships meet with success on May 6 and 11, while career matters shine on the 19th and details flow. Internal customers display their approval and support taking on responsibility for their part in implementing successful action plans.

Relationships

As you head back to the workplace on the first Monday of the month, you are likely to hear from a relative, an old neighbor, or a school contact who wants to connect via a visit to your city or at an upcoming reunion. Shared activities in the workplace receive positive attention, and any meetings around the 19th lead to successful follow-up and new opportunities for involved team members. Schedule a date night with your significant other or pursue a new love interest on the 6th.

Success and Money

The year's first Lunar Eclipse occurs in Sagittarius on May 26 in your solar second house of assets, income, money, resources, and developmental opportunities. Now is your time to shine as the universe points the way to a career or status change, additional studies or a degree program, or a promotion to a higher-paying job.

Pitfalls and Potential Problems

The heavy angle of the Moon in aspect to your Sun on the 4th creates discord in your home-related solar fourth house and affects the mood of family members. Leave the drama at your worksite back at the scene and visualize a calm and caring home environment. Disputes over income or expenses escalate on the 14th. Do what you can to defuse them.

Rewarding Days

2, 6, 11, 19

Challenging Days

4, 14, 25, 26

Scorpio | June

Overall Theme

This month your solar fourth house of home, family, parents, and activity at home base is a hub of activity, highlighting ongoing projects, visitors, emerging plans for household repairs, redecorating, and landscaping. Communication intensifies, and some of it may be highly emotional.

Relationships

By the 2nd, Venus is in Cancer and puts the spotlight on close family members, some of whom may be visiting from long-distance locations. Enjoy the reunion and embrace your connection and fond memories. People who live with you demonstrate feelings and rapport and you gain insight into the maturity and wisdom they now own. Colleagues may be out of sorts on the 4th, and it is tempting but not wise to push for details.

Success and Money

Eclipses travel in pairs, and two weeks after the Sagittarius eclipse on May 26, you experience the first Solar Eclipse of 2021 in your solar eighth house of shared income, money you owe, estate matters, and financial holdings on June 10. This influence stays with you through December 4, creating an opportunity to review your debt load, savings plans, retirement contributions, wills, and important financial documents. Schedule time with your attorney to ensure your holdings are secure.

Pitfalls and Potential Problems

Disagreements with partners flair up over responsibilities and misunderstandings on the 7th. Jupiter goes retrograde on the 20th, possibly leading to the cancellation of a planned trip or purchase. Hold off on a car purchase at this time. Mercury goes direct on June 22, releasing the hold on planned activity and the steady stream of confusing messages.

Rewarding Days

1, 10, 22, 28

Challenging Days

4, 7, 14, 24

Scorpio | July

Overall Theme

Uncertainty over plans you thought were firm early in the month has you scrambling to renegotiate details to ensure you have a clear slate before you take off for faraway places. Interference related to workplace demands slows you down, along with a shortage of staff to cover vacations. Late in the first full week of July, communication improves, eliminating the intensity that kept you grounded. You'll be ready for takeoff early in the day of the Cancer New Moon on the 9th.

Relationships

Personal relationships have a few ups and downs due to a work situation that affects the departure date for a pleasure trip or getaway. You handle the disappointments and find a way to smooth the tension at work and at home base since several affected parties are caught unaware of the shift in activity. Savor the compliments that authority figures dispense on the 8th, and plan on making up for lost time after the 15th.

Success and Money

You're pleased with the payoff rate and balance on a personal loan around the 8th, when you have a chance to review financial papers. At work you find an unanticipated savings in the cost of doing business that could come from an applied discount for volume or a point-earning program. Evaluation for a performance review works in your favor and makes you eligible for a late-year bonus or form of recognition.

Pitfalls and Potential Problems

You may have to cancel a medical appointment, especially if it's for dental work, on the 3rd, a day that just doesn't work well for you. Tension erupts with a loved one on the 5th over disruptions that occurred at the end of the previous week. Study problem areas on the 19th to decide on a smooth course of action after analyzing facts.

Rewarding Days

8, 9, 13, 21

Challenging Days

3, 5, 19, 25

Scorpio | August

Overall Theme

Although the month starts out with conflict and harsh words in your solar seventh house of romantic and business partners, you'll work things out if you dig behind the layer of stubbornness that is in the air and prevents you from getting at the truth. You'll probably scratch the surface during the month, which will give you some temporary relief, but not before discovering another glitch in communication by the end of the month. Patience and resilience work toward healing rifts.

Relationships

You may be able to mend a few fences with your romantic partner if you're able to travel together on a work trip around the 6th that has the flexibility to include a pleasure trip after you conclude the business end of things. Some of you may travel with a coworker and find rapport in how you approach professional problems. Leisurely discussions prime the pump for new partnership ventures.

Success and Money

The greatest successes this month lie in using your penetrating mind to make dead-on analyses about sudden changes in circumstances and applying your considerable decision-making skills to creating solutions. You earn the respect of those in charge and deserve every compliment. Family members show appreciation for your wisdom, even those who would like to see you lighten up sometimes.

Pitfalls and Potential Problems

Be aware that Uranus, the planet of the unexpected, is transiting in Taurus in your solar seventh house and will turn retrograde in motion on August 19. On the 22nd, the Full Moon in Aquarius occurs in your solar fourth house of home. This combination so close together can be volatile and sheds light on why you are experiencing your most intense challenges this month in the partnership arena and at home base.

Rewarding Days

6, 8, 19, 22

Challenging Days

1, 4, 17, 28

Scorpio | September

Overall Theme

This month you seem on edge at home and in partnership areas. The transits of planets in other fixed signs, Jupiter and Saturn in Aquarius and Uranus in Taurus, are chipping away at your inner psyche, creating anxiety. A perplexing relationship matter deserves airing, yet you are not ready to speak up. Tabling the matter may buy you time while you work up the courage to speak up, but it does little for your health.

Relationships

Contacts at a distance and those on teams or in classroom settings provide levity and a sense of appreciation for where you are with goals and plans. Children add enjoyable experiences to the mix and appeal to your nurturing side, helping you assess the value of intimate relationships that are currently in a rocky place. A date night on September 20th could lead to deeper love and understanding. This Pisces Full Moon in your solar fifth house is highly romantic.

Success and Money

You could be traveling for an assignment, a fall getaway, or formal training away from home base. Relatives at a distance contact you to share news, make plans, or invite you for a visit. What you learn about financial matters around the 1st drives your urgent need to understand communication gaps. Your best dates for reviewing plans, looking for solutions, or working on budget matters are September 9–12.

Pitfalls and Potential Problems

Confusion and misunderstandings affect communication and financial dealings on the 1st. Mercury goes retrograde on the 27th, cautioning you not to get carried away with implementing plans or signing contracts. Matters of the heart are painful around the 24th. Distance yourself from those who want to argue or take their frustrations out on you.

Rewarding Days

2, 9, 12, 20

Challenging Days

1, 5, 7, 24

Scorpio | October

Overall Theme

Pull out all the stops. October is here and ready to loosen all the reins that have held up productivity when four planets that have been retrograde move direct. Saturn and Jupiter have been dragging feet at your home base, clogging your spirit and creating friction among family members looking for a clear path to the truth. Take a deep breath the first few weeks of the month and then let the discussions begin.

Relationships

Set aside time on the 15th for a serious discussion. Make the upcoming weekend one to remember by hosting a meal, ordering takeout, playing games, or watching a movie, using icebreakers to ease tension to get to the heart of the friction that has created emotional rifts. Be receptive to listening and giving involved parties a chance to vent. By the end of the month, you should have enough information and understanding to notice a difference in behavior and receptivity. If any blocks remain, consider professional counseling.

Success and Money

Income streams look good, the checkbook balances, retirement funds are growing, and credit cards have a manageable percentage of use. Low self-esteem issues that have surfaced undergo healing by searching for the underlying cause and a win-win solution for addressing rather than burying incidents as they arise. Count on Pluto for a slow-paced but deep release.

Pitfalls and Potential Problems

The first five days of the month are not conducive to scheduling important work meetings or pitching new proposals. An ego problem could be the driver behind lack of receptivity. The Full Moon on the 20th is another day to be cautious about sharing details, especially if someone on the scene is displaying full-on anger.

Rewarding Days

6, 11, 15, 29

Challenging Days

1, 3, 20, 22

Scorpio | November

Overall Theme

Those of you born with your Sun at 11–13 degrees of Scorpio benefit from the New Moon in your sign on the 4th. It's a perfect time to take stock of your successes this year and look ahead to your goals for 2022. The Moon in your twelfth house on November 2–3 indicates you are not ready to reveal plans and want to put more meat on them once you're sure of your new direction. If you're planning on changing jobs or retiring, that is a good strategy. Ditto if you want to sell your home and move.

Relationships

Business relationships are harmonious on the 3rd. Money discussions with family members run smoothly and set the tone for participation in holiday events. Neighbors visit and extend invitations. Date night rocks for you and your loved one on the 14th, setting the tone for conveying deeper romantic feelings and melting the iciness you've struggled with in recent months.

Success and Money

Online shopping for the purpose of obtaining price comparisons and studying the differences and warranties on products yields the highest pay value for intended purchases in the next month. An excellent day to shop or make purchases is the 9th, when you receive attractive offers for desired goods. You are on your game on this date in terms of getting your point across and displaying strong negotiating skills.

Pitfalls and Potential Problems

Look out if you're having an affair, especially if you have not been discreet and confided in the wrong person. The 1st is one date to be aware of untrustworthy associates or members of professional groups. You could be at the wrong place at the wrong time, and those without sufficient knowledge make assumptions about your behavior.

Rewarding Days

3, 4, 9, 14

Challenging Days

1, 11, 19, 23

Scorpio | December

Overall Theme

The final Solar Eclipse of 2021 occurs on December 4 in your solar second house, providing some extra incentive to finish your holiday shopping early and get the best value for your investment. On your travels, you could buy a lottery ticket and visualize a win. The 5th also works for shopping, dining out, or making reservations for holiday attractions. A charitable contribution gives a boost to those who have unmet needs, and the giving appeals to your deep sense of caring.

Relationships

You are sold on entertainment this month to bring relatives and friends together for a fun event. Whether you choose to host a holiday party in your home or buy tickets to a seasonal concert, you will capture the spirit of the season and spread cheer. You and your significant other may celebrate together on the 16th to acknowledge your feelings and the lessons you've learned on your journey to build a stronger partnership.

Success and Money

For many Scorpios, this is the month when you receive a bonus for your many contributions throughout the year. With the second-house eclipse, there may be a surprise element to the size of the bonus. Invest any unanticipated income in debt reduction, savings, and retirement accounts, and use a portion to have fun and purchase a bucket-list item.

Pitfalls and Potential Problems

Venus goes retrograde on the 19th, a day when you should avoid purchasing jewelry or luxury items or traveling on icy roads, since the station occurs in your solar third house of transportation, local roadways, and vehicles. Keep a cool head at home base on the 9th, when a household member is argumentative. Stay patient on the 21st, when you may have to cancel a trip due to weather conditions or an illness.

Rewarding Days

5, 7, 16, 23

Challenging Days

2, 9, 21, 28

Scorpio Action Table

These dates reflect the best—but not the only—times for success and ease in these activities, according to your Sun sign.

	JAN	FEB	MAR	APR	MAY	JUN	JUL	AUG	SEP	OCT	NOV	DEC
Move	13			7				6				7
Romance		14			6				20		14	
Seek counseling/ coaching		2	24	11				19			9	
Ask for a raise					19	10				29		
Vacation						22	9		2			23
Get a loan	24		3				8			11		

Sagittarius

The Archer
November 21 to December 21

Element: Fire

Quality: Mutable

Polarity: Yang/masculine

Planetary Ruler: Jupiter

Meditation: I can take time to explore my soul

Gemstone: Turquoise

Power Stones: Lapis lazuli, azurite, sodalite

Key Phrase: I understand

Glyph: Archer's arrow

Anatomy: Hips, thighs, sciatic nerve

Colors: Royal blue, purple

Animals: Fleet-footed animals

Myths/Legends: Athena, Chiron

House: Ninth

Opposite Sign: Gemini

Flower: Narcissus

Keyword: Optimism

The Sagittarius Personality

Strengths, Talents, and the Creative Spark

Everything must be larger than life to fit comfortably in your world, allowing you to expand the possibilities for success. Your symbol is the Centaur, the sign of the Archer, a mutable-fire member of the zodiac and natural ruler of the ninth house of the higher mind, religion, spirituality, the clergy, advanced education, the law, publishing, in-laws, foreigners, and travel to distant places. Jupiter rules your sign and attracts you to a variety of adventures at home, at work, in sports venues, and in faraway countries and cultures. As a truth seeker, you want to know what gives when you have questions and seldom quit until you find out. People say you're blunt when you tell others exactly what you think, especially if they ask for your opinion. Like your opposite sign, Gemini, many of you are perpetual students who thrive in academia, often obtaining a PhD or multiple degrees or certifications in subjects that interest you and enhance your employment outlook as well as your desire for personal growth. Your workplace is the world at large and what it has to offer in bringing you options to satisfy your desire for recognition, especially if the assignments include travel.

Early in life you gravitate toward careers that offer experimental opportunities in diverse social or cultural settings. You'll accept temporary, part-time, internship,or intermittent assignments with perks that give you the latitude to learn on the job and soak up the vibes of the environment. You're a member of a sign that often has two or more careers, and you cherish what you learn from each. A number of career choices suit you, including journalism, law, medicine, philosophy, politics, religion, teaching, the travel industry, and writing. Many of you excel in advertising, sales, international trade, and social change venues.

Many of your sign have an interest in architecture, home styles, and refurbishing properties. When it comes to selecting a signature palette, no pale or barely there shades will do for you. You prefer rich, deep colors, like bottle green and evergreen, dark blues, browns with a sheen, and majestic purple, and you integrate them into your decorating scheme along with dark wood floors and trims. Lofty, stately trees such as birch, elm, and oak resonate with your sign and accent your landscape. You would rather wait to make purchases for furnishing and sprucing up your home until you find the right accessories and have the budget to make your residence compatible with your comfort zone.

Intimacy and Personal Relationships

A partner for all seasons suits you to a T in your quest for the perfect companion. The person who wins your heart does not have to come from a traditional mold or expect to marry early. This charmer wins your heart by sharing adventures along untraveled paths, sampling exotic foods, adapting to groundbreaking career fields, and living in one-of-a-kind homes. A stay-at-home type or someone too possessive need not apply. You enjoy personal freedom. When you become bored, you drop the relationship like a hot potato. You want a lover with a wicked sense of humor who enjoys playtime, entertainment, abstract films, mental games, sports, and horse races. Your thirst for knowledge leads you to seek a partner who spars with your brain and shares facts, figures, and historical tidbits. Informative discussions keep your relationships at a high level of interest, especially in the early days when you're getting to know whether you could share life with this individual on a daily basis. A person with a sense of humor gets high marks by enjoying comedic interludes, variety shows, and monologues that stimulate your date nights and parties. The thrill of the chase appeals to your heart.

Values and Resources

As a mutable sign, you experience a change in values reflective of the lessons life throws your way, be it in a personal relationship, career challenge, neighborhood environment, or cultural exchange. You eagerly meet travelers along your life path and learn how to survive as you observe what they have to offer and decide what you can readily exchange to bring meaning to the connection. Diversity in relationships is high on your list of preferences, and you keep in touch with others long after you have moved on. You value meaningful work and want to thoroughly enjoy what it has to offer with passion, excitement, and the potential for growth. Education is a lifelong quest for you and is never far from your awareness, whether it applies to you, your significant other, or your children.

Blind Spots and Blockages

Managing time well can be a deficiency in your operating style. You sometimes feel that as long as you show up, why worry? Those who know you often complain about your disregard for schedules when you arrive late for meetings, dates, parties, and work. Doctors' receptionists frequently have to phone you when they call your name in the waiting room at the scheduled appointment time and you're not present. At the workplace, you would rather have a reliable assistant who keeps records, monitors the timeline for due dates, and does the grunt work you dislike. Without support, team leaders often have to chase you down looking for deliverables. Your boss might say that while you have brilliant ideas and make worthy contributions to the organization, you lose track of time, talk too much at meetings, and get off point when making presentations.

Goals and Successes

Although you're likely to change jobs more often than most, it is usually out of boredom that you look into positions that challenge your adventurous mind. Whether you work for a large organization or a small firm, you want a lot of latitude and independence in how you manage your day-to-day interactions. Solutions for world dilemmas appeal to you. These concerns could lead you to a career in air quality management, such as monitoring it, holding others compliant, providing remediation expertise to solve problems, analyzing air quality, or managing related projects. If you're planning to remodel your home or build a new one, look into current green building practices that make effective use of natural resources to improve air and water quality and generate less waste. On the chance that you are looking for a romantic partner, you could meet a gregarious Aquarius on the job who shares your interest in environmental improvement and recognizes the heart awakening that allows the two of you to make beautiful music for life.

Sagittarius Keywords for 2021
Encounter, expansion, experience

The Year Ahead for Sagittarius

Looking for a chance to stand out from the crowd? You'll be one of the signs receiving abundant recognition this year when two eclipses fall in Sagittarius in your solar first house of assertiveness, appearance, passion, and activity. Savor every experience in a phase that has you anticipating opportunities for personal growth and accomplishments. The new eclipse patterns moved into this house last year, as well as into your opposite house, the solar seventh house of partnerships, both of which continue to demand attention in 2021.

One of the most active departments of your life has been your solar second house of assets, income, money you earn, and developmental opportunities. For the last few years, Jupiter and Saturn in Capricorn have grabbed your attention, pointing out opportunities to expand your leadership skills, sending challenges your way in terms of deadlines that demand copious amounts of your time, and shifting the scope and breadth of your responsibilities. You are ordinarily a sign that likes to stay loose and take things as they come, but the intrusiveness of pressing, unanticipated demands from out of the blue, especially from Saturn, has skewed your focus. Adding to the intensity has been Pluto in Capricorn in residence in your solar second house, which hangs around all year, moving slowly but surely to open your eyes to any places where you feel stuck regarding salary, benefits, and the potential for growth.

Jupiter and Saturn in Aquarius are on the scene now, settling into your solar third house of community, contracts, mental state, siblings, and transportation, and setting up encounters with neighbors, relatives, IT specialists, and local authorities. You'll also meet up with Neptune in Pisces all year in your solar fourth house of family, home, and base of operations as you review the spiritual qualities present and neutralize any situations that confuse the quality of communication among residents. Outer planet Uranus, in Taurus all year, tests the stability of your daily environment by jolting the status quo in your solar sixth house of health, organization, routines, and pets. Focus on your goals and give the thumbs-up to those that meet your innermost desires.

Jupiter

In 2021 you have a chance to learn everything you want to know about your neighborhood, community officials, residents, the fiscal health of operating your city, and where to find the most desirable properties. All you have to do is ask and information will flow. Jupiter in Aquarius arrived in your solar third house in December 2020 and will influence the local area, your mind and how it works, reconnection with siblings and cousins, and the quality of communication in your life and how it applies to people with whom you interact. Acquisition of a new vehicle is likely, as is an upgrade to electronic equipment that includes everything from computers to cable, telephone, and televisions. Cutting the cord is a real probability in the ever-improving digital age. Business picks up for those of you who make a living developing and negotiating contracts, writing, or teaching. If you're self-employed, seek the advice of an expert to develop a web presence that attracts more business and offers helpful tips to customers. Chance encounters in your neighborhood lead to profitable relationships.

Saturn

In December 2020, Saturn moved into Aquarius, joining Jupiter in your solar third house of advertising, communication, contracting, education, electronics, mental outlook, neighborhood activity, transportation and machinery, and reconnection with siblings, cousins, or other relatives. At the same time that Jupiter prompts you to expand your field of operations, Saturn prompts you to look carefully at proposals in front of you before taking any serious next steps. The taskmaster planet reminds you to improve relationships with relatives, issue invitations to unite family, and demonstrate a welcoming attitude toward new neighbors. Saturn in Aquarius enjoys a harmonious relationship with your sign and generates encouraging vibes conducive to sealing deals, influencing smooth communication, and stimulating the quality of the written word. Those of you born between November 22 and December 6 experience the most influence from 2021's Saturn transit, especially through May 23, when Saturn turns retrograde until October 10 and challenges you to keep tabs on relationships, contracts, messages, and agreements. Read between the lines if you're going to negotiate terms of important contracts of any type or purchase vehicles, equipment, or luxury items. Focus on details for the most successful outcomes. Identify what you most need to know and gather information, and you'll end the year with a new perspective and a positive attitude.

Uranus

This year Uranus, the planet of chaos, sudden events, and new directions, is in Taurus and your solar sixth house of daily routines, fitness, health, healing, nutrition, organizational style, pets, coworkers, and work life, including colleagues. Back in May 2018, this erratic visitor paid a teaser visit to this important house that drives the operation of all you do in any given day. You were made aware of the need to reset norms to achieve goals that influence the flow of work and lead to desired accomplishments that increase compensation for all you do. This year Uranus will most affect the daily routine of Sagittarians born between November 27 and December 7, shaking up the status quo in both your personal and your business life and rearranging conditions related to health, pets, dietary and medicinal intake, and current healing modalities. Uranus in Taurus won't be silenced when it goes off the grid again in retrograde motion on August 19 for the rest of the year. Don't be surprised if you change jobs, your work world undergoes a reorganization, you have new orders from your physician, you acquire a new pet or one of your pets is ill, or you make a commitment to practice a more effective fitness routine as a result of medical test disclosures. In the sixth house, this erratic planet is a stress inducer that has a surprising way of getting your attention. Stay calm and alert and start your day with a deep breath and a huge intake of optimism, one of your signature attributes that drives the success you attract.

Neptune

I'll be surprised if you haven't been through both the sublime and the ridiculous with the presence of Neptune in Pisces in your solar fourth house of domestic matters, home, family, parents, projects that enhance the beauty of your home from the inside out, and the everyday affairs of those who live with you or for whom you are responsible. The glamorous Lady Neptune has been in this house since April 2011 and is sure to trigger emotions related to dear ones, nostalgic memories of special events and milestones, and romantic interludes. You or someone in your household may be celebrating an engagement, wedding, retirement, or birth of a child this year that brings out the best of Neptune's soft side. Simultaneously, Sagittarius and Pisces create hard aspects to one another, so this transit will bring periods of confusion, misunderstanding, needy people, or prolonged communication glitches. Make sure you steer clear of negativity when moodiness surfaces that could come about through excessive drinking, dependence on drugs, or staying in a funk without help from medical professionals. Those of you born between December 9 and 16 feel the greatest impact from Neptune's presence this year.

Pluto

Your solar second house of assets, income, money you earn and how you spend it, and self-development undertakings has been the site of transiting Pluto in Capricorn since 2008. You have had ups and downs in meeting compensation goals but have managed to rise from the ashes when the chips were down, even when you felt stuck and impatient at the pace of progress. Rather than stick around and take your lumps, you are likely to travel to put distance between problems and realistic next steps. Your second house also received a helpful transit from Jupiter in Capricorn, irritation and eye-opening truths from 2½ years of Saturn in Capricorn, and a few years of eclipses that resulted in shifts in plans, goals, and momentum. Now just ride out what you've been blocking by acknowledging that Pluto is present to help you clean out the closets of doubt and fear that keep you from taking that final leap to success. Acknowledge that you are your own money, and never fear that you'll lack sustenance. Pluto lingers in this house until March 2023, when it makes a brief teaser appearance in Aquarius before slipping back into Capricorn in mid-June. In 2021, those of you born between December 15 and 19 feel the most significant impact from Pluto's presence. Consult financial specialists to address situation-specific conditions that help you shed baggage. Greet the new year with an upbeat outlook and savor success.

How Will This Year's Eclipses Affect You?

In 2021, a total of four eclipses occur. There will be two Lunar Eclipses and two Solar Eclipses, creating intense periods that begin to manifest a few months before their actual dates. Eclipses unfold in cycles involving all twelve signs of the zodiac, and usually occur in pairs about two weeks apart. Think of eclipses as opportunities to release old patterns and conditions that have outlived their usefulness. Have no fear of them, since they can bring you unexpected surprises and windfalls. The closer an eclipse is to a degree or point in your chart, the greater its importance in your life. Those of you born with a planet at the same degree as an eclipse are likely to see a high level of activity in the house where the eclipse occurs.

Sagittarius lands a starring role in the eclipse activity this year. The first one is a Lunar Eclipse in Sagittarius that takes place on May 26 in your solar first house of activity, appearance, individuality, overall health, passion, recognition, self-discovery, and expression. Many of you have been working on personal physical changes for over a year to become healthy and whole and to sculpt a better body with less flab, a toned look, and better posture. This eclipse most affects you if born between November 26 and 28, alerting you to wellness goals and fitness routines you're already undertaking, and perhaps modifying work-related agenda items that call for your implementation and leadership or making changes in your physical appearance that demonstrate your individuality, such as cosmetic surgery, tattoos, weight loss, or a new hair color or style.

On December 4, the last Solar Eclipse of the year takes place in your sign, intensifying activity around the regimens you initiated in late May. You may also be adding travel or a sabbatical to the mix, especially if you are feeling restless and desire a change of pace. Those of you born between December 3 and 6 see increased activity in matters connected to this house, calling for leveraged expansion and compromise.

The year's first Solar Eclipse takes place in your opposite sign, Gemini, on June 10 in your solar seventh house of personal and business partners, the public, consultants, cooperators, and open enemies. You'll feel the greatest effect if born between December 10 and 12 as you examine conditions surrounding spousal relationships, business associates, pending mergers, and activity with medical practitioners or legal authorities. New people who enter your life may be there for the long run.

The last Lunar Eclipse of the year occurs on November 19 in Taurus and your solar sixth house of daily routines, fitness, health, nutrition, organizing assets, pets, and work life, including coworkers, colleagues, and subordinates. Those of you born between December 17 and 19 feel the greatest impact from this eclipse, which calls into play your time-management habits, health and nutrition maintenance, and possibly workaholic tendencies that have surfaced in the past year. As conditions in your routine shift, some of you may decide to seek a new employment arena or change careers. Individuals you have found compatible in the work scene may bail. For other Sagittarians, economic conditions may lead to reorganizations, layoffs, or pay reductions. Eclipses in the sixth house sometimes create new opportunities for advancement. By embracing a new workplace perspective in 2021, you'll celebrate the fulfillment of cherished goals.

Sagittarius | January

Overall Theme

With a big boost from Venus in your sign and Mars in Aries, romance is in the air as the month gets off to a lively start and highlights a perfect time to travel. You may actually feel passionate about creating New Year's resolutions that match your goals and lend support to your fondest desires. Neptune can be tricky, so look out for strangers in your travels or newcomers to your circle on the 4th, keeping an eye on your wallet or other valuables.

Relationships

Happiness and contentment seem to rule the opening days of 2021 when you and your significant other enjoy a romantic and enjoyable time at a well-appointed vacation resort that specializes in pampering guests and adding ambience every step of the way. Bonding occurs and remains strongest through the 17th making this adventurous time a memorable one. The 7th is a perfect time to renew friendships.

Success and Money

Attitude is everything, and when it's filled with optimism and the desire to expand your field of vision, you touch a high note with everyone you meet. Purchasing power works in your favor on the New Moon of the 13th when your solar second house gets a positive vibe about goods or services you are seeking. Make appropriate arrangements to complete your transaction or sign contracts.

Pitfalls and Potential Problems

Wait until after Uranus goes direct in your solar sixth house on the 14th to seal any pending deals or begin travel. Bide your time earlier in the month by researching and comparing options so your discussion points are on the money. Take caution on the 4th and 8th, when you may be unaware of hidden agendas. Avoid starting major undertakings on the 30th when Mercury goes retrograde in Aquarius.

Rewarding Days

2, 7, 13, 17

Challenging Days

4, 8, 25, 28

Sagittarius | February

Overall Theme

The first week of the month gets off to a rolling start with the Aquarius Sun in favorable aspect to your sign showing early lunar aspects in harmony with transiting Venus, Jupiter, and Saturn. You have plenty of energy to burn when prevailing air-sign dominance stimulates your creative thinking process and the stifled momentum of the last few days of January disappears as you promote new ideas.

Relationships

Groups and professional organizations show an interest in your proposals on the 2nd, 5th, and 6th, which are ideal dates to set up or attend meetings. Get a feel for the leading interests of members and the status of progress in accomplishing goals. Offer suggestions when appropriate. Your input may lead to an important role in guiding the organization in a desirable direction. A new position may be on the horizon.

Success and Money

The New Moon in Aquarius on the 11th opens the door to enterprising opportunities in the coming months. You've been feeling restless and desirous of critical change. The prize isn't ready yet, but it is a good time to think about how expanding your vision will meet your needs and give you a chance to showcase the breadth of your experience. The planetary weather looks promising on the 24th, when you find extra cash or savings that benefit your holdings.

Pitfalls and Potential Problems

Keep a low profile on the 4th, when an aura of conflict is in the air and will lead to a stalemate if you pursue it. Wait until Mercury goes direct on the 21st to return to pending projects and ready them for execution in early March. The Full Moon on the 27th is not a good day to make decisions about purchasing costly items for family members.

Rewarding Days

2, 6, 11, 24

Challenging Days

4, 7, 22, 27

Sagittarius | March

Overall Theme

Household activities and interactions with residents are the reason you have little downtime this month. You may be called on to help with a lifestyle decision that involves a personal or career move or a parent's welfare. One or more family members may need medical attention. You could be the one chauffeuring others to doctor appointments or medical tests.

Relationships

The New Moon on the 13th aligns with the Sun, Venus, and Neptune, creating a romantic undertone. You and your significant other seem to be on the same page most of the month, with the exception of the 19th, when the Moon in Gemini generates a standoff over plans, purchases, or a position you take on child-rearing. Clear the air of tension.

Success and Money

You could be one of the designated employees at work selected for specialized training that lasts for a year or more and is likely to include a commitment on your part to stay with the organization for a specified number of years if you accept this benefit. Weigh your options carefully and acknowledge your success.

Pitfalls and Potential Problems

Days when you could be feeling under the weather include the 4th and 17th, when you catch whatever bug others in the family are passing on. Give yourself a day or two to rest, especially if the malady can be passed on to others in your sphere of operation. The Full Moon on the 28th is not particularly beneficial to organizational causes or to hold a vote for changes in the action plan. You'll see plenty of passion on display but no agreement if you decide to push the agenda, which clearly needs a closer look.

Rewarding Days

2, 6, 13, 24

Challenging Days

4, 17, 18, 28

Sagittarius | April

Overall Theme
Time for a spring fling! That welcome tax refund you received has been sitting in your solar eighth house of joint assets, compliments of compatible Jupiter in Aquarius, looking for a chance to buy a little downtime in a refreshing resort area that appeals to your psyche. If you and your partner check your calendars, you can coordinate a delightful getaway to soak up some sun and surf. Include your children if schedules permit.

Relationships
Family members are the stars this month, with opportunities to bond over leisuretime activities, sports venues, a variety of entertainment options, and vacations that offer interesting choices for each person. Parents may visit or invite you to share vacation time with them. Single Sagittarians may experience extra activity in the dating scene or book a singles cruise to meet potential partners.

Success and Money
Work and career goals meet your expectations this month, along with a stellar compensation package. Savings are growing in favorable increments; plan to review your holdings at least twice a year to examine trends. Conditions favorable to your performance take place on the 23rd, an ideal date to share accomplishments and monitor project timelines. The New Moon in Aries in your solar fifth house on April 11 presents opportunities for successful entrepreneurial pursuits.

Pitfalls and Potential Problems
Lie low the first four days of April, when you could feel more tired than usual and sense the need to regroup. Purchases you've been contemplating are less attractive, especially on the 4th, when you feel the price is too high or doesn't have a very attractive warrantee. Those at home base show moodiness and passive-aggressive behavior on the 9th.

Rewarding Days
1, 2, 11, 23

Challenging Days
3, 4, 9, 27

Sagittarius | May

Overall Theme

The planetary activity in May is about to get erratic, starting with Saturn turning retrograde on May 23. The first Lunar Eclipse of the year falls in Sagittarius on May 26, followed three days later by Mercury turning retrograde. The retrograde motion of Saturn sucks the air out of the momentum you gained in implementing strategic plans, while the shift in Mercury's direction in communication-oriented Gemini creates delays in travel and mix-ups in dates and details.

Relationships

Your interactions with accountants, bankers, and financial planners are strong and successful this month, especially before May 23. Family members are in a good place, and coworkers and collaborators work congenially with you and genuinely get along. An enjoyable lunch with a friend in the latter half of the month leads to the discovery of mutual interests that shape future social outings.

Success and Money

A raise or bonus may appear in your paycheck the first week of the month based on successful performance. Purchases made around the 2nd meet your needs, and the price you pay for goods or services is fair and appealing. The excellent vibe of ongoing relationships sends a strong message that you are doing something right. Pay it forward by giving recognition to others for their accomplishments.

Pitfalls and Potential Problems

A message from a partner may tell only part of the story on the 14th. After you have a chance to digest it, ask some clarifying questions. Your feelings are very sensitive on the day of the Lunar Eclipse on May 26. Don't make it worse by knocking the wind out of a partner's sails with insensitive comments.

Rewarding Days

2, 6, 11, 23

Challenging Days

4, 14, 21, 26

Sagittarius | June

Overall Theme

Meetings, timelines, and work-related travel keep you hopping this month. Assignments hold the key to new responsibilities that are likely to come about when key goals are tweaked. Keep your eyes wide open. It's possible that a new hierarchy is moving into place. Serious shifts in planetary direction occur this month, including a Solar Eclipse in your opposite sign of Gemini on June 10 in your solar seventh house of business and personal partners.

Relationships

The favorable momentum between you and your coworkers continues, highlighting professionalism and excellent business practices. You may find that anyone leaving the organization probably earned a reputation for building a better organization. Your spouse could be in the limelight this month and for several additional months. Harmony captures the essence of your communication and rapport this month.

Success and Money

Your checkbook looks healthy now that you've pared down debt, put away extra cash to save for the future, and made a serious effort to talk to your spouse about mutual goals. Performance effectiveness puts the spotlight on you and the work team, allowing you to enjoy well-deserved attention.

Pitfalls and Potential Problems

Jupiter moves into retrograde motion on June 20, possibly delaying a work trip or vacation plans. Relief appears when Mercury goes direct on June 22; early next month you'll catch up on matters you had to suspend in May. Neptune joins Jupiter in turning retrograde on June 25, adding an aura of mystery to some of the activity at home base. Ask questions.

Rewarding Days

7, 10, 13, 22

Challenging Days

3, 17, 24, 27

Sagittarius | July

Overall Theme

The first weekend of the month ends on a playful note as you get ready to enjoy the holiday and possibly take a longer vacation after putting in extra hours and wrapping up loose ends at work. Take time off to enjoy favorite attractions, especially during the first ten days of the month. Go ahead and make those reservations while you renew personal bonds that reflect your adventurous spirit.

Relationships

Spend time with children, partners, sports team members, and lovers who show an interest in the recreation and travel arrangements you've proposed. Enjoy the quality time you set aside for exploring new discoveries and revisiting old haunts with your favorite people. Contact friends and visit out-of-town relatives if your travels take you to their resident cities.

Success and Money

You can count on celebrating the rewards of your accomplishments as the middle of the year arrives and reminds you of your acumen in goal achievement. Those who know you were surprised at how deeply you concentrated your efforts to make things happen without bailing when the going got tough. Compensation for a job well done made a difference in your financial solvency.

Pitfalls and Potential Problems

Demands for your time accelerate in the middle of the month, when extra pressure is on to correct data deficiency. Avoid trying to solve everything in a single day on the 15th or on the 20th, when the quest for a rapid solution falls apart. The Full Moon on the 23rd is a good day to rest and recover your energy after a taxing workweek.

Rewarding Days

5, 7, 10, 22

Challenging Days

4, 15, 20, 23

Sagittarius | August

Overall Theme

The compatible Leo Sun shines in your solar ninth house of long-distance travel for the first part of the month, calling out to your soul to book some exotic travel and give your exhausted brain a rest. An appealing deal is waiting for you if you book your destination between the 3rd and the 14th. A car trip is a fine substitute if you prefer driving and enjoy winging it as you discover new sites.

Relationships

There is an attractive glow around your relationship with your intimate partner as the month begins, and it warms up even more as you make the time to listen, understand, and show how much you care. Authorities at your workplace are high on praise of your talents and spread the word. A new respect comes from coworkers. Your laid-back leadership skills make a difference.

Success and Money

Thanks to your passionate contributions, the work environment takes on a sunny glow. You could possibly find new wealth in a growing investment portfolio that pays off down the road, providing validation to the merit of your initial contribution. A charity drive opens your eyes to local community needs, leading you to volunteer time and money.

Pitfalls and Potential Problems

Uranus in Taurus goes retrograde on August 19 and won't go direct until January 2022. Avoid starting a major undertaking on this day, even though the aspects are largely compatible to your Sun. In-laws or others who live at a distance create a distraction on the 8th, possibly while you are traveling, and could result in a change of itinerary. Children who are not traveling with you could also disrupt your schedule with news of an unplanned occurrence.

Rewarding Days

3, 11, 19, 29

Challenging Days

1, 8, 17, 24

Sagittarius | September

Overall Theme

This month takes on a serious note and reminds you to look closely at personal obligations and take an even closer look at tasks waiting for you in the work environment. If you tackle the household chores first on the 3rd or 4th, you'll have time for a lively weekend respite to celebrate the holiday with family and friends. Business travel is likely by the middle of the month.

Relationships

Early in the month you have a chance to enjoy relaxing time with in-laws or other relatives that prove to be informative and lead to an early discussion of holiday plans. You'll get together with close friends and associates more than once this month, possibly due to a class reunion or milestone birthday celebration. Savor these opportunities, especially if you learn that someone close is moving away soon. You and your romantic partner are in sync after some tension early in the month.

Success and Money

A sense of justice and fair play comes into prominence over pending disputes that result in scheduling extra time to hash out differences. Savvy negotiation saves the day, and involved parties treat results as an all-around win. Juggling workloads and adding members to teams that have urgent deadlines may be necessary to get the job done.

Pitfalls and Potential Problems

You could learn that you need a new heating or air conditioning unit (or another pricey appliance) early in the month. Set up appointments for estimates and be sure to have the installation in place before September 27, when Mercury goes retrograde. On the 20th, steer clear of household friction that has been brewing for a few days. You and a child may not agree with a pending request. Things come to a head around the 23rd. Offer choices and settle differences diplomatically.

Rewarding Days

4, 9, 14, 27

Challenging Days

2, 7, 20, 23

Sagittarius | October

Overall Theme

Both your social life and your interaction with that special someone are the center of attention this month when compatible sign Libra dominates the landscape. Accept an invitation to a party or gala, say yes to a new dress or suit, and log these festive events into your appointment calendar. Ask your partner or a date to accompany you, especially around the 25th, when ideal conditions prevail for engaging in stimulating communication and discussing shared interests.

Relationships

This month you're adapting to differences in outlook expressed by your partner that you never considered before. You just weren't hearing the truth and did not want to open old wounds for fear you'd have to address them. Plan to get away this month to spend intimate alone time with your significant other. Neutral turf allows you to listen intently to your loved one's perspective.

Success and Money

Social interactions bring old friends and new acquaintances together through group meetings, dinners, and milestone celebrations. Partners work their charm on colleagues and members of professional organizations when they accompany you to planned events. Relatives at a distance schedule a visit for the weekend of the 30th and succeed in convincing you to be their tour guide.

Pitfalls and Potential Problems

Once Saturn goes direct on October 10, plans you had on hold get the green light and cooperation from others is a given. On the 18th, Jupiter goes direct and Mercury moves forward again, allowing you to get back on track with schedules and routine business that were hampered by petty annoyances. Lie low on the Full Moon of October 20, when communication falls apart.

Rewarding Days

7, 11, 25, 30

Challenging Days

1, 3, 5, 27

Sagittarius | November

Overall Theme

You could use a few mental health days off this month before the fast-paced holiday season begins. Take the time to revisit old anger issues and release the parts that keep you from fully enjoying cherished relationships. Massage the wound related to work performance that dug into your vulnerable ego. No one is thinking about it but you, so don't bring it up during a review or you'll come across as a martyr.

Relationships

Compliments of the Lunar Eclipse on November 19, your solar sixth house of everyday routines, workmates, and those who influence your daily life play an influential role this month. If you have doctor appointments scheduled, medical professionals may schedule tests or make suggestions for improvement. Enjoy the attention of your significant other, who shows a vested interest in your health and welfare, especially if you've been complaining about a physical ailment.

Success and Money

At the beginning of the month, your pile of money looks good, with expenses surfacing at an anticipated pace. Purchases made around the 9th represent money well spent. Be sure to set aside a fixed amount for holiday spending to avoid going overboard. Plans for holiday decorating fall into place. You snag some elegant accessories at a discount.

Pitfalls and Potential Problems

A surprise on the 1st uncovers an inconvenient slip-up when numbers don't add up or facts are missing from an important deliverable at your workplace. It's all hands on deck to identify the lapse and proceed to the finish line. A doctor visit is likely on the 4th, especially if you've been overdoing it. If you haven't set a limit on purchasing gifts, someone in your household, possibly your partner, goes on a buying spree around the 21st and could throw the budget out of whack.

Rewarding Days
7, 9, 13, 19

Challenging Days
1, 4, 21, 24

Sagittarius | December

Overall Theme

An exciting six months awaits you when the last Solar Eclipse of the year takes place in Sagittarius in your solar first house on December 4, accompanied by Mercury in your sign. Back in May, you experienced the first Lunar Eclipse of the year in Sagittarius, so you know what being in the limelight does for your personal space, and it has been lively. You have much to celebrate with career accomplishments bringing you recognition and monetary rewards.

Relationships

Look back at the inroads you made this year in cementing closer ties with your children and establishing enjoyable, meaningful traditions. Congratulate yourself for healing sore spots with your significant other and growing closer and more in love than ever. Acknowledge your willingness to adapt to and respect others' thinking patterns in the work world, so they feel a sense of camaraderie and ownership in the mission.

Success and Money

The raises and bonuses you received in 2021 are greatly appreciated but pale when compared to the noticeable satisfaction you feel for the high quality of relationships you have in your personal and professional environments. The time you took to focus on improving the level of understanding and reaching out to those who matter increased your regard for humanity.

Pitfalls and Potential Problems

Dark thoughts and doubts creep in on the 2nd; chase them away with music and relaxation. The 19th may be an emotionally vulnerable day for your partner, due in part to a disappointment on that day. Check schedules on the 23rd, when airport pickups are delayed and trains are not running on time. Weather conditions in your part of the country may be a factor, especially if runways and rails are covered with ice.

Rewarding Days

1, 4, 25, 30

Challenging Days

2, 11, 19, 23

Sagittarius Action Table

These dates reflect the best—but not the only—times for success and ease in these activities, according to your Sun sign.

	JAN	FEB	MAR	APR	MAY	JUN	JUL	AUG	SEP	OCT	NOV	DEC
Move		11					5		4			1
Romance	7			11		10			27		19	
Seek counseling/ coaching			6	23			7			25		30
Ask for a raise		24			11			11				
Vacation			24			22				30		
Get a loan	13				2			19			9	

Capricorn

The Goat
December 21 to January 19

♑

Element: Earth

Quality: Cardinal

Polarity: Yin/feminine

Planetary Ruler: Saturn

Meditation: I know the strength of my soul

Gemstone: Garnet

Power Stones: Peridot, onyx diamond, quartz, black obsidian

Key Phrase: I use

Glyph: Head of goat

Anatomy: Skeleton, knees, skin

Colors: Black, forest green

Animals: Goats, thick-shelled animals

Myths/Legends: Chronos, Vesta, Pan

House: Tenth

Opposite Sign: Cancer

Flower: Carnation

Keyword: Ambitious

The Capricorn Personality

Strengths, Talents, and the Creative Spark

"Ageless" may be an appropriate way to describe you, Capricorn, for you are a sign that looks older than your years when you're young and much younger than most when you're old. You may be somewhat shy in your youth and toe the line, obeying rules and regulations, even to the point of not snipping off those tags on furniture you own that say "Do not remove under penalty of law." The ambitious Mountain Goat symbolizes your approach to work and responsibility as you set out to leave your mark on the world. Your first Saturn Return at age twenty-nine often indicates a time of awakening, when you start to blossom and display your many talents, often gaining the attention of those with hiring authority. Organization and thorough research of facts, practical solutions to problems, and the way you develop clear, efficient plans all give you a competitive edge in career matters. You love work and go out of your way to find satisfying outlets for your talents. Some call you a workaholic, yet you believe that if you love what you do, it doesn't seem like vitality-zapping labor.

With your high standards of performance, you're a viable candidate for leadership and management roles, and your many accomplishments put you on a fast track to success. In whatever role or life circumstance you acquire, you like to be in charge, call the shots, and set the agenda. A retentive memory is one of your strongest assets, along with a thorough knowledge of the subject matter in your chosen field. Others recognize your expertise and hold you in high esteem when your methods prove successful time after time, and authority figures trust you to get the job done.

Intimacy and Personal Relationships

As the third earth sign in the zodiac, you seek out a partner who makes you feel emotionally secure in the love you share by demonstrating loyalty, respect, and affection. You're not likely to rush into a relationship, but once you know that you've met "the one," you passionately display your romantic side and seek every opportunity to spend time with them. It helps if your partner has similar financial goals and attitudes toward saving for the future. You enjoy being seen in elegant attire and formal wear, arriving at social events in a limo, making appearances at charity venues, and supporting worthy causes. In public you may be more reserved in showing outward affection, yet you make a loyal life partner to the one you adore. Those who don't know you well may think of you as a working stiff, but you're quite sensual in private and your intimate partner will know this soon enough. A fair amount of scheduling takes place at home base, where the pace is rapid and involves family members who quickly learn the rules about putting chores first and then letting go to have some fun. It's important for you to balance your schedule and offer others the same freedom to enjoy much-deserved leisure time.

Values and Resources

Your world revolves around a serious attachment to achievement, high standards of conduct, meeting goals, and taking responsibility for your destiny. By starting with a well-developed plan, you cover all the bases with projects and proposals that showcase the core mission and your talent in making it stand out. You get along well with all the VIPs in the work world and place a great deal of importance on being recognized and rewarded for your outstanding performance. You enjoy recruiting or working with employees who show commitment to the work and demonstrate excellent work habits, including punctuality, subject matter expertise, and attention to critical deadlines. Accolades that come your way inspire you to give similar recognition to subordinates, peers, and colleagues. You value ceremonies, photo ops, and publicity to elevate the status of the organization, division, or team. You hold your family in high esteem. Your parents and long-standing family traditions mean a lot to you. You may have a special place in your heart for seniors and spend time tending to their needs and honoring their dignity. Volunteering your time at senior centers, contributing to charities that feed people in need, and making sure older people in the community have transportation are some of the ways you can make a difference in caring for others.

Blind Spots and Blockages

Although you value the contributions of others in your work circle, you often show impatience with those who perform at a slower pace or seem to lack the foresight to nip problems in the bud before they escalate. Contacts perceive you as a harsh judge of others' work and as being too picky in pointing out how they go about managing tasks, especially if their methods differ from your own. You didn't get the reputation of being a stern taskmaster by accident and have to learn to be less cold and rigid when situations don't match your expectations. Impatience over delays in getting the work done is one of your sore spots that needs attention, especially since you don't hide it well. Watch your tone of voice and the body language in the room when you emit a vibe that shows you disapprove of the status quo. Be sure you don't criticize others in front of their peers. Those in your circle find your approach miserly when funding awards with token amounts or choosing gifts that have no meaning. Stop holding back, and the loyalty you receive in return will be yours for life. Conversely, you believe you deserve the very best and lobby to get the most you can for yourself. While you are very proud of your children's accomplishments, you can be very demanding as a parent, insisting that you want them to succeed and attract the very best into their lives.

Goals and Success

When you have a profound idea, you are the first to hit the boss's office to make sure there is visibility for your winning solution, workable plan, or image-changing contribution to the organization. With your superior leadership skills, you chomp at the bit to explain the fine points of the big picture and eagerly claim center stage to present details to the VIPs in the chain of command. Climbing the ladder to success is your cherished goal, and you're willing to pay the price with overtime, volunteering for work no one else wants to take on, and learning new skills to integrate into your evolving workload. Continuous improvement of all you represent is your ticket to the executive office or your place in the choir, depending on your chosen life path. Celebrate success with your winning solutions.

Capricorn Keywords for 2021
Reputation, results, rewards

The Year Ahead for Capricorn

The year 2021 could be your breakout year as you bid goodbye to the intensity of the situations you experienced from the dominance of cardinal-sign planets in your solar action-oriented houses. For the last few years, your solar first house of self-interest has been the hub of major activity, with Jupiter, Saturn, and Pluto firmly entrenched there in Capricorn, along with eclipses in Capricorn and your opposite sign, Cancer, the sign on your solar seventh house of partners. Pluto in Capricorn entered your first house in 2008, dropping hints for you to clear away the clutter and the inflexible practices that limit freedom in how you approach the world. Pluto sticks around here until March 2023, when it makes a brief appearance in Aquarius for a few months before edging back into Capricorn to make sure you're karmically free from old garbage before changing signs permanently in early 2024. This year, with Jupiter and Saturn in Aquarius occupying this space, attention falls on your solar second house of assets, income, money, developmental programs and training, financial resources, and the benefits you receive for services you offer. After the hard work and challenges you met recently, you are eager to reap the benefits of recognition and elevated esteem for your accomplishments. You'll catch the aura of mystery associated with transiting Neptune in Pisces in your solar third house of community and mental outlook and gain a new perspective on neighbors and close relatives.

Transiting Uranus in Taurus continues its seven-year passage through your solar fifth house, shaking up your love life, social schedule, attitude toward risk management, and relationships with children for the next few years. Learn more about what gives meaning to your life while you secure your reputation as a reliable mover and shaker. Count on your burning desire for achievement to influence your goals and you'll see successful results in 2021.

Jupiter

In December 2020, Jupiter in Aquarius arrived in your solar second house, where it remains through December 28, 2021. Opportunities abound during this period, offering you a cornucopia of options for earning income through financial choices and investments, business deals, new jobs, promotions, windfalls, and contracts for your goods and services. Look over proposals carefully and choose those that meet your life vision and career goals. Want to travel more? Jupiter in this house just might bring a new position that includes plenty of time in the air or on the road and a terrific compensation package. This year, Jupiter's transit through Aquarius ends temporarily on May 13, when the planet of expansion moves into Pisces. It turns retrograde on June 20, moving back into Aquarius on July 28, covering familiar, already traveled degrees before turning direct in Aquarius on October 18. Take advantage of this lucrative money cycle by reviewing your budget, debt load, long-term investments, retirement funds, and savings accounts. Adjust your financial plan and earmark additional funds for future expenses.

Saturn

Keep your eye on the prize and go after your dreams this year. In December 2020, Saturn moved into Aquarius and your solar second house of money you earn, assets, personal income, compensation for goods and services you provide, commissions, self-development, financial resources, and people affiliated with banks, lending institutions, and investment firms. This could be your year to step into a new arena for showcasing your talents and earning your pay. Although Saturn in the second house highlights restrictions, you're also experiencing Jupiter, the Greater Benefic, moving through this house simultaneously and tempering some of the constraints usually associated with a Saturn transit. Those of you born between December 21 and January 4 experience the most intensity from this transit, especially through May 23, when Saturn turns retrograde until October 10 and challenges you to monitor conditions surrounding your employment, financial outlook, and investments. Look over offers and contracts carefully to make sure agreements gel with offers for your services. It's possible that you could experience delays or disappointments in the amount of money you were anticipating for salary, raises, or bonuses. Gather information, study salary comparisons, and be prepared to negotiate in good faith. You'll also have to keep watch over your spending habits and make sure your budget remains intact. Set aside funds every month to keep building reserves. Your excellent planning instincts should bring you the financial results you desire and strengthen your holdings in 2021.

Uranus

In 2021 you may be wondering what rollercoaster you're riding when the activity in your solar fifth house escalates and either brings new people into your life or sends them packing with little or no warning. By the time you read this passage, you may be remembering how romantic interests popped up in your life in the past few years, stuck around for a hot and heavy fling, and just as suddenly left the embrace of your shocked and tender heart. That's Uranus and evidence of the erratic behavior of a dance-away lover. This year Uranus will most affect the social lives of those born between December 25 and January 5 by shaking up the status quo with children (who could be acting rebellious), lovers (demonstrating fickle vibes), travel companions (wishy-washy about commitments and plans), those you coach or teach (skipping practice or ignoring homework), and speculative ventures (too hot to touch). Uranus enjoys going rogue, especially when in retrograde motion, which this year starts on August 19 and lasts for the rest of the year. Hang on to your hat and don't elope during this period, or the marriage is unlikely to last. Make travel plans with an eye on staying flexible in case weather or interference from third parties interrupts the itinerary. Is Uranus just a bucket of chaos? Some would say yes, although the truth is that you can win big in areas of your life when you least expect it, since Uranus in Taurus is in a compatible sign to Capricorn. Structure goals and plans with a positive perspective and enjoy the benefits that bring you unanticipated reasons to celebrate, along with favorable outcomes.

Neptune

An area of life that may seem confusing to you this year is right in your own backyard, with transiting Neptune in Pisces occupying your solar third house of communication, your mind and how it works, neighbors, the local community, siblings and other relatives, transportation, electronic equipment, and education. Those of you born between January 7 and 14 benefit the most from this transit. Individuals often write beautiful poetry or romantic material during this Neptune passage. Depending on where your birthday falls in this cycle, you may experience more than the usual number of mixed messages from others, errors in written material, confusion over terms in contracts, frustration over neighborhood policies, missing links in educational testing, and interactions with your relatives that leave you puzzled, with no clear understanding of what has been shared. Forgetfulness may crop up more than usual under this transit. Vehicle maintenance could be challenging, creating conditions where you must return to the service department multiple times before the real issue is diagnosed and corrected. Neptune has been occupying your solar third house since April 2011, so you should have a good idea by now of the level of fog that may affect transactions.

Pluto

With your solar first house the site of transiting Pluto in Capricorn for the entire year, you have a chance to identify the scope of undesirable conditions that are clinging to certain parts of your life, especially if you were born between January 13 and 16. Since other Capricorn transits and eclipses passed through this house in recent years, you may have noticed there is less garbage as you enter 2021 and are eager to unload any lingering annoyances. Certain Capricorns may have dealt with serious health conditions or undergone surgery. Others experienced the death or illness of loved ones. During this constructive period, take inventory of any areas that trouble you. Note any recurring themes that pop up and involve anger issues or feelings of abandonment. What complex questions remain unanswered? Have you succeeded in retrieving old wounds and difficult conditions buried in your subconscious mind? Do what you can to eliminate blocks and your health can improve immeasurably, communication may flow more smoothly than ever, and you'll feel the freeing effects of transformation at the cellular level. Pluto is nearing the end of its journey through your sign. In March 2023, Pluto makes a brief teaser appearance in Aquarius before slipping back into Capricorn in mid-June and then embracing its new home in 2024. Until then, create a plan and engage the appropriate experts to help you through the probing excavation of your deep feelings. Let 2021 be the year when you grow in wisdom and celebrate your stellar reputation for meeting your objectives.

How Will This Year's Eclipses Affect You?

In 2021, a total of four eclipses occur. There will be two Lunar Eclipses and two Solar Eclipses, creating intense periods that begin to manifest a few months before their actual dates. Eclipses unfold in cycles involving all twelve signs of the zodiac, and usually occur in pairs about two weeks apart. Think of eclipses as opportunities to release old patterns and conditions that have outlived their usefulness. Have no fear of them, since they can bring you unexpected surprises and windfalls. The closer an eclipse is to a degree or point in your chart, the greater its importance in your life. Those of you born with a planet at the same degree as an eclipse are likely to see a high level of activity in the house where the eclipse occurs.

The first eclipse is a Lunar Eclipse in Sagittarius that takes place on May 26 in your solar twelfth house of behind-the-scenes activity, seclusion, healing, recuperation, meditation, mystical experiences, secrets, hidden enemies, and orphans. An eclipse in this position points out the need for discretion, since it may bring matters you don't want revealed out into the open. You may also formulate plans that you want to keep to yourself, such as scheduling a date for surgery, leaving your company, or getting divorced. This eclipse will have the most impact on you if you were born between December 26 and 28.

The year's first Solar Eclipse takes place on June 10 in Gemini and your solar sixth house of health, daily activity, coworkers, nutrition, fitness routines, and pets. You'll be most affected by this eclipse if you were born between January 8 and 10. You may be undergoing staff changes at work, taking on new assignments, interacting with clients, monitoring timelines, and keeping careful records. Other Capricorns may take cooking lessons, purchase food preparation appliances, or change eating habits as a result of health constraints.

The last Lunar Eclipse of the year occurs on November 19 in Taurus and your solar fifth house of fun, games, children and their interests, dating, romance, social activities, sports, and vacation. It relates favorably to those born between January 16 and 18. Watch for an accelerated round of parties, special events, and invitations that could lead to developing important close relationships. A change of pace may break you out of rigid work routines and show you the light side of entertainment and playful pursuits.

The final Solar Eclipse of 2021 takes place on December 4 in Sagittarius, again in your solar twelfth house of seclusion, confinement, hospitals and institutions, work with charities, management of secrets or private information, meditation, and psychic phenomena. This eclipse may coincide with new work you're taking on (such as writing) that requires a quiet environment to let the ideas flow. The time you spend visiting friends and relatives who are ill could increase, or perhaps it is you who needs recovery time after surgery or an illness. For the overworked, solid downtime gives you a chance to chill and refine your future plans to include more balance. Those born between January 1 and 3 may experience the greatest impact from this eclipse.

Capricorn | January

Overall Theme

Celebrate your essence in this month that captures your finest qualities and lets you shine in the spotlight as you ring in the new year. Some of your finest moments occur with your family at home, visiting relatives, and professional connections affiliated with your work environment. Embrace spontaneity as you enjoy a year free of Saturn conjunct your Sun. Set those goals and soar!

Relationships

People at a distance visit you or issue invitations while they're in town to spend quality time and enjoy your company while catching up on news. Long holiday weekends provide perfect options for a family getaway to visit a playful paradise, a historical site, or a favorite haunt. Sentimental feelings arise to release inner joy.

Success and Money

Everything is coming up roses as you return to the work world and receive an enthusiastic welcome back from authority figures that raises your self-esteem and gives you the incentive to blaze trails. Plan a meeting for January 6 if you have the clout, and include a discussion of goals for expansion, along with emerging roles and responsibilities for the team. A raise may be in your first paycheck for the year.

Pitfalls and Potential Problems

Avoid adding gloom to the celebratory nature of January 1 by criticizing the amount of holiday spending and the culprits who ran up the debt. The Moon makes harsh aspects to transiting planets on the 7th in your solar eleventh house of friendships and groups. Stay in the background as arguments flare. Mercury goes retrograde on the 30th, while the Full Moon on the 28th fuels the flame for talks about the budget.

Rewarding Days

4, 6, 12, 19

Challenging Days

1, 7, 11, 28

Capricorn | February

Overall Theme

Worries related to expenses from last month seem to clear up after you apply the brakes and reduce or pay off the unacceptable balance on your credit cards. Schedule checkups or medical tests around the 9th, making sure to cover any concerns you have with your physician no matter how you're feeling on appointment day.

Relationships

Make plans to celebrate Valentine's Day with your sweetheart when the Moon is in compatible Pisces. Enjoy camaraderie with relatives, neighbors, and internet connections on the 21st, when chatter accelerates, exchanges net valuable information, and rapport leaves you desirous of spending more time with these cherished contacts.

Success and Money

The New Moon conjunct Jupiter on the 11th marks a favorable time to purchase goods you've been contemplating, especially high-end TVs, vehicles (after the 21st is best), and jewelry. Paying down debt has left you feeling more secure and pleased with recently implemented monetary strategies. A savings plan you've invested in shows promising results.

Pitfalls and Potential Problems

Remember to pay yourself first, and that means adding to savings accounts every month. A day when you might be lax in monitoring finances is the 4th, when aspects show arguments over purchases or lapses in good judgment. Home base may be turbulent on the 17th, so wait until the 21st for a more harmonious communication phase. Sharp exchanges with a partner on the 27th over family issues curb romantic gestures. Apologize if you've been crotchety.

Rewarding Days

2, 9, 11, 21

Challenging Days

4, 17, 24, 27

Capricorn | March

Overall Theme

Education and continuous improvement could be high on the agenda as the month unfolds. The early part of the month, especially the first week, benefits from work-related travel and possibly attendance at a seminar on team building. Enjoy the momentum and internalize the information each employee brings to the table to experience a more powerful message from this training module.

Relationships

Work colleagues, bosses, and members of professional organizations dominate the landscape early this month. Opportunity increases to build solid rapport, exchange critical information, and strengthen commitment to goals. Family and intimate partners claim your attention during the second half of the month, with an emphasis on handling responsibility judiciously and balancing work with playtime.

Success and Money

Progressive ideas bring attention to your standing in the company from those who oversee your work. A bonus or unexpected raise could be part of the acknowledgment late in the month. Domestic affairs and plans for adventures, outings, or vacations increase excitement at home base, especially around the 14th. Decisions over spending quality time together as a family are appropriately nurturing and lead to healing emotional rifts, resulting in an outcome that money simply can't buy.

Pitfalls and Potential Problems

Board members, best friends, and group affiliates are in a scrappy mood around the 4th, suggesting that you settle into observation mode and let the fur fly without your input. One of the more challenging days for early-born Capricorns is March 22, when the Moon tangles with fragile emotions and opens old wounds with your significant other. The Full Moon on the 28th brings criticism from those in charge.

Rewarding Days

2, 8, 14, 24

Challenging Days

4, 6, 22, 28

Capricorn | April

Overall Theme

Late-born Capricorns feel the shift in direction when Pluto goes retrograde on the 27th. In the early part of the month, tension forces you to soothe ruffled feathers and hurt feelings at home base and help children navigate challenging waters. Take a day off on the 2nd to do some soul-searching and behind-the-scenes planning as you jump-start the fast-paced month ahead.

Relationships

You hit the jackpot on the 1st with members of clubs, groups, or professional organizations who want to hear your thoughts and pick your brain. Your contributions could lead to an invitation to consider holding an office in the group or chairing a committee. The New Moon on the 11th enhances rapport with family members and adds fun, excitement, and creative tension to the mix.

Success and Money

Scheduled travel leads to highly productive business meetings with desirable results that elevate your work status and give your reputation for analyzing the big picture a boost. A pleasure trip this month with family or friends nets you a terrific package deal in a location that satisfies everyone's preferences and is pocketbook-friendly.

Pitfalls and Potential Problems

Sometimes the Moon in your sign gives you low energy due to aggravating circumstances, especially when the Sun is in Aries. This month, the draining energy takes place on the 5th, so don't plan any big undertakings that day. A child's issue may keep you off your game and disrupt your work day on the 14th. Asking the right questions instead of making assumptions brings satisfying rewards.

Rewarding Days

1, 2, 11, 23

Challenging Days

5, 14, 19, 27

Capricorn | May

Overall Theme

The focus this month is on the movement of several planets and the year's first Lunar Eclipse on May 26 in Sagittarius. Saturn in Aquarius and Mercury in Gemini both go retrograde in motion on May 23 and May 29, respectively. Demands on your time dominate the landscape, especially related to communication, contracting, and children's needs.

Relationships

If it isn't neighbors knocking on your door asking for help with neighborhood fundraising drives and community projects, it's your siblings and cousins calling you to ask for help in finding solutions to vexing problems. Meanwhile, workplace demands revolve around contract negotiations, electronic equipment purchases, and new employment policies. Children shine in school activities, and you proudly support their achievements.

Success and Money

Additional cash comes your way compliments of your partner's raise, bonus, or windfall. You'll celebrate with the goodies and bank the rest in your rainy-day fund. Recognition comes to your family in the form of sports achievements, academic excellence, an engagement, or an entrepreneurial venture. As a proud parent, you'll book entertainment and amusement venues to reward the family.

Pitfalls and Potential Problems

Make no major purchases on the 4th, when planets gang up on price options and fail to disclose hidden costs. Lie low on the 26th, when the Lunar Eclipse could trigger a headache and send you to the sofa. Don't start a trip on the 23rd or sign a real estate deal or a contract for a new vehicle. Mercury's shift to retrograde motion on May 29 delays plans in the workplace and contributes to confusion.

Rewarding Days

2, 7, 11, 17

Challenging Days

4, 8, 21, 26

Capricorn | June

Overall Theme

Local travel and communication accelerate this month, and you'll have little downtime from the volume of work and home demands that stimulate a hectic pace. The year's first Solar Eclipse occurs on June 10 in your solar sixth house, highlighting shifts in your daily routine and schedule accommodations. Jupiter turns retrograde on the 20th in your solar third house, along with Neptune on the 25th, while Mercury goes direct in your solar sixth house on the 22nd.

Relationships

Happy times unfold as you enjoy children and their interests, leisurely outings with your family, and favorite recreational pursuits. Schedule get-away time for you and your significant other around the 12th to attend special events like weddings, graduations, anniversaries, or reunions. Work teams enthusiastically celebrate productivity milestones.

Success and Money

Diplomacy pays off in your career when your insightful observations save the day around June 20–22 and you come to the aid of the brass over availability or reliability of presentation materials or important papers. You will be purchasing a greater number of gifts than usual this month and will look for value and unique ways to honor recipients.

Pitfalls and Potential Problems

You can be a harsh disciplinarian at times when something catches you unawares. Pay attention to what happens around the 4th when someone's sensitive feelings show the bruises at home base and communication breaks down. The gist of a message is lost on recipients on the 18th, resulting in confusion and critical reactions. Be prepared for the fallout if you're one of the problem-solvers.

Rewarding Days

3, 7, 12, 20

Challenging Days

4, 10, 18, 24

Capricorn | July

Overall Theme

July could be one of your more romantic months, with the love planets Venus and Mars in Leo and your solar eighth house of intimacy and deep feelings. Rewards in the love arena are yours for the asking. When the Moon moves into Leo on the 10th, this passionate mood accelerates, creating the perfect conditions for a memorable honeymoon or anniversary celebration.

Relationships

The sunny beach, majestic mountains, and pristine parks beckon. With the Sun in Cancer shining brightly in your solar seventh house of partners during the last part of the month, your main squeeze and children might be on board for a well-deserved vacation. Be sure to include family members, especially those who live with you or those whose company you enjoy. Make beautiful memories while positive aspects prevail from the 2nd through the 15th.

Success and Money

Your reward for managing debt wisely pays off this month. An offer for an attractive mortgage interest rate comes through based on your excellent credit scores. The New Moon on the 9th positively affects your cash flow. If you are on vacation or planning one, you could net some attractive perks and comps on entertainment and meals.

Pitfalls and Potential Problems

A face-off with a stubborn child or romantic interest leads to nasty exchanges and hurt feelings. Don't be surprised if you hear the words "you don't understand me" more than once, especially around the 5th or the 8th. Say no to a major purchase on the 25th to avoid missing the fine print and having to return the product later.

Rewarding Days

2, 10, 12, 23

Challenging Days

5, 8, 16, 25

Capricorn | August

Overall Theme

Although still retrograde, be glad that Jupiter has traveled back into your solar second house of money and assets in Aquarius, where it joins transiting Saturn in this sign. The Full Moon in Aquarius joins them on the 22nd, alerting you to the possibility of unexpected expenses or a delay in obtaining a loan, approval to travel, or money for education. Ride it out until clearer details emerge.

Relationships

The social side of connections heats up this month, paving the way for pleasurable interludes. Schedule a date night with your spouse or romantic partner on the 6th, when conversation gives your spirits a lift. Accept a good friend's invitation for a weekend getaway or say yes to lunch with club members around the 16th. Join work colleagues for a barbecue or picnic on the 31st, and talk about personal interests rather than what you left behind at work.

Success and Money

Money matters unfold along prosperous lines as long as you don't rush deals before they're ready. An unexpected gift from a kindred spirit brings a tear to your eye and appreciation for unconditional love. Pay it forward by paying the bill for an unsuspecting stranger when the opportunity arises. Watch for those smiles.

Pitfalls and Potential Problems

Steer clear of hotheads on the 1st, when impulsive actions lead to outbursts, reckless driving, or unexpected tirades. Uranus is at work plucking your nerves with students if you teach, athletes if you coach, or your children. Disagreeable political discussions could be part of the environment on the 26th when a group gathers in your home. Use discretion.

Rewarding Days

6, 8, 16, 31

Challenging Days

1, 17, 22, 26

Capricorn | September

Overall Theme

You're looking for a couple of highly productive work days to start the month so you can take time off for a much-anticipated long holiday weekend of fun and games. Cooperation hits a high note in the work scene, with everyone on the same page and passionate about meeting goals. Everyone at home base is in sync too, except for on the 2nd, when upcoming plans need clarification before everything is a go for travel. By the 3rd you're on your way to relaxation and adventure.

Relationships

The New Moon on the 6th in your solar ninth house has a unifying effect on collaborative plans for future travel to vacation spots and lifts spirits. Siblings weigh in this month, planning visits and family get-togethers, especially those at a distance. An important community-based meeting delivers news about improvements and available funds. You could be asked to take a vote on suggestions.

Success and Money

Organizational goals are a major focus at your workplace and are tied to competition and incentives. Your feedback seems essential to developing components and adds a new dimension to your responsibilities. Around September 9, a critical meeting highlights the agenda and looks at leadership and the makeup of the team. Consider this an invitation to show your interest in an emerging position.

Pitfalls and Potential Problems

Financial opportunities emerge on the 5th with little notice, suggesting that you pass on this round and do your homework before parting with hard-earned cash. Mercury heads into retrograde territory in Libra on the 27th, urging you not to sign documents or make executive decisions on this day.

Rewarding Days

1, 3, 9, 20

Challenging Days

2, 5, 14, 27

Capricorn | October

Overall Theme

This month several planets move forward in direct motion: Pluto in Capricorn on the 6th, Saturn in Aquarius on the 10th, Jupiter in Aquarius on the 18th, and Mercury in Libra also on the 18th. You'll want to push hard to get it all done. Grab your calendar, look at your deliverables timeline, and settle into a productive, accomplishment-oriented month. No burnout allowed!

Relationships

The vibes right now are excellent for experiencing stellar work dynamics with key players and strengthening group rapport, especially on the 7th through the 13th. Family members show the love and spread the cheer on the 19th through the 21st. Discussions revolve around children's activities, sports events, and amusement. Don't rock the boat on the 1st, when your significant other runs out of patience.

Success and Money

Connections with bankers, realtors, and investment experts net favorable terms for savings, home purchases, and interest rates. You could find the perfect property and have your lender ready to fund the deal on the 31st. Checking options leads to unexpected discoveries related to up-and-coming neighborhoods.

Pitfalls and Potential Problems

No matter how tempting, don't put pen to paper on the 3rd, when challenging planetary aspects skew the integrity of a contract, plan, or policy. You'll need a day to recover on the 14th after a week of intense interactions with those in your business environment. The 30th starts out well but quickly morphs into confusion and misunderstanding. Watch your food choices.

Rewarding Days

7, 13, 19, 31

Challenging Days

1, 3, 14, 30

Capricorn | November

Overall Theme

What results are you expecting as the holiday season unfolds, bringing anticipation and excitement? Do you want to play host to display your exceptional flair for setting a splendid table and presenting elegant meals? Just ahead of November's holiday, the last Lunar Eclipse of the year occurs on November 19 in compatible Taurus, reminding you to ask guests to share something for which they are grateful as they present you with a wish list to help you shop for cherished gifts.

Relationships

The New Moon on November 4 highlights social activities with friends, groups, and professional organizations. Why not lock in that date to catch up with colleagues and learn about ongoing personal and work changes? Networking pays off. You could meet new people and expand your field of contacts. Single Capricorns have options for meeting potential partners on the 24th.

Success and Money

Hard work pays off on the 3rd when accomplishment results receive recognition, some of which may come with a pay raise in coming weeks. Business partners deliberate over strategy options and decide on a winning solution by month's end. A marriage proposal is in the works for a member of your circle during the last few days of November.

Pitfalls and Potential Problems

Protect your reputation on the 1st when contacts in distant places drop hints about personal troubles that are not based in fact. Mars blasts Uranus conjunct the Moon on the 17th, bringing a testy close to the workweek. Differences of opinion clash and call for a diplomatic intervention to ease tension.

Rewarding Days

3, 4, 9, 24

Challenging Days

1, 11, 15, 17

Capricorn | December

Overall Theme

Transiting Jupiter in your solar second house of money and assets brought you opportunities to increase your financial holdings during 2021. Your stellar reputation earned you entry into previously closed circles after you worked industriously to build impressive credentials that qualify you for raises, bonuses, and desirable career perks. Time to visit your mentor—you're ready for the promotion.

Relationships

Join work-related groups for holiday parties and celebrations during the first few weeks of the month. Affiliations with charitable organizations have your attention around the 4th, the date of 2021's last Solar Eclipse. Help those in need with gifts, food, and shelter. In-laws and relatives at a distance gather after the 26th, adding sparkle to holiday festivities. Host visitors with favorite entertainment and dining venues.

Success and Money

You get some much deserved time off after the 15th, so plan wisely and enjoy the change of pace as you complete holiday plans and shop for last-minute gifts. Productivity and patience pay off between the 8th and the 14th, when critical challenges land in your lap related to costs and availability of goods. Your astute negotiating skills bring you the successful outcome you desire.

Pitfalls and Potential Problems

Neptune in Pisces turns direct on the 1st, replacing fuzzy thinking with practical insight. Keep an eye on luggage at the airport. The Full Moon in Gemini on the 19th creates tension in work circles if you work on the weekend or with your health if you've been fighting a lingering ailment and need a few days in bed to heal. Venus in Capricorn goes retrograde on the 19th, disrupting the flow of plans or schedules. Don't begin a vacation on that date.

Rewarding Days

1, 4, 7, 26

Challenging Days

8, 14, 19, 21

Capricorn Action Table

These dates reflect the best–but not the only–times for success and ease in these activities, according to your Sun sign.

	JAN	FEB	MAR	APR	MAY	JUN	JUL	AUG	SEP	OCT	NOV	DEC
Move		21			7				1			
Romance			24	1		12	23	16			4	
Seek counseling/ coaching	19			23						7		1
Ask for a raise		11				20		8			9	
Vacation	4				17				20			26
Get a loan			2				12			31		

Aquarius

The Water Bearer
January 19 to February 18

Element: Air

Quality: Fixed

Polarity: Yang/masculine

Planetary Ruler: Uranus

Meditation: I am a
wellspring of creativity

Gemstone: Amethyst

Power Stones: Aquamarine,
black pearl, chrysocolla

Key Phrase: I know

Glyph: Currents of energy

Anatomy: Ankles, circulatory
system

Colors: Iridescent blues, violet

Animals: Exotic birds

Myths/Legends: Ninhursag,
John the Baptist, Deucalion

House: Eleventh

Opposite Sign: Leo

Flower: Orchid

Keyword: Unconventional

The Aquarius Personality

Strengths, Talents, and the Creative Spark

The symbol for your sign is the Water Bearer, known for favoring humanitarian endeavors and optimism, a trait of your intellectual air element. As the fourth fixed sign of the zodiac, you are the natural occupant of the solar eleventh house of associations, friendships, goals, groups, your employer's resources, hopes, global initiatives, leadership in organizations, motivations, mutual interests, new trends, unorthodox methods, wishes, and sudden revelations or change. Any planets you have residing in this house in your birth chart showcase your creative leanings and how you wish to interact with diverse groups. Spontaneous Uranus is your sign ruler and helps you connect with others in a variety of social settings, adding new insights to your sphere of influence. Joining groups to support mutual interests appeals to you and satisfies your need for impersonal togetherness. Collaborations are your jam, attracting you to a cause, purpose, or principle that allows you to band together in unity and create your niche in the world. You enjoy breaking down old ideas and giving them a modern spin by daring to be unconventional in your approach.

As one of the most analytical signs in the cosmos, you take pride in your application of innovative problem-solving skills that work especially well when you remain flexible and impartial to input from others. Aptitude in personal, organizational, and social problems places you in the spotlight in arenas that improve conditions for humanity, strengthen management development, and promote safety in electronics technology. Your more altruistic side shines when you demonstrate commitment to the improvement of relationships in both personal and professional settings. You're proud of your many affiliations and excel in the role as a change agent or internal consultant in many high-profile organizations. It is not unusual for you to have an astrologer or two in your life through friendship or information seeking. You may even become a serious student of astrology, if not a practitioner.

Intimacy and Personal Relationships

Communication and networking influence your dating style. A talker is a good match for you because you want to test your profound thoughts on someone who understands your complex mind and listens to your take on life. A loving partner is just what you need to be less abstract and more connected to your deep emotions and touching romantic expression. You are blessed with charisma that draws intelligent, inspiring companions into your circle. You need a soul mate who loves your creative mind and charming disposition and doesn't mind sharing you with the rest of the world. Your wish for the perfect partner is someone who understands your mindset and shares your views on politics and social justice and your outlook on the acquisition of timesaving gadgets, ownership of innovative phones, and installation of cybersecurity equipment.

Values and Resources

When your world revolves around making choices that come from a strong internal desire for change, your fondest hopes and aspirations open up to many possibilities. The urge to improve the profile of the planet or your network of friends runs deep and comes from your perception of what makes others tick. Information seems to flow to you from diverse sources, yet you maintain a sacred hold on revelations about your personal life, keeping most friendships on an impersonal level, with no emotional investment, a strong eleventh-house trait. To get mushy over a cause means to lose control in your eyes. You prefer to shape and effect change within a structure by examining existing conditions and offering compromises or forming new alliances. Group goals inspire you, politics fascinates you, and meeting others halfway spells success. A fascination with all things unique leads to selection of one-of-a-kind home purchases, the new car nobody else has, and vacations to exotic lands. Cookie-cutter residences or predictable careers paths are not for you. Aquarians are known for setting up unusual living arrangements and putting up with inconvenient conditions for much longer periods of time than most others would tolerate.

Blind Spots and Blockages

Bringing relationships to a close when they have outlived their meaning or usefulness is difficult for you. You don't let go easily because you feel that something advantageous may pop up and make you sorry you walked away. Often you just want to be friends after the romance has lost its bloom or the friendship cools. With the inner detachment you possess, clinging to a person or group can be a matter of convenience to you, often a monetary one, until you open your eyes and see that you are limiting your options and becoming resentful. When you lose interest in people or undertakings in your daily environment, you become peevish and cynical. At times you may not recognize that you have become depressed. Critics say you can be manipulative with colleagues and pit competitors against one another. Those who observe you say that when life bombards you with lemons, you sound angry all the time, getting up on a soapbox to complain bitterly about people or conditions yet not necessarily addressing what is actually on your mind. Learn to make a pitcher of lemonade.

Goals and Success

One of your exceptional gifts is experiencing out-of-the-blue revelations that showcase your flair for defining unique possibilities for implementing change. You have outstanding analytical skills and easily integrate them in a variety of consulting venues. Most likely your career history reflects an array of ticket-punching assignments and a collection of work titles designed to broaden qualifications that give you the edge in a talent manager's collection of dream profiles. If you're in a job-seeking phase or in search of a trendsetting new venue, 2021 could be your year to shine. Seek out preferred options that reflect future growth for the planet, community enterprises, humanitarian causes, or products that could benefit from creative or more efficient use, or explore the world of electronic communication, an enterprise that matches your innovative, solution-oriented mind. Your networks include acquaintances from all walks of life who are the sources of leads and open the doors for social and scientific opportunities. Scope out these beneficial affiliations to maximize the use of your progressive thought patterns and celebrate the journey of unprecedented diversification.

Aquarius Keywords for 2021
Feedback, friendship, future

The Year Ahead for Aquarius

After experiencing a pileup of Capricorn energy in your solar twelfth house for the last few years and feeling unsettled over the way problem areas converged to demand your attention, you feel relieved that your internal desire for change has been met in most ways. The bottleneck started with Pluto in Capricorn entering this twelfth house of seclusion in 2008 and applying pressure on you to change outmoded attitudes about people and conditions in your life. Vision seemed blocked and you seemed to go around in circles revisiting the same negative patterns. Then restrictive Saturn in Capricorn joined the party in December 2017 and created a stronger holding pattern in critical areas that tied your hands and your soul to undesirable and exhausting situations. Eclipses in Capricorn and opposing ones in Cancer in your solar sixth house found a strike zone and kept you chained to old issues. You sometimes felt like you were in prison. Instead of speaking out, you held your tongue and seethed in silence. A part of you felt unprepared to take the big steps to embrace your future until Jupiter in Capricorn arrived, opened doors, and offered a way to liberation and a brand-new life direction in 2020.

Now the focus is on you, Aquarius, with both Jupiter and Saturn in your sign in 2021 and occupying your solar first house of action, attitude, and self-expression. This position speaks to moves—physical, career, or relationship changes. If you haven't already done so, set your sights on new environments. Eclipses light up your solar eleventh, fifth, and fourth houses in 2021. Say goodbye to old work mates, bosses, living quarters, and partners as you embrace a new phase of life. Let go of fear and anger and make what resonates to your purpose count the most. If you've been honest, you have the tools to create a better world in the year ahead.

Jupiter

All Aquarians benefit from this year's Jupiter transit, which touches every degree of your sign through December 28. You only get to experience this enjoyable benefit every twelve years, when the planet of expansion and confidence building lands on your Sun and sends a bit of prosperity your way. Luck follows you wherever you go while Jupiter in Aquarius occupies your solar first house all year. No doubt you will take pride in your physical appearance, develop new goals, call attention to your master plan, and share expectations in collaborative ventures with important groups. Jupiter in this house increases your net worth and encourages you to make changes in your financial holdings. Adventure awaits you wherever you go. Travel is part of the scene for both business and pleasure, with plenty of opportunities to eat too much. Consuming rich foods, eating out more than usual, or attending banquets is tough on your waistline, so put down your fork to control weight when Jupiter moves through this house. If you've been rebuilding your body to a healthy state while showcasing your assets, you'll have the passion and energy to enjoy the attractions that distant locations have to offer. Get to know the fine points of your new residential location if you've moved, and build in time to enjoy vacation destinations of choice. Some Aquarians buy a home this year, find true love, or change careers. Currently Jupiter enjoys the company of Saturn in Aquarius in your action-oriented solar first house. Shape your world with cherished wishes.

Saturn

When 2021 dawns, Saturn occupies the first degree of Aquarius in the company of transiting Jupiter in early Aquarius in your solar first house of assertiveness, character, individuality, mannerisms, passion, and self-discovery. In this location, Saturn offers opportunities to shine, yet not without restriction until the planet of limitations is sure you're ready to take the leap into the void. Ideas will flow, as will the subsequent discovery of overlooked details and missing information, which is delicious food for thought for your voracious, analytical mind. Since you are a joiner, check out new networks that welcome your gregarious personality and value your management acumen. Compare the goals of groups that improve conditions for humanity, and volunteer your time for a worthy cause. Timing is everything when you have an agreement or contract for employment to sign. Note that Saturn is direct until May 23, when it goes retrograde and then resumes forward motion on October 10. Those of you born between January 20 and February 3 feel the deepest impact from this transit. Have you noticed any difference in physical stamina lately? Is your work environment less energizing for you, or are you bored with your job? Saturn moving through your first house can zap your energy or draw attention to every ache and pain and make you sensitive to colds and flu bugs. Working overtime makes you less tolerant of stress and begs you to get more sleep. Be sure to monitor health and nutrition and balance your daily routine with exercise.

Uranus

When 2021 begins, retrograde Uranus in Taurus will be navigating your solar fourth house of home, family, foundation, emotional makeup, parents, privacy, and your physical space. Uranus here spells trouble, possibly interfering with your need for security and your preference for not rocking the boat in domestic circles. In this action-oriented house,

Uranus could play to your eccentric side and stimulate your interest in laying down new rules with no warning, restricting the purchase of foods you don't consider healthy anymore, or redecorating your home with striking patterns and pop art that jar your partner's sense of equilibrium. Look at some of these areas where Uranus is likely to strike for clues about how this transit will play out. In the sign of Taurus, this rebel planet is not particularly friendly toward Aquarius, as it creates harsh aspects and could upset the applecart at home base, preferring chaos to mellow moods. Examine family relationships for clues. What could you do to stabilize them? Use fusion to unite forces rather than divide members by coercing them into choosing sides. On January 14, Uranus turns direct in motion and most affects those of you born between January 26 and February 4 before going retrograde again on August 19 and resuming direct motion in January 2022. Enjoy love and congeniality as you express your views, stimulate productive conversation that encourages sharing, and build a stable environment with just a tad of the unexpected thrown in to keep you in your comfort zone.

Neptune

With Neptune hanging out in your solar second house of assets, income, money you earn and how you spend it, and developmental opportunities, you have experienced confusion and some unfavorable deals in money transactions. Value may not have met your expectations for your purchases, draining your hard-earned cash with slippery deals. You've probably had a few pity parties since Neptune entered this house back in April 2011 and you found out that purchases cost more than advertised, careless accounting mistakes drained your funds, and salary increases were not what you expected. Review disappointing outcomes that have occurred. In what ways have you not spent your money wisely or spent too much of it? With Neptune in your money house, you have to make sure no one steals it or gives you a dramatic sob story so you part with your cash, or you lose it due to identity theft, a stolen wallet, or a bad investment deal. This transit of Neptune calls for maintaining a clear head in all financial dealings by taking your time, checking facts, and coming out of the fog to review clauses, contracts, and proposals. Those of you born between February 6 and 13 experience the most impactful side of Neptune's 2021 journey.

Pluto

How is your judgment these days, and what do you do when you're sitting on some hot information that is just not ready for public disclosure? Pluto has been holding down the fort in your solar twelfth house since 2008, working on your psyche, your dream state, and your inner barriers to test how well you keep secrets and suggesting when it is okay to release them, along with the accumulating guilt that makes you wary of others' reactions. You value discretion, Aquarius, and realize that suppressing information is not your bag. You struggle with keeping facts to yourself that you would very much like to share with the universe. Part of you knows that not everyone can handle the truth, and you check the rule book for lessons in using tact and diplomacy. Pluto in the twelfth house influences your thinking patterns and your style in unloading the accumulating garbage. Don't back away from what you need to get off your chest. Talk to others with a fair and open mind, using a winning solution where everyone speaks their truth and has a stake in the outcome. In 2021, those of you born between February 13 and 19 feel the greatest impact from this Pluto transit. Consult your most astute advisors to discuss specific steps that will help you shed fear. Maintain an upbeat attitude and celebrate success in the new year.

How Will This Year's Eclipses Affect You?

In 2021, a total of four eclipses occur. There will be two Lunar Eclipses and two Solar Eclipses, creating intense periods that begin to manifest a few months before their actual dates. Eclipses unfold in cycles involving all twelve signs of the zodiac, and usually occur in pairs about two weeks apart. Think of eclipses as opportunities to release old patterns and conditions that have outlived their usefulness. Have no fear of them, since they can bring you unexpected surprises and windfalls. The closer an eclipse is to a degree or point in your chart, the greater its importance in your life. Those of you born with a planet at the same degree as an eclipse are likely to see a high level of activity in the house where the eclipse occurs.

Aquarius, get ready, because two eclipses take place this year in your solar eleventh house of associations, friendships, groups, goals, shared causes, and wishes. The first one is a Lunar Eclipse in Sagittarius on May 26 that relates to activity in organizations that hold your interest—

leadership, mission, and values. What role do you wish to occupy in a group like this where you share common interests and are willing to work for its success? This eclipse may also prod you to look closely at friendships that have been largely impersonal. Some may grow stronger, while others drop further out of sight as you realize the glue is not there to build closeness.

The second Sagittarius eclipse is a Solar Eclipse on December 4, where you could find yourself in the limelight, in demand to take the helm of a leading initiative or humanitarian project. You could learn a great deal about your employer's resources and how well they will cover planned projects in the coming year. An action related to this house that you began in May is ready for your final touch and an acknowledgment of achievement.

The first Solar Eclipse of 2021 takes place in Gemini on June 10 in your solar fifth house of adventure, children and their interests, entertainment, risk-taking, romance, speculation, sports, and vacation. Depending on other planetary relationships in your chart, you may be looking at a new romance and passionately pursuing the object of your affection. An engagement may be in the works. With an eclipse in this house, you could welcome the birth of a baby or share more than the usual amount of activity with children, students, or those you coach. Perhaps travel for pleasure keeps you hopping, or you socialize more with favorite friends.

The final Lunar Eclipse of 2021 occurs on November 19 in Taurus in your solar fourth house of the home and family, where it keeps company with transiting Uranus in Taurus, further highlighting the spontaneous and unpredictable nature of activity in this house. When Uranus passes through the fourth house, it often results in a physical move, sometimes because of new job opportunities, the forces of nature via storms or environmental conditions, or ruptures in intimate connections. Study the energy and the relationships with family members who live with you for clues about what needs attention and is likely to come to a head. Then bombard yourself with optimism as you address the elephant in the room and present options so everyone has a chance to work out their differences. Your quick wit and way with words should break the ice and send the message that behind the criticism lies deep love and caring.

Aquarius | January

Overall Theme

Dream big in 2021! With Jupiter and Saturn in early Aquarius as you start the year, whatever you want to accomplish is yours for the asking. Take inventory of your assets, qualifications, and desired salary for a new job. Start out by contacting your networks, letting leaders know of your interest and availability for a new assignment. Your ruling planet, Uranus, goes direct on January 14, giving you the go-ahead to move forward with your goals.

Relationships

Friends and mentors hold the cards to introducing you to prospective employers. Accept invitations to lunches, dinners, or meetings where power brokers gather and you have a chance to pass out your business cards or lobby for interviews. Your social life picks up around the 25th, when rapport and compatibility shine.

Success and Money

You start off the year with a healthy wallet and little debt from holiday shopping, a plus for you with all the temptations Neptune in Pisces presented in your solar second house of money. Conservative financial management has paid off, especially with your astute plan to make automatic deposits in high-yield accounts.

Pitfalls and Potential Problems

Avoid relationship hotspots on January 1, when partners are on edge and seem volatile. Bite your tongue as well with household members as conflict comes to a head on the 21st. You won't see eye to eye with your business associates on the 28th and will learn you have much more to discuss when cooler heads prevail.

Rewarding Days

4, 10, 14, 25

Challenging Days

1, 5, 21, 28

Aquarius | February

Overall Theme

Four planets line up in your sign this month. Among your best days are those that host air-sign Moons and also the 6th, when a fiery Moon gives you a dose of passion for managing your priorities. Mercury in your sign highlights stimulating conversations, provocative debates, and excellent feedback results, despite Mercury being retrograde until the 20th.

Relationships

Score a win with Venus in your sign on Valentine's Day, joined by Jupiter conjunct Mercury and Venus. The Moon adds harmonious notes to your celebratory mood as well. The 7th is perfect for dates, hosting a party, or gathering for a social event. Children may be at the center of attention.

Success and Money

Enjoy the New Moon in your sign on the 11th when you unveil plans for your home projects and business investments. The money is available and the terms are easily met. The 21st is a perfect day to get together with friends, visit the country club, take in a show at the theater, or catch a quirky movie you can discuss afterward over a meal.

Pitfalls and Potential Problems

Arguments at work with authorities revolve around money matters on the 4th and need better data before decisions can be made. Avoid making investments on the 1st and 27th, when the Moon makes hard aspects to transiting planets. There's a tempest in the teapot at home base on the 18th, when dialogue centers on bad habits, rude behavior, and missed deadlines among family members.

Rewarding Days

2, 6, 7, 21

Challenging Days

1, 4, 18, 26

Aquarius | March

Overall Theme

The planets of prosperity line up to give your monetary power a boost. You'll be able to pay your bills and stick to your budget this month, with enough left over to add to savings or put aside to fund a big-ticket item you plan to purchase in the near future. You still have some leftover birthday cash to put toward a spring vacation.

Relationships

This month, relationships are generally harmonious at home base and with your significant other. Those of you who are dating have excellent prospects for meeting new people on the 6th. Make time for children and their interests and join them for fun and games. Just be sure to find out details related to entertainment expenses to avoid a few surprises.

Success and Money

With Venus in Pisces conjunct the Sun in your solar second house of money this month, you should be able to cut favorable deals and get excellent discounts on purchases. The New Moon on the 13th also falls in your second house of income and brings attractive offers to expand your career horizon if you're looking for a change. Jupiter and Mercury in your solar first house are magnets for positive financial news.

Pitfalls and Potential Problems

Skip the 28th for meeting a love interest for a weekend getaway. The vibes are sketchy and the Full Moon does not cooperate in creating the romance you desire. Work problems come to a head on the 4th, and cooperation fades as the day goes on. Club meetings or spectator sports events are disappointing on the 20th due to a lack of coordination and a mix-up in arrangement details.

Rewarding Days

6, 13, 18, 25

Challenging Days

2, 4, 20, 28

Aquarius | April

Overall Theme

The New Moon in Aries on the 11th puts communication and your neighborhood in the spotlight. You'll join neighbors for get-togethers, a community event, or a dinner party. Welcome newcomers with a thoughtful gesture to ease uncertainty in new surroundings. Enjoy the private time and the clear thinking that surrounds you on the 6th to ponder over options for decisions you'll be making in the next few months.

Relationships

You can't go wrong this month with the surge of rapport and teamwork that filters through your workplace. You'll hear from cousins and siblings via phone, text, or a visit in the middle weeks of the month and realize it's good to stay connected when you hear about all that has happened since the year began. Make plans for spring events that unite relatives who cherish these bonds.

Success and Money

Group synergy from the 17th to the 20th gives you an enthusiastic boost in confidence for special causes and strengthens the bonds of friendship. Celebrate the fusion of contributions from those in your talent pool who bring their best game and display a high degree of professionalism in a major undertaking. A winning attitude prevails and seeds the enthusiasm for the next phase of action.

Pitfalls and Potential Problems

You could be double-booked on the 3rd if you're not careful with scheduling and will disappoint a loved one who's counting on your presence at a special event. Pluto in Capricorn turns retrograde for the next six months on the 27th in your solar twelfth house, and you postpone a contemplated undertaking until you clear up uncertainty.

Rewarding Days
1, 6, 12, 17

Challenging Days
3, 5, 14, 27

Aquarius | May

Overall Theme

More than a few cranky people come your way this month, especially after the 20th. Look to the cosmos for answers. Uranus stomps along in your solar fourth house of home and family, contributing to the chaos. In addition, two planets turn retrograde and the first Lunar Eclipse of the year occurs in your solar eleventh house of associates and friends. Use humor to get individuals who are out of sorts back into a lighter mood.

Relationships

Thank the New Moon in Taurus on the 11th for sending in an unexpected and loving vibe to bring peace and optimism to the home front. Children, romantic interests, and your social contacts claim your time on May 14 and 15, when you find that diverse activities fill every free moment of your calendar. Have fun while you can. Save space for a romantic interlude with your significant other on the 19th and express devotion for the cherished bond you enjoy.

Success and Money

Your money goes far with recreation and amusement venues and even sporting events, where you successfully land entertainment discounts, cheap tickets for travel, and coveted concert bookings. With Jupiter transiting your solar first and second houses this month, you could win a contest or receive a large refund from a major purchase.

Pitfalls and Potential Problems

Saturn turns retrograde on May 23 in your solar first house, contributing to the tired feeling you've been battling all month. Take time to rest and don't work overtime. Mercury goes retrograde on May 29, signaling delays in accomplishing tasks, mixed messages, and canceled appointments. The Lunar Eclipse on May 26 highlights activity with friends and groups. Wait until the impact fades before starting travel.

Rewarding Days

7, 11, 13, 19

Challenging Days

4, 21, 25, 27

Aquarius | June

Overall Theme

The first half of the month is a bonus for romantics, with Jupiter in early Pisces in harmonious aspect to Venus in Cancer. Mark those dates and have a blast enjoying a respite from excessive mental pressure. Creative ventures lead to successful outcomes when your talent matches the goals of a potential employer. Follow up on entrepreneurial leads.

Relationships

Connections you meet through work could be the reason that your heart feels lighter this month. If you're single, you'll want to know more about an intriguing new person who comes on the scene. Romance plays a prominent role now whether you're married or single. Home and family relationships are congenial for most of the month, except for the 15th, when a blowup may occur with your partner.

Success and Money

Although your schedule has little downtime, surprise your family by finalizing plans for a summer vacation, making sure that your getaway location has something for everyone to enjoy. Offer young children options for enjoying attractions. Meet project deadlines by the 22nd and celebrate milestones with the work team. Mercury goes direct in your solar fifth house on the 22nd, suggesting that you resume negotiations for speculative deals in the following week.

Pitfalls and Potential Problems

With Mercury, Saturn, and Pluto all retrograde and soon to be joined by Jupiter on June 20, you could easily misinterpret the motives of a love connection or close acquaintance. Check out facts before leveling unfounded accusations, especially after Mars enters Leo on June 11. Partnership communication is testy on the 15th. The Moon conjunct Saturn opposes Mars on the 27th and suppresses conditions for driving an agreeable bargain.

Rewarding Days

1, 8, 10, 22

Challenging Days

6, 15, 18, 26

Aquarius | July

Overall Theme

Although some of you landed a new job or retired from one in the last year or so, you're feeling restless and want to find something new. Hold on! The timing is not right for a career move. Retirees among you might volunteer for a charitable cause or use your expertise to find a part-time opportunity that showcases your skills. Your need for benefits drives the decision to reenter the workplace.

Relationships

Venus and Mars oppose your Sun and transiting Saturn right now and contribute to a bit of friction between you and your significant other, possibly due to your doubt about staying the course in your present work arena. Close relatives may be part of the holiday scene when you host festivities and invite family and friends to celebrate. Cordial relationships dominate the work scene, especially mid-month.

Success and Money

With Jupiter galloping back into your sign at the end of July, money continues to reward your efforts in the form of bonuses, raises, and unexpected recognition. Members of professional organizations reach out for your opinions on evolving initiatives and scope out your interest in taking on more responsibility as a member. Feedback is your jam and it hits the right zone on the 21st, eliciting gratitude from contacts.

Pitfalls and Potential Problems

Look before you leap into a no-win situation with your partner or family member on the 4th, when the Taurus Moon feels the energy of hard aspects from Venus, Mars, Uranus, and Saturn. Differences that flared up over the weekend need resolution. Don't dismiss them as unimportant. Get a second opinion from another medical professional if a diagnosis feels shaky on the 16th .

Rewarding Days

2, 7, 19, 21

Challenging Days

4, 12, 16, 25

Aquarius | August

Overall Theme

Earth and air signs dominate the planetary landscape this month, with a bit of fire and a pinch of water thrown in to anchor your psyche. You won't get the long vacation you desire, with earth beating the drum to complete pressing tasks and air complaining about the deluge of unnecessary demands that hinder performance. Schedule a vacation during the last half the month, after Venus moves into Libra on the 16th and favors your social life.

Relationships

Work connections hum along productively, encouraging you to take pride in the brilliance and efficiency of colleagues. You and your partner find bliss as you wrap up obligations in preparation for some much-deserved vacation time. Respect from authority figures makes your self-esteem soar and makes you rethink any doubts you have about moving into a new work arena. Parents or in-laws may join you for a few days of your vacation for a pleasant interlude of fun and sun.

Success and Money

The New Moon on the 8th favors collaborative efforts with business partners and others who support your work. Intimate partners acknowledge your smarts and your caring attitude in getting the job done so you have quality time to enjoy travel plans without disappointing your boss.

Pitfalls and Potential Problems

Stay away from any contentious subjects at home base unless you research their origins before you discuss them, especially around the 1st. You're better off skipping a conference or meeting scheduled for the 17th since you may not be prepared to discuss agenda items due to pressing work deadlines.

Rewarding Days

6, 8, 16, 29

Challenging Days

1, 17, 22, 23

Aquarius | September

Overall Theme

For the third and final time this year, Mercury turns retrograde, this time in Libra on the 27th, putting the spotlight on people at a distance, medical and legal practitioners, writing and publishing ventures, long-distance travel, and philosophy. Professional obligations and program reviews may take you away from your home base to foreign countries or temporary duty in another state.

Relationships

Beautiful momentum with work partners, collaborators, and bosses continues as others seek your expertise and load up your daily agenda with increasing obligations. You get along well with individuals from foreign countries who do business with yours, and you may be motivated to study another language to enhance communication.

Success and Money

The good news is that extra assignments bring increased compensation for your performance. A far-away trip around the 9th introduces you to new people and a different work culture. You're a hit with the brass in this location, who pick your brain for management solutions and pass along positive feedback to your work leader. Your money situation is prosperous and allows you to afford the finer things in life.

Pitfalls and Potential Problems

Relationships with siblings or cousins could get off track around the 2nd, when travel plans may be canceled or misunderstood. Harmony on the home front is in jeopardy on the 5th, when the Moon directs hard aspects to Jupiter and Neptune. Engage in a straightforward discussion and admit that you didn't want to accept a social invitation.

Rewarding Days

3, 7, 10, 20

Challenging Days

2, 5, 18, 25

Aquarius | October

Overall Theme

October is a high-action month. A number of retrograde players are coming home to roost: Pluto in Capricorn moves direct in your solar twelfth house on the 6th, followed by Saturn in Aquarius in your solar first house on the 10th, Jupiter in Aquarius also in your first house on the 18th, and Mercury in Libra in your solar ninth house on the 18th. Say goodbye to seemingly endless delays and hello to a month of accelerated activity with work assignments and professional contacts.

Relationships

Interactions with teachers, tutors, or coaches increase due to your shifting interests, enrollment in a class, or children's activities. A number of you will be attending family reunions around the 9th. Enjoy the bonding and endearing discussions that make it worthwhile to travel while you reconnect with favorite people and cherished memories.

Success and Money

An exceptional credit rating gives you access to the sought-after loan rate you desire to buy or refinance your home. Lenders compete for your business and tempt you with more money than you actually need. Borrow what you need and avoid taking out an overly generous home equity loan for household improvements.

Pitfalls and Potential Problems

You and your partner argue over the purchase of a luxury item for your home or vehicle. Don't make a decision about this on the 3rd, as it will be reversed. The 29th is another prickly day for domestic bliss, with individuals competing for dominance in hopes of winning the "I was right" war. A friend wants to argue on the 20th; don't take the bait.

Rewarding Days

5, 7, 9, 15

Challenging Days

3, 8, 20, 29

Aquarius | November

Overall Theme

The good news is that an aura of determination and grit is everywhere, giving the impression that an individual's commitment is solid and you can rely on the spirit of intent. The other side of the coin is that with an intense display of fixed-sign energy right now, including yours, power struggles, stubbornness, and arguments dominate the landscape. The last Lunar Eclipse of the year occurs in still another fixed sign, Taurus, in your solar fourth house of home.

Relationships

People at a distance play an important role in your life right now. Interaction with business contacts escalates the volume of travel, conference calls, and distance learning. You may pack your bags with little notice, especially at the beginning of the month and at the very end, when demand for your services increases. Children and their interests are a high priority from November 20 to 22.

Success and Money

Enjoy the letters of commendation, awards, and extra cash that flow into your personal file and your bank account around the 14th. Savor the demand for your time and contribution to modern productivity. The sought-after expertise you have perfected puts you out in front of the competition for emerging assignments. Expect a raise!

Pitfalls and Potential Problems

Don't spread yourself too thin on the 1st, when several annoying setbacks crop up that are out of your control but require your services to solve them. Realistically assess the timeline and analyze the major problems, delegating less exasperating snafus to other team members, especially on the 11th, when you need some help to meet a major deadline by the 15th.

Rewarding Days

3, 14, 20, 30

Challenging Days

1, 4, 11, 19

Aquarius | December

Overall Theme

The month starts out with the final Solar Eclipse of the year on the 4th in Sagittarius and your solar eleventh house of friends, hopes, wishes, and affiliations, putting the spotlight on goals you set for the past year, how well you met them, and your expectations for accomplishments in 2022. This New Moon Eclipse is conjunct Mercury, setting an anticipatory tone for upcoming seasonal celebrations, just as soon as you can break away from the influence of obsessive Mars in Scorpio demanding that you finish every delegated task before you party.

Relationships

Early holiday gatherings bring folks together in the spirit of appreciation for professional contributions, teamwork, and rapport. Plan on attending events hosted by company executives, friends, and relatives. The passion for expressing joy and happy wishes to others spreads to neighbors, relatives, and family by the 13th, when Mars moves into adventurous Sagittarius and adds extra sparkle to your mood.

Success and Money

Achieving career goals and meeting strict deadlines are priorities from the beginning to the end of the month. Authority figures express confidence in the continuing high level of performance, share compliments putting the spotlight on achievement, and provide bonuses or promotions to those who earn them, including you.

Pitfalls and Potential Problems

Duck the whip that someone wants to crack on the 2nd to prod you to complete an assignment—you're in the clear, but it may not be evident until the 3rd. Be alert to package delivery theft or a neighborhood problem on the 14th. Venus turns retrograde on December 19 in Capricorn, indicating a need to check jewelry or luxury item purchases carefully for flaws before your wrap them.

Rewarding Days

3, 4, 7, 30

Challenging Days

2, 14, 15, 20

Aquarius Action Table

These dates reflect the best—but not the only—times for success and ease in these activities, according to your Sun sign.

	JAN	FEB	MAR	APR	MAY	JUN	JUL	AUG	SEP	OCT	NOV	DEC
Move		2		12		8			10		3	
Romance		7			13		7	8				7
Seek counseling/coaching	14		13	17			2			7		
Ask for a raise			6			22				5		4
Vacation								29			20	
Get a loan	4				7				20			

Pisces

The Fish
February 18 to March 20

♓

Element: Water

Quality: Mutable

Polarity: Yin/feminine

Planetary Ruler: Neptune

Meditation: I successfully navigate my emotions

Gemstone: Aquamarine

Power Stones: Amethyst, bloodstone, tourmaline

Key Phrase: I believe

Glyph: Two fish swimming in opposite directions

Anatomy: Feet, lymphatic system

Colors: Sea green, violet

Animals: Fish, sea mammals

Myths/Legends: Aphrodite, Buddha, Jesus of Nazareth

House: Twelfth

Opposite Sign: Virgo

Flower: Water lily

Keyword: Transcendence

The Pisces Personality

Strengths, Talents, and the Creative Spark

The symbol of your sign has a deeply spiritual connotation: two Fish swimming in opposite directions that signify your desire to understand differences in others, a quality you compassionately demonstrate and thoroughly appreciate. Yours is the only mutable water sign in the zodiac and the owner of a well-developed sixth sense that seldom steers you in the wrong direction when you're pursuing the truth. Behind your dramatic eyes lies a probing mind that values personal space. Mystery, romance, and adventure appeal to you while you absorb the details and note the actions and words of those close to you. Yours is one of the most complex of the twelve astrological signs. When searching for a new perspective, you retreat into the private sanctuary of your mind to process what you know. Although Pisces is closely affiliated with the twelfth house of seclusion, retreat, and regrouping, you enjoy personal freedom and share your generous spirit with loved ones. Neptune is your sign's ruler and is the natural occupant of the twelfth house of secrets, planning, and behind-the-scenes activity, and so many other themes that make it difficult to define all of your interests.

Some of you are gamblers and enjoy playing the lottery or making trips to Atlantic City, Reno, and Las Vegas. You are likely to gravitate toward careers that give you plenty of privacy, such as work in hospitals, institutions, healing or rehabilitation facilities, or prisons. If you enjoy working with computers, telecommuting is a perfect match for your skills. Those of you adept with numbers excel at accounting, bookkeeping, and teaching math. Learn to say no to anything that bores you.

Intimacy and Personal Relationships

In the love department, you're the type of person who longs to have your dream of the perfect partner come true. You relish happy endings, poetry, romance, love at first sight, and tender stories about how lovers met for the first time. Most of you won't quit if you don't get the marriage right the first time and will persist even if it takes multiple unions, always feeling sure the perfect match is just around the corner. The search for your soul mate is unending. You tend not to see the faults of lovers and could be taken advantage of, especially in your early life. Your heart is totally ruled by your emotions, unless you have strong earth or fire planets present in your birth chart. In that case, you may be attracted to a mate with one of those signs or to another water sign. You freely give support to family and close friends and champion the underdog. Compassion comes easily, unless you discover that someone you adore has not been truthful. While you generously open your door to visitors and make them feel welcome, you may not want to cook meals, preferring to host a catered dinner or treat your guests to a restaurant meal. Remember to change your routine to change the dynamics of your love life.

Values and Resources

One of your mantras is "I'm dedicated to the one I love," and you go out of your way to show devotion and care to those you cherish. You often sacrifice a great deal for loved ones, stopping only when you realize that certain individuals are not pulling their own weight, don't care, or have been untruthful. You value personal space and plenty of alone time. At times, people call you a loner. You can be a fireball at work, but once you check out of the duty zone, you want complete control over your downtime to pursue hobbies and recreational interests. Many a Pisces relishes a good movie plot—adventure, mystery, or romance. Reading is another favorite pastime. You may have accumulated your own personal library and often spend a long weekend curled up with an interesting book. Living near water or enjoying the beach has always attracted you. One of your favorite meals is a succulent seafood feast served with spicy condiments and an extra-large glass of iced tea.

Blind Spots and Blockages

Those who know you say you balk at incorporating new technology into your work routines that might include system training, installation of equipment upgrades, or reorganization of practices. Some of you succumb to the old Neptune fog and spend too much time daydreaming, especially when receiving unpleasant assignments that don't match your skill set or interfere with the timeline you've set to finish your work. Other Pisces individuals ignore opportunities for self-development, always stating a reason why they don't want to consider additional education, formal classes, or certificate programs to feed your mind and seed your qualifications for future opportunities. At times bosses call you inefficient in carrying out the work, especially if you have trouble meeting deadlines. As kind and considerate as you are under normal circumstances, you're known for making snappy retorts that others interpret as defensive when someone blindsides you with an unexpected comment, question, or request. Some of you can't balance a checkbook and shy away from money management. Certain Pisces drink too much or rely on recreational substances that can get out of control at various life stages and call for admission to a rehabilitation or medical facility.

Goals and Success

Expertise at journaling keeps your goals close and helps you monitor steps you'll need to take to bring them to fruition. Use your creative imagination to develop a vision board to highlight possible careers that interest you or list dreams you have for your future. Update it as you develop each new passion. Apply the excellent tool of mind mapping to list your plans and link your ideas together as you build an intuitive framework. Just like your kindred water signs, Cancer and Scorpio, many of you are drawn to the world of metaphysics, including psychic phenomena, mediumship, clairvoyance, tarot, runes, and numerology. More than a few Pisces use these or similar skills in their professional practices. Meditation and chakra-clearing techniques relax your body and mind, allowing you to practice healing techniques instead of escaping from problem areas. You are one of the signs that opts for multiple careers to take advantage of your diverse interests, and enjoys two or more retirements. You thrive on the security of having several pensions or retirement funds.

Pisces Keywords for 2021
Emancipation, enchantment, ESP

The Year Ahead for Pisces

With a pragmatic and sometimes intense gathering of Capricorn planets in your solar eleventh house over the last few years, your zone of groups, friends, and goals has been a hub of activity. The bottleneck started in 2008 when Pluto in Capricorn entered that house, joined in late 2017 by Saturn in Capricorn and late last year by Jupiter, which wrapped up its tour in November 2020. Pluto is still around to help you break up the stuck places that affect your affiliations and inhibit execution of your plans.

This year, attention centers around your solar twelfth house of secrets, healing, and behind-the-scenes activity, with Jupiter and Saturn taking up residence in Aquarius. They'll team up tentatively at first, blowing off steam when they get on each other's nerves, because Jupiter wants to go big or go home and Saturn wants to call a halt to any risk-taking before doing a careful assessment of the pros and cons of any undertaking. Transiting Neptune in Pisces will continue its journey through your solar first house, tempting you to stay put in the aura of an idyllic daydream instead of wandering into uncharted waters.

Jupiter

What were you doing on December 19, 2020, when Jupiter in Aquarius jogged into your solar twelfth house of atonement, charity, hidden matters, and psychological health? How were you assessing your status in life? Opportunities rapidly surface to accentuate circumstances that stimulate conditions to show compassion for others, lend a hand to those less fortunate, complete a phase of recovery for afflictions to your physical or mental body, and use introspection to work on career and life plans. The rapid Jupiter-in-Aquarius transit ends temporarily on May 13, when the planet of luck and expansion moves into Pisces and samples the outlook in your solar first house of self-interest to hint at probable changes after completing its Aquarius cycle on December 28, 2021. Jupiter was the old ruler of your sign before Neptune took over the honor. While these two planets have similar interests in savoring travel and the sea, Jupiter wants to pack a suitcase and hit the road instead of hanging out in the attic in self-imposed confinement.

Although it won't always be fun for Jupiter to hang out in your twelfth house for a year, its presence helps you heal and replenish your energy. Jupiter turns retrograde on June 20, moving back into Aquarius on July 28 to cover familiar, already traveled degrees before it turns direct in Aquarius on October 18. Use this time wisely to sort through major issues that have been troubling you. Separate situations where you can confidently display sound judgment from those where you're tempted to come up with illogical solutions that hinder progress and block clarity. This cycle of healing, redemption, and taking control of your well-being has the ultimate effect of improving the quality of your relationships, starting with the one you have with yourself.

Saturn

Your solar twelfth house of seclusion has no lonely corners this year since transiting Saturn moved into Aquarius on December 16, 2020, and quickly invited jovial Jupiter to share your ultra-sacred space while you broaden your view of responsibility. If you've had a blah feeling and show signs of withdrawal or depression after juggling health issues, personal disappointments, or wandering thoughts, it's time to break out of the rut and work on a new plan. Focus is key, and that concept is balm to Saturn, who likes nothing better than to put you back on track to succeed by fulfilling your dreams. First, you have to get rid of the nightmares. Enter Jupiter, your temporary roommate who lobbies for clear head space and plenty of room to loosen the restrictive zone you've built to keep out prying eyes and probing inquisitors determined to crack the code to figure out how you got into this mess. Patience pays off after all of the boxes are ticked with Saturn, the astrological culprit who makes you pay your dues in a seemingly endless 2½-year cycle before releasing you to fully enjoy your next reward. Note that Saturn is direct until May 23, when it goes retrograde and then resumes forward motion on October 10. Those of you born between February 19 and March 4 feel the greatest impact from this transit. Keep an eye on your physical stamina and any mental fatigue. Presumably you are ready for complete emancipation. Make rest a priority while you recharge your batteries, and embrace comedy, dancing, and yoga to keep the blues at bay.

Uranus

In 2021 you'll entertain the provocative nature of Uranus in Taurus in your solar third house of communication, contracts, education, electronic equipment, local travel, neighbors, relatives, and your state of mind. Activity in this area of life is off the charts, with increased frequency of conversations, correspondence, visits, phone calls, and messages from diverse contacts. Oddly, increased communication benefits you, even if you balk at the volume of chatter and demand. You tend to keep much information to yourself, more than you realize. This habit is often detrimental when you tell only half the story or leave out critical facts that would facilitate understanding of situations. Although some of you can be terse on paper, you tend to cover much more in writing than you do in discussions, often feeling that words fail you when you need to jog your brain. Hang on, because remaining silent won't be easy this year. Uranus begins 2021 in retrograde motion and goes direct on January 14. Pisces born between February 23 and March 5 are most affected this year in the area of communication, when Uranus shakes up conditions related to contracts, orders, purchases, school papers, and transportation. Uranus will grab your attention provocatively on August 19 when it goes retrograde again and stays in this provocative state until early 2022. Keep your eye on the performance of equipment, appliances, and vehicles, and watch weather patterns when starting travel. Uranus is in a sign compatible to yours, so anticipate enjoyable get-togethers and reasonable success with your goals.

Neptune

Since April 2011, Neptune has been a steady occupant of your solar first house of action, assertive behavior, physical body, passion, personality, self-image, and temperament. Those of you born between March 7 and 14 benefit the most from this inspirational and romantic passage that encourages you to learn all you can about your soul and the gifts contained within it. You probably need no reminders that your talent as a psychic, intuitive, or interpreter of dreams suits you well and gives rise to some fascinating conversations in your circle of friends. Neptune in the first house makes you a tenderhearted being, aware of every nuance and shift of energy that crosses your path, even if you are stoic in your outward expression and sometimes forget to protect yourself from the psychic vampires that roam the planet. This is a time to dissolve illusions and get rid of addictions that interfere with your plans and zap your funds, such as alcohol, drugs, shopping, gambling, overeating, or television. Redirect your subconscious to stay aware of vulnerabilities—everyone has them—and create a safe haven conversing with those you trust. Neptune goes retrograde on June 25 and moves direct in motion on December 1.

Pluto

While Pluto spends yet another year in Capricorn in your solar eleventh house, you gain tremendous insight into the inner workings of your associates, friends, members of clubs, professional organizations, and peer groups, with this planet taking stock of the power struggles and stressing the need to clear away the dead weight. Perhaps you've questioned why you're still paying dues to an organization that you seldom interact with because the environment is stale. When you find yourself going through the motions, doing things by rote, and feeling like you're getting nowhere with your goals, your path points to attracting associates whose views offer a fresh perspective and whose values you share. Think of what you could build for your future with a shot of innovation and a project that addresses worthwhile causes in a venue that offers an opportunity to lead with conviction in the years ahead. Pluto completes the final leg of this journey in the next few years before settling down in Aquarius in early 2024. This year, those of you born between March 13 and 17 feel the greatest impact from this transit and long to shed any old wounds connected to group activities and unfulfilled goals. In the sign of Capricorn, Pluto offers compatibility and closure to your enchanting soul. Celebrate your awareness.

How Will This Year's Eclipses Affect You?

In 2021, a total of four eclipses occur. There will be two Lunar Eclipses and two Solar Eclipses, creating intense periods that begin to manifest a few months before their actual dates. Eclipses unfold in cycles involving all twelve signs of the zodiac, and usually occur in pairs about two weeks apart. Think of eclipses as opportunities to release old patterns and conditions that have outlived their usefulness. Have no fear of them, since they can bring you unexpected surprises and windfalls. The closer an eclipse is to a degree or point in your chart, the greater its importance in your life. Those of you born with a planet at the same degree as an eclipse are likely to see a high level of activity in the house where the eclipse occurs.

The first one is a Lunar Eclipse in Sagittarius that takes place on May 26 in your solar tenth house of ambition, authority figures, career, status quo, and success. Your long-held quest to find the perfect job may be within your grasp this year, as your outstanding performance grabs the attention of hiring executives. You've done the work to become more competitive and earned credibility for your rapport with the team. This eclipse strongly relates to those born between February 22 and 24, alerting you to put your best foot forward and grab the brass ring.

The last eclipse of 2021 is a Solar Eclipse on December 4 that occurs once again in Sagittarius and your solar tenth house, highlighting the qualities of leadership, strategic wisdom, and fair management that you demonstrate and the professionalism that you bring to the workplace. Toast new opportunities to succeed if your birthday occurs between March 1 and 3.

The first Solar Eclipse of 2021 takes place in your solar fourth house on June 10 in Gemini, shedding light on the activity at home and the people who live with you. What has been percolating at home base? Has the environment been calm and bright or testy and confusing? Where are the hot spots? If you haven't identified them yet, you will shortly, because an eclipse in your fourth house of home and family sheds light on any occupants in a state of flux. You could be a major contender for action since this eclipse is in harsh aspect to your Sun, especially if you were born between March 8 and 10. Examine conditions surrounding your close relationships.

The last Lunar Eclipse of the year occurs on November 19 in Taurus in your solar third house, the temporary residence of transiting Uranus in Taurus. You've already had your hands full with incidents that have jarred the tranquility of your neighborhood in the form of noisy construction, redirected traffic, or inconsiderate neighbors who have moved in and routinely violate community norms. You'll be most aware of any eclipse side effects if you were born between March 16 and 18. Keep an eye on computer equipment, educational materials, sales agreements, and vehicles. Periodically check in with siblings and cousins to keep up with family news and make arrangements for visits and vacations. Enroll in classes that complement your interest in hobbies. Challenging your mind is one of the most stimulating perks in the coming year. Perhaps the insights you gain will lead you to collect your thoughts and write your memoirs.

Pisces | January

Overall Theme

Your planetary ruler, Neptune, travels in harmony with the Sun for most of the month, generating enjoyable social opportunities. Give yourself a few days to recover from the New Year's celebrations and return to the work world with renewed enthusiasm. Check your calendar carefully to make sure you don't miss invitations for important personal or business events.

Relationships

The New Moon on the 13th falls in your solar eleventh house of friends and associates, opening doors for meeting inspiring individuals at special gatherings. Many in your circle are enthusiastic about networking and learning about unfolding career and professional meetings. You and your partner cherish special times together early in the month and may schedule a winter weekend vacation on the 9th.

Success and Money

You get a chance to communicate your creative ideas and share information with interested parties in both your work world and your social arena. Be at the top of your game with your message. The middle of the month brings news about financial offers and positive feedback regarding loan or refinancing options.

Pitfalls and Potential Problems

Ground yourself as Uranus in Aquarius moves direct in your solar twelfth house of seclusion on January 14. Wait until the following week to sign important papers. Be sure you have all legal documents in order before Mercury goes retrograde in Aquarius on the 30th. Avoid arguments at home base on the 25th when fragile feelings surface. Lie low on the 1st when extra rest is soothing and you enjoy an understated welcome to the new year.

Rewarding Days

4, 9, 13, 17

Challenging Days

1, 11, 20, 25

Pisces | February

Overall Theme
The New Moon in Aquarius on February 11 falls in your solar twelfth house of seclusion, along with Mercury, Jupiter, and Saturn, giving your mind a workout and your soul an awakening of consciousness. Enjoy those big dreams and create a pathway to prosperity that allows you to offer them to the right bidder. Spend quiet time working on options for showcasing your talent.

Relationships
The Valentine's Day Moon is in romantic Pisces. Treat your loved one to a celebratory meal and serve up tender caresses for the perfect dessert. Relationships with household members as well as siblings at a distance are cordial and caring. Treasure them.

Success and Money
An early review of your financial picture on the 3rd paints a positive outlook for the stable landscape on display in your savings and debt management arena. Hats off to you for exceeding your goals. Excited by the flow of entrepreneurial ideas you've had this month, you're ready to bring them to the highest bidder among hiring authorities. The pace picks up especially during the week of the 21st, when the Sun is in Pisces.

Pitfalls and Potential Problems
Steer clear of professional differences at your workplace when tension escalates around the 7th. Executives are unprepared for the fallout and have to schedule a private discussion to look at the cause of the disagreements. A faceoff of opposing viewpoints flares up among coworkers on the 25th, in the aftermath of earlier revelations that were never resolved.

Rewarding Days
3, 11, 19, 21

Challenging Days
7, 14, 19, 28

Pisces | March

Overall Theme

How do you feel about romance? If you're anticipating shifts in the status quo, watch the lunar activity this month, which is perfect for announcing an engagement, getting married, or celebrating a relationship milestone. This month's New Moon in your sign takes place on the 13th in the company of Venus in Pisces conjunct that other expressive love planet, your ruler, Neptune. March 23 is also a date with positive Moon-Neptune aspects.

Relationships

Step up your social life with bonding events that include friends, amicable groups, individuals you're dating, and those with whom you'd like to share a long-term relationship. Conversations are stimulating, and a few may surprise you with the depth of feelings expressed. You could be walking on air all month.

Success and Money

You could sail through an audit or get good news from your accountant over the estimated amount you owe on your taxes. The 2nd is an excellent day for a meeting to discuss details. Be sure every form or receipt is ready with appropriate signatures before you file.

Pitfalls and Potential Problems

In-laws or contacts at a distance share disapproval of impending plans, which could include the scheduling of surgery, business travel, or vacation dates. Make no decisions on the 4th, as the plans will not stick. Arrange a video phone conference for better communication. Clashes with coaches, teachers, or law officers are possible on the 6th. Be diplomatic and listen to strategic details before you judge an action.

Rewarding Days

2, 7, 19, 21

Challenging Days

5, 12, 16, 25

Pisces | April

Overall Theme

Restlessness catches up with you this month just in time for a spring vacation, so you can feed your soul with self-love and appreciation for the unrelenting commitment you demonstrate in the work world. Spread the seed of optimism where it counts, with your family members and contacts you plan to visit while traveling. The little things count—show appreciation for kind gestures that come your way.

Relationships

Happily, most relationships are cordial this month, especially the one you have with your intimate partner. Discuss an entertainment venue that means a lot to both of you and book reservations. You'll visit relatives at a distance and rekindle bonds that are strong and remind you of the joys of childhood, prompting you to stay in contact more frequently by sharing hosting duties.

Success and Money

The New Moon on the 11th shines prosperously in your solar second house of income and assets, throwing a spotlight on cash flow, money you received as a tax refund and how you used it, and your plans for allocating a larger portion of income to savings accounts. This Aries Moon connects with Venus and highlights spending for a special gift such as jewelry or a decorative accessory for your home.

Pitfalls and Potential Problems

Obey all the traffic rules if you're traveling on the 3rd, a date that indicates a conflict with an authority person. Communication could be frustrating on the 5th when group discussion generates conflicting opinions. Due to incomplete information in an invitation, an argument may emerge over who picks up the tab for a restaurant meal.

Rewarding Days

1, 7, 11, 23

Challenging Days

3, 5, 14, 27

Pisces | May

Overall Theme

The year's first Lunar Eclipse occurs this month on May 26 in Sagittarius in your solar tenth house of career and status, putting matters of ambition, family, leadership, and achievement in the spotlight. You could be juggling dates, adding meetings and business travel to your calendar, and looking closely at prospects for scheduling a summer vacation.

Relationships

Connections with friends, professional organizations, and neighborhood groups are in excellent shape, and they resonate favorably with family members on the 1st and 2nd. The health of a family member comes to light, leading to a discussion of concerns among relatives. You may be called on to introduce the parents of team members to neighborhood newcomers.

Success and Money

Your warmth and focused leadership have made a difference in the dynamics of a favorite organization or charity, and you may be asked to serve as an officer. Your negotiating skills get a workout during discussions to schedule construction work on your home. Do this before Saturn goes retrograde on the 23rd and Mercury does the same on the 29th.

Pitfalls and Potential Problems

Pay close attention to attitudes around the time of the Lunar Eclipse on May 26, when tension in your workplace could be high before and after the event over staffing changes and contentious decisions. Bring out the lavender oil on the 4th so you don't have to experience a sleepless night, possibly over promises you can't keep. A similar scenario builds on the 21st when you squabble with your significant other.

Rewarding Days

1, 2, 7, 13

Challenging Days

4, 21, 26, 29

Pisces | June

Overall Theme
The first Solar Eclipse of 2021 occurs in your solar fourth house of home and family on June 10 in Gemini. By now you'll have a fresh perspective and information on the health of an older family member. You often worry without knowing all the facts. Breathe, let go of unnecessary tension, and look optimistically at finding treatment solutions.

Relationships
What a plus for relationship compatibility when the Moon joins Jupiter on the 1st and brings long-desired invitations your way. Venus joins the group too, giving you a reason to dress up and leading to some lively talks in your home. Savor the communication harmony.

Success and Money
You have the money to outfit the entire family in new clothing for a special event. Purchase these party clothes on the 6th, when your money goes further than anticipated thanks to a timely sale. Right after the eclipse on the 10th, a close relative could ask you to witness a will and then ask you to keep a copy of it. Make sure you make an additional copy and store it in a safe place.

Pitfalls and Potential Problems
Mark the 15th as a day when something could be lost, broken, or stolen in your everyday environment. If it is workplace equipment, you're at the mercy of repair associates to get the item up and running. If the breakdown occurs at home base, it may take a few days to book the appropriate repair team, causing upsets through the 17th.

Rewarding Days
1, 6, 10, 29

Challenging Days
3, 15, 17, 21

Pisces | July

Overall Theme

Holiday fun and happiness define what you experience in your solar fifth house of entertainment, recreational activity, and vacations this month when the compatible Cancer New Moon on July 9 shines its nurturing light on your plans. Be sure you include parties in the mix or a day trip to the beach, one of your favorite relaxation spots. Feast on shrimp and crabs to satisfy your pescatarian palate and call the outing a success.

Relationships

Among your children, students if you teach, and your traveling companions, it's a thumb-up for the month as you synchronize calendars and plan some mutually agreeable play dates or schedule favorite entertainment venues from the 2nd through the 10th. Everyone is in the mood to chat, even the less talkative individuals, and excitement picks up as departure dates near. You and your spouse explore favorite haunts and savor quality adventures on the 15th.

Success and Money

The seed money you socked away in the spring easily covers vacation and holiday expenses. You may even see a raise or a performance award in your paycheck. Your workplace is increasingly productive. Be proud that your contributions make a difference after adding specialized training to your developmental plans.

Pitfalls and Potential Problems

Misunderstandings over communication or instructions that surface on the 5th could result in a "he said, she said" situation. Keep a calm head and look for a solution, sticking with the truth. Confusion over responsibilities at the workplace affects organizational tranquility on the 23rd. Intervention saves the day, along with relevant research into assignment protocols.

Rewarding Days

2, 9, 10, 15

Challenging Days

5, 8, 21, 23

Pisces | August

Overall Theme

The Aquarius Full Moon on the 23rd joins Jupiter and Saturn, the other two planets that are transiting this same sign and your solar twelfth house of seclusion. You're in search of relief from the stress you're experiencing in the aftermath of acquiring new duties at work resulting from unexpected personnel shifts. You're prepared to accommodate the change and may decide to telecommute a couple days a week to stay on top of the work.

Relationships

Outstanding relationship dynamics continue between you, your spouse, and your children as you free up weekend space to enjoy amusement parks, summer sports, and state fairs. A midweek date night is a solid hit with you and your significant other on the 11th. Locally based siblings invite you for a get-together or mini vacation before the children return to school.

Success and Money

The New Moon on the 8th in your solar sixth house puts the spotlight on the efficiency associated with accomplishing work projects. You may have a hand in organizing a seminar to bring everyone in the work group up to speed. New equipment and shared educational tools enhance the implementation of innovative management practices.

Pitfalls and Potential Problems

Mixed signals on the 2nd confuse the message in project instructions. A few of the staff with answers are missing for a critical meeting, leading to a delay in starting assigned work. Although not a total bust, hard attitudes surface at home base with a member of the younger set. The Moon transiting your solar tenth house of career bears down on a Mercury-Mars standoff, sending confusing signals to the team when management backs away from a solution.

Rewarding Days

6, 8, 11, 29

Challenging Days

1, 3, 17, 22

Pisces | September

Overall Theme

When the Sun occupies your opposite sign of Virgo, you often feel a bit drained of energy. It's a Pisces thing to take a vacation with your spouse or best friend in September when the crowds have thinned out to recharge your batteries and visit a favorite leisure spot. Rent a beach cottage or hang out at a cool mountain retreat from the 11th through the 14th so you return with a positive outlook and a golden glow.

Relationships

You'll have abundant contact with friends, coworkers, family, and especially your partner with the New Moon lighting up your solar seventh house on the 6th. It's always nice to feel in sync with others, and this month resonates with the energy of showing appreciation for the special people who light up your life.

Success and Money

A critical time to show you've got what it takes to run a project successfully is the middle of this month. Accolades come to you around the 14th when your innovative spirit outshines the competition by demonstrating how effortlessly you meet deadlines, use new methods to resolve roadblocks, and more quickly disseminate information to key stakeholders. If only they knew about your ESP!

Pitfalls and Potential Problems

It wouldn't be normal to have a month completely free of challenges, yet this one is much more manageable than usual. There's a communication glitch over canceled plans with a social contact on the 3rd. An accounting error in your personal financial records prevents you from balancing the books on the 10th, and the Full Moon in Pisces on the 20th depletes your energy.

Rewarding Days

6, 11, 14, 30

Challenging Days

3, 10, 20

Pisces | October

Overall Theme

If emancipation from gridlock in executing plans is your goal, this month spells relief. Planets emerge from their retrograde states: Pluto goes direct in Capricorn on the 6th, Saturn in Aquarius on the 10th, Jupiter in Aquarius on the 18th, and Mercury in Libra also on the 18th. Air planets dominate the landscape, indicating clear communication and the use of advanced technology to meet pressing timelines.

Relationships

Take a bow in the relationship department this month starting with spontaneous actions compliments of your significant other, who showers you with attention on the 4th. In-laws surprise you with a generous gift related to the arts and entertainment. Unconditional love affects family interaction as you witness a more giving and caring spirit in the household, with members looking out for one another.

Success and Money

Your face lights up when your usually aloof boss recognizes the intensity of meeting a challenging deadline by treating the team to a festive lunch in a show of appreciation. Purchasing power goes far this month as you buy discounted summer furniture and barbecue equipment at bargain prices, negotiating for free delivery and takeaway charges.

Pitfalls and Potential Problems

You may be forced to work on Saturday the 2nd even though you had plans to attend a sporting event with friends. Monday morning blues hit the work space on the 11th over incomplete information, but by noon the issues are resolved. Stay away from shopping on the Full Moon of the 20th, when bargains are hard to find and the ATM is out of cash.

Rewarding Days

4, 9, 10, 25

Challenging Days

2, 11, 20, 27

Pisces | November

Overall Theme

The deep, rich earth of November strikes a chord in your psychic soul and leads you toward manifesting your destiny when the Scorpio New Moon on the 4th appears in your solar ninth house of the enlightened mind. A feeling of gratitude engulfs your sensitive heart as you spend most of the month thinking of loved ones, planning holiday get-togethers, and shopping for special gifts.

Relationships

Thoughts turn to people at a distance who travel to see you for seasonal visits or invite you to share holidays with them over the next two months. Parties or special lunches with friends take place around the 10th, and you receive an invitation to a celebration a week before the Thanksgiving holiday. You review the relationship you have with yourself and vow to get along better with friends and relatives whose philosophies are different from yours.

Success and Money

Financial investments look solid on the 6th and the 30th, when you congratulate yourself for putting money aside to cover holiday expenses without tapping into savings or running up credit card balances. Leads from your networks provide links to positions that are opening up in the near future. Do your homework if a job change interests you.

Pitfalls and Potential Problems

The month gets off to an annoying start with signs of friction between you and your partner on the 1st. Everything falls into place by the 2nd. A neighbor shows signs of hostility on the 19th, the date of the Lunar Eclipse in Taurus in your solar third house. Avoid arguing with a bully on the 27th, especially if the contentious behavior takes place in your home.

Rewarding Days

4, 6, 10, 30

Challenging Days

1, 7, 19, 27

Pisces | December

Overall Theme

The Sun, Mercury, and Mars pass through your solar tenth house this month, reminding you to tackle any pending chores that free up your calendar for the downtime you need to work on holiday preparations. Joining these planets is the last Solar Eclipse of the year in Sagittarius on December 4, an event that resonates for the next six months and signals welcome changes in your career outlook and achievement of your goals.

Relationships

You've got the attention and support of the executives who manage candidate selection for upcoming position openings. Early parties to celebrate the holidays include favorite friends and esteemed networks around the 7th. Toast your family and cherish your significant other on the 25th, when the Moon stimulates lively conversation and heartfelt praise for the special people in your life.

Success and Money

Your financial picture looks rosy in 2022 after the praise you receive in a performance review. Update your resume and get ready to apply for the plum job that is on your radar screen. Plan the perfect getaway for departure around the 30th to ring in the new year, possibly while visiting relatives in another country or a distant location. Acknowledge the gratitude you feel for life's rewards.

Pitfalls and Potential Problems

Hump day on the 1st brings a few unanticipated financial problems to the surface. Be alert and check figures. In view of disappointing news you receive on the 11th, stay calm and don't read more into the information than is necessary. Watch expenses on the 14th and also on the 19th, when Venus goes retrograde in Capricorn until the end of January 2022.

Rewarding Days

4, 7, 25, 30

Challenging Days

1, 11, 14, 19